A HISTORY

OF

MARLBORO COUNTY,

WITH

TRADITIONS AND SKETCHES OF NUMEROUS FAMILIES.

REV. J. A. W. THOMAS,
AUTHOR.

A wonderful stream is the river Time
As it runs through the realms of tears
With a faultless rhythm and a musical rhyme,
And a broader sweep and a surge sublime
As it blends with the ocean of years.
—TENNYSON.

ATLANTA, GA.:
THE FOOTE & DAVIES COMPANY,
Printers and Binders.
1897.

Copyright 1997
Heritage Books, Inc

A Facsimile Reprint
Published 1997 by

HERITAGE BOOKS, INC.
1540E Pointer Ridge Place
Bowie, Maryland 20716
1-800-398-7709

ISBN 0-7884-0713-9

A Complete Catalog Listing Hundreds of Titles
On History, Genealogy, and Americana
Available Free Upon Request

DEDICATION.

To the People of Marlboro, Who Have
Uniformly Shown Their
Appreciation,
Love and Esteem for the Author.
J. A. W. Thomas,
This Work is Affectionately Dedicated.

PREFACE.

As stated elsewhere, the author found it very difficult to secure material for the History of Marlboro. Years ago he conceived the idea of leaving such a work as a legacy to the people. But the slow responses to his request for data and facts as to family history and the vast amount of research necessary to finish the historical part caused long delay. His friends will remember, too, that any additional literary work was but adding to the burden of a life already full of study and duties, and was therefore done at long intervals. So it was not strange that his hand was stilled before the task was completed which affection had prompted him to undertake. For the more perfect completion of the work it is to be greatly regretted that it has fallen to the lot of others to finish it as best they could. To a fond son it has been a labor of love, though attended with many difficulties and responsibilities. He is indebted to Judge Hudson, Hon. H. H. Newton, Capt. T. E. Dudley and other friends for facts and data. Special thanks are due Capt. John R. Parker for the map of the county.

It is sad to know that many who were living when the work was commenced, and who, in many instances, gave information to the author, have passed over the river.

Many have dropped by the wayside who would have found pleasure in perusing these pages, for the sake of the author as well as for the contents. But the indulgent friends who tarry yet for a little while, will, it is hoped, pardon mistakes, omissions, and shortcomings. Much of this is due, not to the conscientious, loving author, but to the fact that his work was transmitted to the far less capable, but willing hands of his son,

W. E. THOMAS.

CONTENTS.

	PAGE.
INTRODUCTION.	
By Judge J. H. Hudson, Bennettsville..................	11
CHAP. I.—MARLBORO COUNTY.	
The Aboriginals—Among the Records—The Mace and Sword of State	15
CHAP. II.—FIRST EARLY SETTLERS.	
Craven County—The Welsh Colony—Their Names—The David Family and Connections............................	20
CHAP. III.—EVANS, AND OTHER FAMILIES.	
Judge J. J. Evans—Col. Tom Evans - Col. Wilds—The Hodges—The Irbys—The Pegues......................	26
CHAP. IV.—OTHER EARLY SETTLERS.	
The Rogers Family..	32
CHAP. V.—OTHER BROWNSVILLE FAMILIES.	
Brown—Magee—Carloss—Mason Lee—The Coxe Family —Townsend....	39
CHAP. VI.—PEARSON FAMILY AND OTHERS.	
Henagan, Bruce and Others—Peter S. Ney...............	46
CHAP. VII.—INDUSTRIAL AFFAIRS OF THE EARLY SETTLERS.	
Wild Horses and Cattle—Primitive Means of Transportation—Military Affairs—Some of Their Grievances........	51
CHAP. VIII.—FAMILY OF COL. KOLB AND THEIR NEIGHBORS.	
Pouncey, Cochrane, Spears, Vining, etc..................	60
CHAP. IX.—REVOLUTION DRAWING NIGH.	
Causes Which Led Up to It—Grievances—Eloquent Words From Judge and Jury	65
CHAP. X. SEVERAL OLD FAMILIES.	
Terrell—Dr. James H. Thornwell—Gillespie—Ellerbe—Forniss—Pledger....	72
CHAP. XI.—PROGRESS OF REVOLUTIONARY SENTIMENT.	
Crisis Approaching—The Battle of Lexington—Troops Ordered from the Pee Dee—Patriotic Sentiment—Declaration of Independence—Charleston Threatened	78

CHAP. XII.—THOMAS, PARKER AND OTHERS.
Major Tristram Thomas—Robert, the Grandfather—Moses Parker—Twenty-two Children—Joshua Ammons—Joshua Fletcher—Twenty-two children—Traditions—Some Scotchmen—Easterlings...   85

CHAP. XIII.—PROGRESS OF REVOLUTION.
Events of 1780—Marlboro Troops on the March—Fall of Charleston—Tory Bandit—The Ayers—A Fort Armed with Wooden Cannon—Defeat of Gates at Camden   95

CHAP. XIV.—TRADITIONS FROM COL. JOHN COVINGTON.
Hebron—The Covingtons—A Long Horseback Ride—The Edens—Meekins   100

CHAP. XV.—OPERATIONS ON PEE DEE, 1781.
Col. Kolb—Murder of Harry Sparks by the Tories—Death of Col. Kolb—William Adams—Battle of Eutaw Springs—Surrender of Cornwallis—Triumph of the American Cause   105

CHAP. XVI.—BISHOP GREGG.
His Wife, Miss Charlotte W. Kollock, a Marlboro Lady—Lawyer, then Preacher   114

CHAP. XVII.—TRADITIONS FROM ALFRED PARISH.
Several Families—The Fuller "Ginger Cakes."   117

CHAP. XVIII.—AFTER THE REVOLUTION.
Shouldering Responsibilities—Establishment of County Courts—Naming the Counties—Some of the First Representatives in the Legislature   121

CHAP. XIX.—PROMINENT MEN AFTER THE REVOLUTION.
Governors Furnished by Marlboro—B. K. Henagan, John Lide Wilson, Robert and John Campbell—Baron De Poelnitz—The Introduction of "Nut Grass" in the County   128

CHAP. XX.—MEMBERS OF THE LEGISLATURE AND OTHER OFFICERS.
Members of the Legislature from the Revolution to Date—Clerks of Court, Sheriffs and Ordinaries   132

CHAP. XXI.—SCOTTISH SETTLERS.
McColls - McLaurins—John L. McCall   137

CHAP. XXII.—CLIO.
Joe Ivey—The Father of Senator Joseph H. Hawley, of Connecticut—The First Merchant—Hawleyville—"Muster Day"—Other Early Merchants - T. C. Weatherly, John A. McRae, W. A. Hinshaw—The Old People Living Near—Robert Purnell   144

Contents.

CHAP. XXIII.—SCOTTISH SETTLERS (Continued).
McRaes—McLeods—Laird McLeod—D. McD. McLeod—McLucas.. 152

CHAP. XXIV.—THE "OLD COURT-HOUSE."
"Marlboro Old Court-house"—Its Location—The Old Judges and Lawyers, Chancellors, Solicitors—The Lawyers of Marlboro....................................... 159

CHAP. XXV.—REMOVAL OF COURT-HOUSE TO BENNETTSVILLE.
Causes Which Led to the Removal—Act Passed Dec. 14, 1819—First Court-house at Bennettsville Completed 1824—Name Selected for the Town—Second Court-house at Bennettsville Built 1852—Third one 1884—Its Dedication—The Programme.. 167

CHAP. XXVI.—BENNETTSVILLE.
Its First Beginning—Named for Governor Bennett—First Houses—Pioneer Merchants—Earliest Citizens—Bennettsville Prior to the War—Since the War............ 170

CHAP. XXVII.—BRIGHTSVILLE.
Named for Charles Bright E. W. Goodwin—The "Stage Road"—Odoms and Others—Joel Hall—Stubbs Family—Moores—A. C. McInnis—Captain Thomas W. Huckabee.. 181

CHAP. XXVIII.—BLENHEIM.
Its Name—Donald Matheson—"Mineral Spring"—Summer Residents—Some of the Old Farmers Who Lived Near By—250 Bushels Corn Per Acre......................... 190

CHAP. XXIX.—THE CONFEDERATE WAR.
Secession—"Grim-visaged War"—Eight Full Companies from Marlboro—Full Lists of Officers and Men, Showing Promotions and Casualties............................. 193

CHAP. XXX.—EARLY MINISTERS.
James—Williams—Bedgegood—Pugh, etc............... 228

CHAP. XXXI.—BAPTIST CHURCHES.
The "Old Welsh Neck," the Mother of Churches—Brownsville, Salem, Beaverdam, Bennettsville, and Others—J. A. W. Thomas.. 232

CHAP. XXXII.—METHODIST CHURCHES.
Beauty Spot, the Mother of Churches—Hebron, Parnassus, Bennettsville, Boykin, Pine Grove and others—Circuits and Preachers.. 241

CHAP. XXXIII.—PRESBYTERIAN CHURCHES.
Bennettsville—Great Pee Dee—Red Bluff—Other Presbyterian Churches 258

CHAP. XXXIV.—MCCOLL.
Named for D. D. McColl—Principal Merchants—The McColl Manufacturing Company—Some of the Places Around Tatum.. 263

CHAP. XXXV.—ADAMSVILLE.
Prize Farming—Fine Farmers—J. B. Breeden—Sketch of the Adams Family.................................... 269

CHAP. XXXVI.— EDUCATIONAL MATTERS.
Early Interest in Education—The Old Academies in Bennettsville—Some of the Old Teachers—Bennettsville Graded School.. 274

CHAP. XXXVII.—THE COLORED PEOPLE... 279

CHAP. XXXVIII.—1886 284

CHAP. XXXIX.— DOWN TO THE TWENTIETH CENTURY 286

INTRODUCTION.

BY

J. H. HUDSON.

The author of this volume of local history died before its completion, under circumstances touching and significant. On Saturday August 1st, 1896, he attended the annual reunion of the Confederate veterans of Marlboro at Tatum, where he delivered to the assembly of veterans and citizens a feeling and eloquent address. On the Sabbath following, he preached in the forenoon at McColl, and in the afternoon at Tatum, with his usual fervency and zeal. Returning home, he ate his supper, held family prayers, retired to his couch, and fell calmly into that sleep which knows no waking.

For several years he had devoted his leisure moments to writing the history of Marlboro, but before finishing it for the press was called to his home above. His son has prepared this volume for the press, and now presents it to the people the author loved so dearly, and to whose temporal and spiritual welfare he devoted a half century of his laborious life.

In gathering the material for this history, he omitted no source of information available, but sought aid from all records and all classes of the community. It was the aim of Capt. Thomas, in writing this history, to make it so full in the matters of tradition and genealogy as to leave no room for complaint, but in spite of his zeal, industrious inquiry and research, he was unable to procure from some families, facts and data, whilst some others were unable to give information sought, having preserved no family records, and having no traditions stored up in memory. For any omissions in the work in this regard, the blame must rest where it properly belongs, and must not be cast upon the author, whose work was a labor of love and whose sole aim was to do full justice to the people of Marlboro, their noble ancestry, and beautiful region of country. He loved his native land with a patriotic devotion, and loved the people of his native county as a father loves his children. To the labors of Bishop Gregg, Captain Thomas was largely indebted, and drew from the "History of the Old Cheraws" much valuable material, pertaining to the history of Marlboro, for which he gives full credit to that accomplished writer. No section of South Carolina, distant from the sea-coast, is richer in Revolutionary tradition and deeds of high renown, than the region of the Old Cheraws on the upper Pee Dee, in the heart of which is Marlboro. Much of her history is forever lost, and for such as has with difficulty been rescued from oblivion, the residents owe a debt of gratitude to Gregg and Thomas, worthy sons of a proud ancestry and faithful laborers in the vineyard of our Saviour.

It is sad to know that much of the history of South Carolina has been entirely lost or remains unwritten through the indifference of her citizens. Efforts to perpetuate her proud record were made by Moultrie, Ramsay, Drayton, Johnson, Carroll and Simms, in none of whose histories was a full record made of the memorable deeds of prowess done on her soil, and least of all, of the valorous deeds of the men of the Pee Dee region, not because of indifference or partiality of the writers, but solely from the scantiness of information furnished. This induced Bishop Gregg to write the "History of the Old Cheraws", after years of assiduous labor in gathering material from every available source, and the same patriotic motive induced the Rev. J. A. W. Thomas to write this piece of local history of a people loyal to the State, valorous in war, law abiding, industrious and thrifty in time of peace. The people of Newberry owe a debt of gratitude to O'Neal and Chapman for their local histories, and to Gregg a like debt of gratitude is due from the people of upper Pee Dee, whilst to our author the citizens of Marlboro should feel deeply indebted for the history of the people who have ever been true to themselves and their State in time of war, and who, in peace, by quiet industry and exemplary thrift have made Marlboro the garden spot of the State.

CHAPTER I.

Marlboro County.

"Sit at the feet of history—through the night of years, the steps of virtue she shall trace and show the earlier ages."—Bryant.

The region of country, the history of which these pages is designed to treat, is called Marlboro. Marlboro County (first called District) was established by law, March 12, 1785. It takes its name from John Churchill, Duke of Marlborough, who died in the early part of the 18th century. He was an able English statesman, a successful politician and one of the very few generals, who through a lifetime of war, never met defeat. It is situated in the northeastern corner of South Carolina, and bounded north and northeast by North Carolina; south and southeast by Marion County, and west and southwest by the Great Pee Dee river. In the northern part of the County there are three small creeks rising in the sand hills and flowing in the Great Pee Dee, namely; Beaverdam, Phills and Naked. Crooked Creek, a considerable stream, rises in the extreme northeast and, flowing in a southwesterly direction empties into the Pee Dee river. In the southern part of the County, are the Three Creeks; and two others, designated by the name of Muddy. These various streams, with their smaller tributaries, afford ample drainage for the entire County. The area of the County is about 480 square miles. The surface is slightly undulating, the soil fertile, and largely open, and in a fine state of cultivation. Corn, cotton, oats, wheat, potatoes, rye, rice, tobacco, sugar cane, hay, melons and fruits all yield a rich and bounteous harvest to the intelligent labor of the husbandman. Marlboro County is the pioneer county in South Carolina in the intensive system of agriculture. Improved methods,

implements, seed, stock, drainage and buildings are every
where supplanting the inferior. The population is about
25,000. The whole County is teeming with busy, industrious, prosperous people, in large degree employed in
agricultural pursuits. But tradesmen, merchants, manu-
facturers are all favored in their callings, while medicine,
law, and religion are all honored in the men who represent the learned professions.

One hundred and seventy-five years ago, so far as can
be ascertained at the present time, there was not a white
man living in what is now Marlboro. According to the
conclusions of Bishop Gregg, of Texas, after a research
which has left nothing for the discovery of writers who
came after him, this whole Pee Dee region was held by the
aboriginal red men, until about 1730. He supposes that
a numerous tribe called "Cheraws" ranged the forests
from the Cape Fear to the Pee Dee, and from the Atlantic
coast to the mountains; that smaller tribes occupied more
limited bounds within this vast area; and that upon the
middle Pee Dee region a tribe known as the "Pee Dees" had
their favorite hunting grounds, and from these wild men
the two Pee Dee Rivers took their names. The men yet
live who remember to have seen the evidences of a former population, in the mounds, the arrow-heads, pottery
and pipes found in various localities in the valley of the
Pee Dee. No more sad and mournful requiem can be any
where chanted over the dead, than could be imagined by
kindly sentiment at the disappearance of these children
of the forest, endowed by nature with certain noble characteristics, yet always weakening and deteriorating when
brought into contact with the "pale faces." They have in-
variably disappeared before the tide of emigration and
civilization, until what were once strong, numerous tribes
have dwindled and faded, till many are extinct and the
remnants seem doomed to perish. But however sad this
first chapter in all the history of all parts of this country

may be, truth demands the record that these strange people were here, sole proprietors of the soil, the forests, game and waters of the land, when our ancestor first landed upon the shores of the new world. The marvel is not that they sometimes gave trouble to the whites that came among them, but that those troubles were not tenfold more terrible and protracted than they were. When they saw their forests falling before the axe, their streams being ponded upon their hunting grounds, the graves of their dead turned by the plow-share, it is not strange that they should look upon the newcomers as invaders of their rights and their homes. It is almost too late for "pity for the poor Indian," but not too late to bless the expiring years of his existence with whatever of help and comfort a generous people can give a dying race. How long they trod on plains, climbed our mountains, and paddled their light canoes upon our waters, no man knows; but the statesman and Christian alike must see that if anything is done for he betterment of their condition, it should be done quickly. Hitherto, there has been a wild West, to which their steps could flee before the tide of the white man's enterprise: but now the iron horse and the lightning messages are running from shore to shore, and the wild hidings of the Indian are disappearing forever. With him it is civilization, Christianization, or annihilation.

Among the musty record may be seen at the State House in Columbia a literary curiosity in the shape of a treaty or covenant made between certain aboriginal tribes who once owned the wide forests of this State, and some of the Lord Proprietors who sought fortunes in the new world. It dates back to 1675, or thereabout, and describes certain lands upon the Edisto River and its branches which the Indians sold to the Englishmen, conveying the rights and titles to the forests, the streams. the lands, the hunting grounds; the consideration being "cloths, hatchets, beads and such like trinkets and goods." The con-

tract is signed on the one part by the purchasers, and on
the other by the Indian settlers; the chiefs and leaders of
the tribes, of course all making their own peculiar "marks."
But what is especially remarkable, is the fact that several
"women captains" signed this treaty, or at least made
"their marks," and while the chiefs each made a
mark peculiar to his own hand, every woman made her
mark in the shape of a serpent, not all horizontally, but
some perpendicularly and others diagonally across the
page, but every one is a crooked serpentine line, some even
giving the larger head and small neck. That the Indian
savage allowed a dower to their women seems to be im-
plied, but why this peculiar signature? Did it signify a
claim to superior subtility and cunning? Did it indicate
her peculiar power to hurt and destroy? It has long been
a mystery and is yet. But a few years ago, while the late
Major Leitner was the Secretary of State, he called the
attention of Chief Morrison of the Catawba tribe to these
ancient signs and solicited an explanation of the mystery
and there is pinned upon the page in the handwriting of
the Secretary, the explanation of the chief; it is in sub-
stance as follows: The Indians have a tradition which they
claim to be five thousand years old. That a woman from
whom they are descended met in the forests a singular
serpent whose antics so pleased and charmed her, that she
was induced to break a solemn pledge to which her troth
had been plighted, and in punishment for her crime, an
awful curse befell her; and ever since, when an Indian
woman would make the most solemn vow of which she is
capable, she puts herself under the sign of the serpent,
calling down upon herself the malediction of the perjuror,
a punishment similar to that which befell the mother Indian who was betrayed into falsehood. As Chief Morrison explained it, the sign of the serpent indicates the most
solemn oath a woman can make. You who will may
speculate about the meaning of this singular relic of the

past, and find a better explanation than that given by the civilized chief of the remnant of a once powerful tribe. And alongside this there is another curiosity. The old mace presented to the colony, ornamented with the crown, its globe, its cross—symbol of royalty. And to this day along with the "broad sword" of State it is borne before the chief magistrate of a free people as he is conducted to his inauguration and oath of office. It may mean nothing to us, but did mean much to the old colonists, who received it from the mother country.

CHAPTER II.

First Early Settlers.

In the early division of the Province of South Carolina, this whole Pee Dee region seems to have been embraced in what was called Craven County; named, it is supposed, in honor of William, Earl of Craven, one of the first Lord Proprietors. Its immense area stretched from the Santee River to the North Carolina line, and from the seashore to the mountains. While some measures were adopted at an earlier date looking to its organization into parishes, and near the coast some settlements were made, yet not until about 1730, did the authorities take any active steps encouraging emigration to this part of the colony. About this time, however, several townships were marked out. One was laid off near the mouth of Little Pee Dee called Queensborough; and settlers were encouraged to occupy it, by the offer of "fifty acres of land to each soul that would settle and improve the grant." But not yet did this bring settlers, permanent residents at least, to that portion of country included in the present limits of our county. It was not until 1736, or early in 1737 that any permanent settlement was effected. That first settlement seems to have been so manifestly directed by Providence, and so fruitful in results, important and lasting, as to justify special notice.

The recital must take us back to the beginning of the century, and to the principality of Wales. "Several Baptist people, pining for larger religious liberty, living in the counties Cairmarthen and Pembroke, in the year 1701, resolved to remove to America." And as one of their number, by name Thomas Griffith, was already a minister, they were advised to be constituted a church emigrant. The names were as follows: "Thomas Griffith, Griffith

Nicholas, Evan Edwards, John Edwards, Elisha Thomas, Enoch Morgan, Richard David, James David, Elizabeth Griffith, Lewis Edmund, Mary John, Mary Thomas, Elizabeth Griffith, Tennant David, Margaret Mathias and Tennant Morris." These sixteen persons met at Milford Haven in the month of June, 1701, and embarked on the good ship William and Mary, and on the 8th day of September following landed at Philadelphia, and first settled about Penepeck, but finding certain inconveniences there, "in 1703, they took up land in New Castle County, about 30,000 acres, and built a little house of worship." This Welsh Tract, as it was called, was in Pennsylvania, but by a change of boundary fell into Delaware. Gregg still further records that the first visit from this colony to the Pee Dee appears to have been made in 1735, or early in the following year; that it led to a remarkable act of favor on the part of the Colonial Council to induce the Welsh to come. That act was an order to admeasure and lay out for these Welsh families 173,840 acres of land situated and being in Craven County.

In 1736, or early in the following year, a portion of this original colony from Wales, or their descendants came South, and at first stopped near the mouth of Catfish Creek, in what is now Marion County; but having much sickness there, they remained but a short time, and most of them removed about fifty miles up the Pee Dee River, and settled in what has ever since been called the "Welsh Neck;" a district embracing the lands on the east side of the river from the mouth of Crooked Creek to the Red Hill or Hunt's Bluff. Upon the bank of the river, a few hundred yards above the Society Hill Bridge, this colony of Welsh people met and organized themselves into a Baptist church in January, 1738, calling it Welsh Neck. These are the names: James James and wife, Phillip James and wife, Daniel Devonald and wife, Abel James and wife, Thomas Evans and wife, John James and wife, David

Jones and wife, Thomas Harry and wife, Daniel Harry and wife, John Harry and wife, Samuel Wilds and wife, Samuel Evans and wife, Griffith John and wife and Thomas Jones and wife. But these are not all who came. Bishop Gregg in his "History of the Old Cheraws" mentions a number of others as coming about the same time, such as "Thomas James, Griffith John, Wm. James, John Newberry, Wm. Evans, James Rogers, David James, Samuel Sorency, Evan Vaughan and Wm. Terrell." We are not to suppose that all these settled on the east side of the river, in what is now Marlboro. Now are we to infer that none others than the above mentioned came. Some settled on the west side of the river, and others outside the Neck, above and below.

The names of Owen and Jenkin David are mentioned in connection with the settlement at Catfish, and it is quite well established that both these brothers were early upon Marlboro soil, here lived and died, and have had in all the years an extensive and respectable posterity in the country. Indeed, it is doubtful if any of our old families have so clear and satisfactory a genealogy, or one so ancient, as this family. The writer had access to an "Old Family Bible" in which the record goes back through several generations in Wales, before the coming of Owen and Jenkin to the Pee Dee. The father of these, it is recorded, was John David, of Wales, and wife Ann, and John was the son of David and Lydia his wife; David was the son of Thomas, who was the son of David Bevan. Before coming to America. Owen married Catherine Vaughan of Wales, who died childless. He then married Dinah Underwood, who became the mother of Joshua, Josiah, Benjamin and Sarah. These three sons were soldiers in the Revolution. Joshua and Benjamin were both wounded, Benjamin in the head, and Joshua in the hand, at Eutaw Springs. Joshua married Lucy Hodge, daughter of Thomas Hodge, who was also a soldier in the

War of Independence. From this marriage came John H. Sarah, Joshua, Welcome, Jesse, Dinah and Betsy. John H. married Mary, the daughter of Shadrach Fuller, who becsme the mother of thirteen children. Lucy, Ann, James E., John O., Mary, Alex. H., Evander, Sarah, Joshua, Charles, Elizabeth and William J. Of these, James E., the first son, represented his people in the State Senate and House of Representatives. John O. and Alex. H. were well-known citizens for a long time; they sleep in Marlboro's sacred soil, and are represented by sons and daughters in the County. Dr. W. J. David died at Dillon in 1895, Evander past 80, yet lives in North Carolina.

Capt. Joshua David the second son of the first Joshua, was for many years a civil officer in Marlboro, as sheriff, clerk and ordinary. He was correct, honest, truthful; and no man has left more beautiful penmanship, or a clearer record upon the books. He ultimately married his cousin, Miss Susanna David, and their only son, Joshua, died soon after reaching manhood. Welcome, another son of Joshua the first, has descendants among us yet. Jesse, the third son of Joshua, reared a large family by his two marriages; first with Miss Harry, and then with Miss Webster. Joseph H., James F., and A. Judson David are sons of this good man, and Mrs. J. S. Liles, a daughter, while Mrs. Barnes and a number of others are among his grandchildren. Josiah was the son of Josiah, who was the second son of Owen, previously mentioned, and has descendants among us, but none bearing the David name, except Wm. R. David and his children, who maternally descended from Josiah. Benjamin, the other son of Owen, went West many years ago.

Jenkin David, who came from Wales with his brother Owen, had four sons, John, Azariah, Owen and Jenkin, Of this old man it is upon record that he was a soldier under General Wayne, in the French and Indian wars;

that he married Miss Rachel Rogers, daughter of Nicholas and Martha Rogers. Of his sons Owen and Jenkin nothing is known, except that they left the country at an early period. Azariah, a faithful soldier, also soon disappeared. John, however, remained, was a soldier and non-commissioned officer, and rose to a lieutenant in Marion's Brigade. He was five times married. His first wife was Sarah Booth, became the mother of three children and died; his second wife, Mary Jones, lived but three months; his third wife was Isabella Allison, and the mother of five children; his fourth wife was Sarah Stephens, who had two children and died. His fifth marriage was with Mrs. Mary Stubbs, the daughter of William Bridges, and widow of John Stubbs. One daughter was the fruit of this last marriage. Of these eleven children, all except two died unmarried, and most of them when quite young. The two who survived were both daughters. Mary, whose mother was Miss Allison, became the wife of Lemuel Pearson. A daughter of this pair, Rachel by name, became the wife of Meekin Townsend, and the mother of a large family. Her sons are R. E., C. P. and Walter Townsend. She died only a few years ago. Another daughter of Mrs. Pearson was the wife of the late Joel L. Easterling. An only son, William Pearson, who went to his reward a number of years ago, was the father of the late John D. Pearson, Mrs. J. F. Breeden, Mrs. J. L. Stubbs and Mrs. W. Bennett.

Eliza, the other daughter of John David, was the fruit of the union with the widow Stubbs. Mr. David was sixty-two, and Mrs. David forty-six when the babe was born and both lived to see her a full-grown woman, and the mother was for many years an inmate of the daughter's house after she had become the wife of Wm. D. Bridges. To Mrs. Bridges the Lord gave no children of her own, but many another's child had reason to love her and honor her memory. She passed to her reward, in the eightieth year of her life.

So that so far as this writer knows there is no descendant of Jenkin David, the progenitor of this branch of the family in Marlboro, bearing the David name. All bearing the name are descended from Owen, and yet the descendants of both Owen and Jenkin are numerous. Many interesting traditions of the family must, for lack of space, be omitted from these pages, but in connection with the David family another name deserves to be mentioned. It has been stated that Joshua David, of revolutionary fame, married Lucy, a daughter of Thomas Hodge. Londen Harwell, another soldier of the Revolution, married her sister Mary. Both were natives of Robertson County, North Carolina, and after marriage removed to Marlboro. Londen Harwell, at the age of thirteen years, became a soldier of Marion's Brigade in 1777, and remained steadfastly with him until peace was declared, when he returned home, married Mary Hodge and settled in Marlboro. An only son was born to them, Londen Harwell, Jr., who married Mary Britton, a daughter of John Britton (called Jacky) a soldier of Marion's, and a member of the family who lived in Britton's Neck. Of this marriage the only child was Elizabeth, who married Philip Miller from Frankfort on the Main. The old soldier, Londen Harwell, died in July 1838. Mrs. Miller, his granddaughter, is now eighty-three years old, and the mother of nine children, Mary, wife of ex-judge J. H. Hudson; Anna; Martha, wife of John R. McKellar; Lizzie, wife of J. B. Adams; Sue, wife of J. R. Newton; and four sons, John, Henry, Philip and George. John and Henry each lost a leg in the late war, John at Chickamauga and Henry at Knoxville, worthy descendants of good Whig ancestors. Narcissa, the oldest daughter of J. H. Hudson and the wife of Dr. J. L. Jordan, is the mother of Mrs. Mary West, who is also the mother of an infant, Annie, thus making the unusual record of five living generations.

CHAPTER III.

Evans, and Other Families.

There is need to still linger among the old Welshmen, who first planted civilization and Christianity upon the banks of the Pee Dee. There are several names in the list of the first settlers, as given in a former chapter, that have been prominent in the history of the country, and exercised a large influence in guiding public affairs. Among these, Thomas Evans is worthy of mention. He had a son Thomas, who was called "Old Col. Tom" Evans, who lived on the road from Long Bluff to the Marlboro old Court-house. He was a prominent soldier of the Revolution, a member of the Legislature, and was the father of that incorruptible jurist and statesman, Josiah J. Evans, than whom Marlboro has had few sons more justly honored and revered. Judge Evans was born upon Marlboro soil in 1786. He was among the early students of the South Carolina College, graduating in the third class in 1808. Three years later he was admitted to the bar; was made Commissioner in Equity for Cheraw District in 1812, and in the same year was elected a member of the House of Representatives for Marlboro District. After the expiration of his term of service he married Miss DeWitt, at Society Hill, and became from that time a citizen of Darlington, and soon had a large practice in his profession. In 1816 he was elected to the Legislature from Darlington, and in the year following was made solicitor for the judicial circuit in which he lived. In 1829 he was elected a circuit judge, and continued to preside in the courts of the State with eminent dignity, courtesy, and legal knowledge and accuracy, until 1852, when he was elected to the United States Senate. If wise and pure as a judge, he was not less faithful and true as a Senator. Senator Hale, of New Hampshire, widely differing from him in political opinions, said of him, "that he realized to his mind more fully than any other man whom he had met on the floor of the Senate, the ideal of an old Roman Senator." His career in the Senate was suddenly cut short by the stroke of death on the 6th of May, 1858. His practice as a lawyer, his duties as solicitor and judge, and a large planting interest in Marlboro, brought him frequently among the sons and daughters of his old neighbors. So that we never lost our interest in him, and when death struck him down, Darlington, his adopted home, was scarcely more bereaved than Marlboro. Since his death, although for a time none of his sons or grandsons were residents of the county, yet, their large planting interests within it has brought some of them into such constant contact with our people that they have felt almost like citizens, while in the late years several of the grandsons have become citizens, and one of them, Mr. W. DeWitt Evans, has served his constituents, first in the House of Representatives, then as Senator, and now as Railroad Commissioner.

Judge Evans had a brother, who came to be known as "Col. Tom" Evans, whose name is entitled to appear among the historic names of the County. Col. Evans saw active service in the war of 1812, and was for some time in active duty as Major in Col. John Rutledge's 3d Regiment of State troops, and upon the retirement or transfer of Col. Rutledge he was placed in command of the regiment. He also rendered civil service to his country, having served a term in the Legislature.

The name of Samuel Wilds appears among these early settlers. From Bishop Gregg we learn that he "had two sons, John and Abel. The latter was known before the Revolution as old Col. Wilds. His residence was on the east bank of the river, nearly opposite Long Bluff. John, the other brother, was the father of John and Samuel, The latter became the distinguished Judge Wilds, a man of remarkable character and brilliant talents." "His brother, John, who died prematurely, was considered even more talented." Judge O'Neal, in his "Bench and Bar," presumes that Judge Wilds was born in Darlington, but Gregg, in his history, makes him a native of Marlboro. Nor need our honored sister Darlington grudge us this distinction. She did have his residence and brilliant life —his accomplished daughter, Mrs. R. D. W. McIver, for some years, and his noble widow, who afterwards became Mrs. Dr. Smith—to adorn her best circles as patterns in all that was good. And if our Darlington cousins will allow it, let them be reminded that Peter Wilds, a scion of the same stock, transplanted from Marlboro, a flower that bloomed out for Darlington a precious fruitage not yet ceased bearing; and that Darlington has been greatly since honored, in giving birth to another Samuel Wilds, in the person of that noble, polished, valiant soldier, who led one of her first companies into the war between the States, and who rose to be the beloved Major in his regiment, and, scarred and wounded returned, to his hospitable home, to see his property swept away, and his country reduced and impoverished; yet lived only long enough to prove that he had gone through the struggle, and come out, the same pure-minded, splendid gentleman that went in. Scorning anything low or wrong, and then while yet in his prime, like his distinguished kinsman, fell asleep. lamented by all, and by none more than his comrades in arms.

Among the first members of the old church at Welsh Neck were three Harry's, Thomas, Daniel and John, with their wives, and in a parochial election held in 1768, Gregg gives in the list of voters, Thomas and two David Harry's. It is inferred therefore that one or more of them lived and reared families on Marlboro ground,

It is known that the late Mrs. Samuel Sparks was Miss Ann Harry, that her father died when she was a child, and his widow married David Mandeville; and the first wife of the late Jesse David, as we have seen, was a Miss Harry, and a sister of hers was married to Mr. Sam Crosland, who went to Kentucky, and these latter ladies were not sisters to Mrs. Sparks. It is therefore likely that there were more than one of these Harry's among the early settlers of Marlboro. The name is extinct here now.

It is said that the father of Judge Evans married Miss Elizabeth Hodges, who was a sister of Captain George Hodges, of lower Marlboro. There seems to have been a large family of Hodges upon the Pee Dee. Few families gave more soldiers to the Revolution than this one. We have already seen that the maternal ancestor of the present David family in the county was of this name. Capt. George Hodges married Sarah, a daughter of George Cherry, who was a prominent citizen of Marion county, then called Liberty. The writer has a distinct recollection of Captain Hodges. He commanded a company in the same regiment in which Evans was major in the War of 1812. My friend, Dr. J. H. Lane, placed in my hands a manuscript record of courts martial and general orders, extending from July 15 to October 22, 1812, in which the names of Evans and Hodges frequently occur as members of these courts, and as otherwise connected with the affairs of the regiment, and in a careful reading of the entire record no mention is made of either that would indicate the slightest suspicion of any dereliction of duty: and of the captain, as well as of his company, which was partly at least of Marlboro men, no member is named as having been arraigned before a court martial during these three months; while a good many of other commands were tried, convicted and sentenced; and whatever other sentence of punishment was imposed by the courts, they seldom failed to order that the "daily grog ration" should be withheld. Was it that Hodges' men so loved "grog" that no misdemeanor was indulged in lest the precious ration should be withheld? or are we to infer that the behavior of his men was superior to others? or was it that his discipline and administration of affairs was so sound, that there was no occasion for punishment? The testimony of tradition says, that while firm and strict, he was kind and indulgent, and commanded the respect and affection of his men. If his men feared his displeasure as the boys did, when he shook his gray locks at us for any misbehavior in church, good order would reign in his presence at least. He was spared to see a large family grow up to maturity. Mrs. Hodges and one of the young ladies returning to their home from a visit in the neighborhood were dashed against a tree by a frightened horse, and Mrs. Hodges was killed and the young lady injured. The "old captain," heart broken, lingered a few months in his sorrow and joined his companion in the beyond. The young men in the Brownsville community of this name, and Messrs. P. A. and J. L. Hodges are grandsons of this excellent pair, and so, likewise, was R. H. Hodges, who was a member of the recent Constitutional Convention, and who died while the Convention was in session.

A daughter of "old Col. Tom" Evans and a sister of the Judge, Miss Rebecca, married Charles Irby, who was also a prominent member of the Brownsville community. About 1826 Mr. Irby was elected a member of the Legislature. The writer, though but a boy, can remember the sudden death of the grand, portly old man, and how the neighborhood was moved in sympathy with his large family of sons and daughters in their bereavement; and how they were missed in society and schools of the neighborhood, when, a few years later, the family removed to Alabama. The oldest son, John, married Miss Catharine

Allison, and soon after died in the prime of his young manhood, leaving an only child who grew to womanhood, and became the first wife of the late Henry Rogers, and mother of Thomas Irby Rogers, of Bennettsville, and several other sons and daughters. Mr. Irby's widow, after some years, became the first wife of John C. Bethea, of Marion, and the mother of the well-known excellent farmer, of the Buck Swamp region, Ed. C. Bethea.

Another sister of Judge Evans married Christopher Pegues, from whom descended a numerous connection, and whose influence tended largely to shape affairs on the upper Pee Dee, in the neighborhood of Cheraw. The grandfather of Mr. Pegues, named Claudius, "came to Pee Dee about 1760, and settled on the east side of the river, not far below the State line; was of French descent, married a Miss Butler in Charleston, moved first to Georgetown, and from thence came to this region, and at once took an active part in the affairs of the country." His two sons, Claudius and William, reached manhood. The latter married Miss Elizabeth Murphy and settled on the the west side of the river. His second wife was a Miss Gardner. He is said to have been a man of cultivated tastes, and a staunch Whig and suffered much from Tory hate and robbery. Claudius married Miss Marcia Murphy and settled on the Marlboro side of the Pee Dee. He, too, was a man of fine character, active in all that pertained to the welfare of his country; was a captain in the war for independence, an ordinary for the district of Cheraw, more than once a representative in the Legislature, and a county court justice for Marlboro. This family has, from their first settlement in the country, been prominent in every laudable enterprise. Two sons of this name have been honored ministers of the South Carolina Conference. Randolph, noble soul, of manly bearing, gentle spirit, in the prime of his usefulness, was "gathered to his fathers." While Wesley, an older brother, with silvered locks, stood yet longer on the heights of Zion and warned men to repent. A number of young men bearing the honored name live among us, to yet reflect luster upon their worthy ancestry

CHAPTER IV.

OTHER EARLY SETTLERS.

In 1743, a name appears among the early grantees of land in the Welsh Neck which was destined to be prominent in the history of Marlboro—Nicholas Rogers, a Welshman. He died in 1759, but left a son Benjamin, who lived on the west side of the Pee Dee, a few miles below Cheraw—an ardent Whig, of excellent character, and held in high esteem by his neighbors. Of his sons, mention may be made of two as prominent citizens of Marlboro. Of a third, Nicholas, we have heard, but know nothing. A daughter married a Mr. Pearson, and lived some miles above Cheraw. John Rogers, a son of the first Ben, married Miss Mary Griffin, and lived and died at what is now known as the Dr. McLeod place. He was a member the Legislature, 1808-1809. The fruit of this marriage was three sons, and as many daughters. The first of these daughters married Dr. Francis Lee, and went West. Another was the first wife of Gen. McQueen, who was a lawyer at Bennettsville, and a member of Congress for several terms, and resigned his seat when the State seceded from the Union. A third daughter, Miss Martha, a lady of splendid form, fine character, and superior intellect, became the first wife of Dr. Alexander McLeod, a native of North Carolina, a successful popular physician, a member of the Secession Convention, the father of several sons, and a daughter who became the wife of Capt. C. M. Weatherly. The sons of Mr. Rogers were John M., Benjamin and Robert. John was talented and popular; elected to the Legislature in 1828, but in the midst of his career of promise he was stricken in death. Robert, also, was a noble, brilliant young man, just grown, when, by an accidental shot from his own gun, he was instantly killed. Hardly any young man in the community was more beloved, or could have been more sincerely mourned. The other son, B. N. Rogers, married Miss McQueen, of Chesterfield.

The good man left a family of sons and daughters to mourn his departure to a better state.

Another son of the first Benjamin Rogers was Col. Ben, who resided in Brownsville. By his first marriage he became the father of nine daughters, and nine sons were given him as the fruit of a second marriage with Mrs. Wickam, who also had a daughter by her first marriage. This daughter first married John C. Ellerbe, of Marion, and after his death she became the second wife of Dr. B. K. Henagan. Most fondly does the writer remember the manly form of Col. Ben Rogers, as the neighbor of his father and a friend to all the boys; universally respected, full of energy and push, even in his old age. He was an early sheriff of Marlboro, a Colonel of Militia, a State Senator, a patron of schools, a friend of the churches, and beloved by his servants. He was young in years when the struggle with the mother country came on, but with the ardor of youth and the enthusiasm of an impulsive spirit he drew his sword in the cause of liberty, and to his dying day his face beamed and his eye kindled with an ardent devotion to his country's weal. He was killed at last by a falling tree, the felling of which he was himself directing for plantation purposes. Noble, polite, generous, public spirited, grand old man, we saw him buried, and it is a sad, yet precious privilege, occasionally, to visit his tomb at old Brownsville, where he sleeps between the bodies of the two women whom he loved with the tenderness and devotion that was the admiration of all who knew him in his hospitable home.

His first born son, whom we called "Major Ben," sleeps in that same consecrated plat of ground. He was for awhile in command of the "Lower Battalion" of Marlboro militia. A man of calm, cool temperament, highly respected by his neighbors, they induced him to stand for a seat in the State Legislature in 1846, and he was elected and served; but he would consent no more to ask his countrymen to send him to Columbia, preferring the enjoyments of his own comfortable, hospitable home to the turmoil and excitement of political life. B. B. Rogers, courteous friend, successful planter, his death made a sad void in the community. "Where are the nine?" One only at this writing remains above the earth, Col. John Rogers, of Florence. His silken hair of snowy white proclaims him an old man. Like most of his brothers, he is remembered as a splendid specimen of manhood, the pride of his parents, the soul of politeness, the life of his circle. When he shall rest in the tomb the last of his generation will have gone. But another generation is already upon the scene, doing credit to the name they bear. The present Sheriff of Marlboro (1890) bearing the family name, Ben, is the first born of Maj. B. B. Rogers and Miss Elizabeth Allison, a beautiful woman, the youngest of four sisters. The others were Eliza, who became the second wife of Maj. Rogers; Catharine, who first married John Irby, and after his early death, became the wife of John C. Bethea; Caroline, who married Charles Brown, and became the mother of Mrs. T. L. Crosland. Mrs. Allison was Miss Betsy Whittington, and first married a Mr. McTier and had two sons, William and Robert, and a daughter, Mrs. Henry DeBerry, who, for a long time, lived at Parnassus. Both McTier and Allison are extinct names in Marlboro. There was a young son, Tom Allison, whose death in his brilliant boyhood profoundly grieved the hearts of his comrades and kinsmen.

The Sparks name is to be set down as one of the earliest in this region. Four brothers, Daniel, Charles, Samuel and Harry, are said to have come from Virginia to the

Pee Dee. Harry, a noted Whig, was killed by a band of
Tories in the swamps of Three Creeks. Daniel, the eldest
brother, settled at first not far from and on the east side
from Bennettsville, but afterwards moved to Red Hill. He
married Miss Martha Pearce, a lady of fine character, who
lived to old age, retaining both her mental and physical
vigor in a marked degree. Full of good works, she ultimately sank into the grave lamented by all. Three sons
and four daughters blessed the lot of this pair.

Samuel, who spent his four-score years and more in
Marlboro, first married Miss Allison, and had a son,
Charles, who died young. His second wife was Miss Ann
Harry. Two children were born to them, the late Capt.
A. D. Sparks, and Mrs. Keitt, whose brave husband, L.
M. Keitt, poured out his life's blood upon the red soil of
Virginia in the late war.

One sister of Mr. Sparks married John Crosland of
Marlboro. Another (Lucy) first married Alex Stubbs
and afterwards Thomas Stubbs, and a daughter, Mrs. E.
W. Goodwin, was the fruit of the latter union. A third
sister married William Pouncy, as stated elsewhere in these
pages. Martha, the other sister, died unmarried.

The Crosland family is another of those which dates
back to near the middle of the last century. Edward
Crosland, an ophan boy, of Virginia, thrown upon his
own resources, devoloped an enterprising, adventurous
spirit. He came to Carolina about 1760, and united himself with a party of kindred spirits in the central part of
the province, and traveled extensively in North Carolina,
went across the mountains into Kentucky, from thence to
the Ohio river, down that stream to the Mississippi and
thence to New Orleans. Returning to North Carolina
Mr. Crosland married a daughter of Samuel Snead, and
settled near the boundary line. Subsequently he came to
Marlboro and settled not far from Gardner's Bluff and
reared a large family. His sons were John, Samuel, Dan-

iel M., Israel, David, George, Philip and Dr. William and several daughters. A number of his descendants are now numbered among the respected citizens of the County, while many more have yielded to the inexorable law of destiny, and have gone to people other more western States and build up other communities towards the setting sun.

Another name no longer found in Marlboro is entitled to mention, not only because of the part the family bore in the early history of the country, but because the blood has coursed in veins that have borne other names and made honorable records on history's page. In 1758 Thomas Ayer came to Pee Dee. A native of Ireland, he spent some time in Virginia before coming to Carolina. It is said that he settled on the east side of Pee Pee river a little below Hunt's Bluff, set up a trading establishment and made money. An ardent Whig, he risked life and fortune in the cause of liberty. Lewis Malone, the father of the late Gen. L. M. Ayer, of Anderson, and of Mrs. Judge A. P. Aldrich, was a son of the grand old Irish patriot. So also was the venerable Hartwell Ayer, who lived at the place where J. B. Breeden recently died. Hartwell Ayer had a son, William, who left a family near Fayetteville, N. C., and three daughters, Mrs. Long of sainted memory, Mrs. J. B. Breeden and Mrs. Marshall; noble women of noble deeds, farewell!

There were a number of other families that settled on the Pee Dee about the middle of the eighteenth century, who contributed their full quota to the civilization and opening up of the country, and have left their impress upon its welfare, but in most instances the names have become extinct, although in some cases the blood flows in their descendants of other names in Marlboro; in other instances the names no longer known here are honorably borne in adjoining counties or distant States. Bishop Gregg has done a good work in recording them in his history. His name, among them, is worthy of enduring remembrance, alongside such as Murphy, Hicks, Wilson, Lide, Robertson, Allison, Bedgegood, Lewis, Luke and others as worthy of mention. Pioneers in a new land, they lived in troublous times, and the hardships of subduing an unbroken forest to cultivation, opening roads, building bridges, erecting churches and school-houses, and preparing the way for liberty, prosperity, education and religion to take root and thrive in the new world as it had never done in the old—is never to be forgotten by a grateful posterity.

CHAPTER V.

Other Brownsville Families.

Since reference has frequently been made to this ancient community it is fit that we linger among some of the older names that impressed themselves upon its society. With the main body of Welshmen, or soon after, came John Brown, born near Burlington, N. J., and brought up near Frankfort in the neighborhood of Philadelphia. He came South and united with the colony about the Neck. He was ordained to the gospel ministry May 7, 1750, and succeeded Philip James as pastor of the church at Welsh Neck; but, for some reason did not continue long in that relation, but devoted his ministry to other regions, and was instrumental in organizing a church at Cashway Ferry, with a membership on both sides of the river. Either he or his son, Samuel, had settled on Muddy Creek and built a mill some years before the Revolutionary War began, and near the mill, on both sides of the Creek, a number of prosperous families were settled. Ardent Whigs, it soon became a stronghold of liberty, and the prominence of the Brown family about this time gave name to the Brownsville community. It is not known how many sons the old pastor had, or when he died: It is, however, a well-established tradition that the prominent family of this name on the west side of Pee Dee in the Mars Bluff and Florence region are descended from this old Welsh preacher; and that John and Jeremiah, grandsons of his, moved to Alabama and became prominent in that State. William, another grandson of the old pastor, and a son of Samuel, lived and died near the mill and in sight of the old church, which, after the war, was moved out to the present location. Mr. Brown had four sons and a daughter. The daughter marrried a Mr. Law, of Darlington. The four sons were young men of excellent character. Samuel died unmarried. James lived but a short time after his marriage and left no son. William Brown, one of my early schoolmasters, went West. Charles Brown married Miss Allison, and in the person of Mrs. T. L. Crosland and her interesting young family, alone flows the blood of the men whose characters and influence gave name to an extensive township of lower Marlboro.

William Magee, or as the name was sometimes spelled, McGee, was an early settler in this portion of country. A daughter of his, Martha, became the wife of Rev. Evan Pugh and a daughter by this marriage, Elizabeth by name, was the excellent wife of Mr. Hugh Lide, of Darlington, from whom a splendid family descended. Another daughter of Mr. Magee was the mother of the late Capt. Hodges, of Marlboro. James, a son of Mr. Magee, lived at what has since been known as the Bruce place, about a mile below the site of the old Brownsville church, and there reared a large family. A son, Hartwell, moved into the upper part of the State. Another, Zacheus, went West. The youngest daughter was the first wife of the writer's father, William Thomas. And among the relatives of the first family of children, who sometimes visited us, Rev. William Kennedy, a noted preacher of the S. C. Conference, is remembered. A son of his, the polished F. M. Kennedy, was not less distinguished at a later date. Mr. Magee was noted for his correct Christian character, was a conscientious Whig, and a member of Marion's brigade. He came near losing his life on the day after Col. Kolb was killed, being on the road from his home to Long Bluff on a military mission to the Colonel when Lewis M. Ayer, whose sister Mr. Magee married, at the risk of his own life, and with a narrow escape, intercepted and saved. He lived to see the opening years of the present century, and died suddenly, sitting in his chair with the open Bible upon his knee.

The magistrate of the community and the State Senator, seventy years ago, was Robeson Carloss. He came from Virginia about 1790 and settled on the Pee Dee and married the beautiful and accomplished daughter of Baron Poelnitz, who was at the time, the young widow of Col. Evans, and had been the wife, first of Charles Stuart. The Carloss name is extinct in Marlboro, but through the late Mrs. Light Townsend, the blood flows in the veins of several of our excellent families, viz.: J. R. Townsend, John Irby. T. E. Dudley and F. W. Kinney. So, too, the name of Poelnitz is unknown among us only as it is represented in the above good people. It is fit that another name should be mentioned in connection with Carloss, not because there was any kinship, but because 'Squire Carloss exercised a large influence over Mason Lee, the greatest oddity of his day, and was the executor of his will, if not the writer of it. Lee was a bachelor of considerable property, owning a large plantation on the river just below Cashway Ferry. His will directed that the principal part of his property be given to the States of Tennessee and South Carolina. That if the Wiggins, his natural heirs at law, should contest the will, his executors should employ the best legal talent in the State to defend it, and never allow the Wiggins to have any part of it, "so long as wood grew or water ran." The will was contested upon the ground of mental imbecility, and such "legal lights" as Chancellor Harper, Wm. C. Preston, Judge Evans, Col. Blanding and Col. J. R. Irvin exercised their great powers on the one side or the other in the trial, a record of which is "in the books." The case terminated at last in the establishment of the will. The grave of Lee is another spot at the "old Brownsville graveyard," where memory lingers. It was covered over with brick made in the neighborhood about 1820, and fifty years ago a tree, nearly a foot in diameter, which had been killed by lightning, fell diagonally across the grave, displacing a few but not breaking any bricks, and to-day those old brick lie in good shape, firm and strong above the dust of Mason Lee. Such were his singularities, and so much was said of him in my boyhood days that it seems to me as if I used to see him ride past the door on his way to Carloss' on a mule whose "ears had been shaved off at the skull," seated upon a saddle "hewed out of a hollow gum," his feet in "grapevine stirrups," a blanket "tied over his shoulders," with a "coon skin cap upon his head," and yet Lee was buried two or three years before I was born. The earless mules, once his, did survive their old master for years, and their appearance upon the road was real.

Let us linger yet longer among the old families of this ancient community. Emanuel Coxe came at an early day, long before the war with the mother country and when the conflict came, himself and several sons enrolled themselves on the side of liberty. Bishop Gregg mentions James, John, Josiah, Samuel and William. The tradition as received from our fellow citizen, Mr. James E. Coxe, names all these except Josiah, but mentions three others as sons of Emanuel and as having been soldiers of the Revolution, viz.: Ezekiel, Jesse and Benjamin. It may be that the name Josiah, as given by Gregg, is a mistake, and ought to be Jesse, or one of the others. It is inferred that whoever was meant by Josiah, means a son of this old Brownsville patriarch, because he is enrolled as a member of Capt. Moses Pearson's company, who was himself a resident of this community. However that may be, it is beyond question that few families in the Pee Dee region, numbering no more men has furnished a larger proportion to the cause of independence. Samuel Coxe, the son of Emanuel, and the grandfather of our friend, Jas. E., was quite noted for his valor and services. Crossing over Brown's mill-dam one night a Tory tried to shoot him, but his gun missing fire, Coxe arrested and carried him a prisoner to the American camp. Mr. Coxe lived to a great age, until most of his comrades were gone. His neighbors on the fourth of July sometime in the forties, honored him with the first place at a barbecue. This was his last dinner, for in the afternoon he mounted his horse, and crossing over the same mill-dam, where his Tory neighbor had sought his life, he had nearly reached his home a mile or so beyond, when his horse took fright and the old patriot fell off, and in a few days was no more. Two of his sons, Capt. Moses E. and Ezra, were soldiers of the war 1812-14. The former never married, but was an excellent citizen, who lived to see yet another war of greater dimension, and died a few years after peace was made. Ezra married Miss Ann B. Bass, of Marion, and was the father of James E., Dr. Robt. A., and Edwin M., noble boy who fought his way through many a conflict in the late war till he was made a prisoner, and died at Newport News only the day before he was to have been released from his captivity.

John Coxe, another son of Emanuel, married a Miss Mixon and was the father of eight children. A daughter, Fanny, married John Hood and became the mother of a large family of that name yet represented in the old neighborhood. A son, Eli, first married a Miss Stroud and raised a large family. Charles, Daniel and Hugh all growing old, yet survive. His second wife, Miss Ann Haskew, yet lives, but had no children. Eli Coxe also rendered faithful service in the war of 1812, in the company of Capt. Tristram Bethea, and if he saw no bloodshed he retained a vivid and intelligent recollection of events connected with his soldier life. Honest, truthful and correct, he went to the grave respected and lamented by his neighbors. A brother of his lived just across the creek and raised a large family also, and left a blameless reputation behind him when he died.

William Coxe, another son of Emanuel, was perhaps more distinguished for his revolutionary record than either of his brothers because his services were more continuous. He was one of those patriotic "sons of liberty" who could not be content at his fireside so long as the enemy trod the shores of the New World. If not needed in one place, he would get a transfer to a more active sphere. And yet, when the war was over no man more loved the sweets of peace. No more inoffensive man has lived upon the waters of Muddy Creek than he. He was twice married and was the father of twenty children. Two sons and nine grandsons of his had places in companies raised in Marlboro for Confederate service, and no one knows how many more from among those who had made their homes in other States of the South. A son-in-law, Jeremiah Coxe, a grandson of the venerable Samuel, went into the Seminole War of 1835 and died in the service away from his home, in the savannas of Florida. The late Michael Coxe, a fine workman in iron especially, and who made some excellent improvements in the plow, and was well and favorably known in Masonic circles for a long time, was a son of this venerable patriarch and soldier of 1776. The Mr. James Coxe who married Miss Hubbard and raised a family in the Brightsville region, was a grandson of old Mr. Samuel Coxe. His father's name was Aaron, who married a Miss Spears, aunt of Lewis and Harris Spears, of Hebron. There were other children who went West.

The Townsend family, which has been prominent in Marlboro for many years may also be placed among the original settlers of this portion of the country. The first to come, so far as our information goes, was Light, who is put down as an active soldier of the Revolution. He is said to have been the father of two children, John and Rhoda, both of whom the writer distinctly recollects as among the old people, in the days of his youth. Light

Townsend was the only son of John who remained long in Marlboro. He was a man of indomitable energy, and large native intellect. He gathered a large fortune by his industry and skill, and left his young family in comfortable circumstances. Another son of old John was long and favorably known as a member of the South Carolina Conference and left a family in the upper part of the State. The late Mrs. Kinney, mother of Capt. Frank Kinney and his excellent sisters, was a daughter; and the second wife of Jabish N. Townsend was another. Besides these there were other children born to "Uncle John and Aunt Kissy," as the venerable couple were familiarly called, who moved West. The larger portion of this numerous connection, however, are descended from Rhoda, through the three sons, Benjamin, Jabish and Samuel. The former was the ancestor of the young men of the name now living a few miles above Bennettsville. The brilliant Col. Knox Livingston, of Bennettsville, is a grandson of Samuel Townsend, who lived for a long time in the very heart of the Brownsville community, and when an old man removed to Florida with a large family of sons and daughters. Jabish Townsend, the other son of Rhoda, married Bettie Spears and a numerous family came from this union. Meekin, the father of Judge C. P. Townsend, and others, was a man of keen intellect, popular manners, and great energy. He served his people quite acceptably as sheriff and died in the strength and vigor of manhood. Maj. B D. Townsend, so long and favorably known in Bennettsville as a merchant and patron of temperance, and afterwards as a citizen of Society Hill and a successful railroad president, was also a son of Jabish T. Townsend. So, too, was Samuel J., who successfully practiced law in Bennettsville and was elected to the Legislature. Of quick mind and ready speech, he seemed capable of large attainments, but was cut off in the midst of his career by the relentless reaper. Jabish N., father of John C. and others, was also a son of this old man; another son went West. Besides these the Galloways and some of the Pearsons are descended from the same source. It is indeed amazing how many of our people, and how many others, West and South, may trace their lineage back to Hilson's Bay and to the first Light, who left but two children to bear his name, to the generations coming after him.

CHAPTER VI

Pearson Family, and Others.

We begin this chapter with the name Pearson, which has been largely represented in all the years of our history. The first was Aaron, who came from one of the English settlements of Virginia in colonial times. He was the father of two sons, Aaron and Moses. The latter owned, and lived upon, what was called the "big plantation," now known as "Lowdon." He was prominent in Revolutionary affairs. First, as Lieutenant in Hicks' Regiment in 1780, and in the two following years a captain in Benton's Regiment. After the war his name frequently appeared upon the records of the old Brownsville church, as well as upon those of the county courts. He was one of the first justices of Marlboro and seems to have presided over the court, and before the county was organized he held position and took part in judicial affairs in the old district of Cheraw. He is said to have been the father of fifteen children, eight sons and seven daughters. One daughter became Mrs. Haskew, another Mrs. Galloway, and the Johns are some way connected with this old family. Thomas, one of the sons, was the ancestor of the Messrs. Moses and Zacheus Pearson. Mrs. Joel Easterling, John D. Pearson and Mrs. Rachel Townsend are descended from another.

Aaron, the other son of Aaron the first, was also a soldier of the Revolution. He married a Miss Spears and another Aaron was the fruit of this marriage. He in turn married Miss Ann Vining, who became the mother of several daughters and two sons, Thomas, who moved to Alabama, and the late John Pearson, of Bruten's Fork, who, at an advanced age, passed away only a few years ago. It is fit that credit be given him for much information embodied within these pages. His health was remarkably preserved, and his vigor of body and mind, when past four-score, was a marvel. Not only did he love to live over in thought the scenes and enjoyments of his earlier years, and to tell of his experiences as a soldier of the war of 1812, but he manifested a lively interest in passing events, and the employments of people of another generation.

The Haskews mentioned in connection with the Pearsons are worthy of a more special notice. Two of these old men are remembered. John is entitled to a place among the old heroes of the Revolution. His name is upon Marion's muster roll as "John Askew," the initial H omitted, and yet no difficulty was found in proving his claim to a pension when so many living witnesses were found to testify to his presence and services. Quiet, inoffensive old man! At a great age he was thrown from a vehicle in which he was riding and received fatal injuries. Thomas H. Haskew is a grandson. Zacheus was the other brother, a younger man than John, and more successful in the affairs of this life. He was the father of the excellent ladies, Mrs. Donaldson and Mrs. Bruce, from both of whom many good young people have sprung. A sister of these old men married a Mr. Britton, a son of whom, Hugh Britton, is remembered as one of the fine-looking young men of Brownsville society in the thirties.

In 1756 James Sweeny is supposed to have come to the Pee Dee. In some way the name was subsequently changed to Henagan. James Sweeny had a son, Barney, who had two sons, Darby and John. Darby was the father of B. K., Ephraim L. and Mrs. McCollum and Mrs. Lewis E. Stubbs. Dr. B. K. Henagan was not only prominent as a practicing physician fifty years ago, but as a politician also. In 1834 his people elected him to the State Senate and the Legislature elected him Lieutenant-Governor, and upon the death of Governor Noble, he was sworn in and filled out the unexpired term. He subsequently moved to Marion and was sent to the legislature again. Dr. Henagan's first wife was a Miss Gibson, an excellent lady, who became the mother of four sons and two daughters. One of these became the fourth wife of the late A. G. Johnson. The other married a Mr. Northrop. Only one of the splendid sons remains, Robert, who resides in the Florence neighborhood. Ephraim L. Henagan, a brother of the Governor, was in his day one of Marlboro's most popular men. He served a term in the office of sheriff and never sought position any more, but retired to his farm and devoted his great energies to the education and maintenance of his large and interesting family. His wife was Miss Nancy McInnis. Noble woman! Well she filled her place.

The first son in this family was John W., who never asked a position of the people that was not given him. He was sheriff of the county and a member of the Legislature in 1860–61, and in the militia had risen to a brigadier's commission when the war between the States came on; and at the first organization of the Eighth Regiment of South Carolina Volunteers he was elected Lieutenant-Colonel and at the reorganization became Colonel. In one of the engagements in Virginia he fell into the hands of the enemy and, like thousands more, died a prisoner. True to his country, beloved by his command, respected by his superiors, his death was a loss to his people. Other members of this family live to honor the name.

Connected with the Henagans, in the writer's memory, was Capt. Francis Miles, then an old man, in 1830. His wife, Mrs. Lucretia, was an aunt to the Henagans. This ancient couple had but a single child who bore the father's name, Francis, a gifted, modest young man capable of filling any position, but his great diffidence held him back.

When past the meridian of life he married his cousin, Amanda Henagan, and an only daughter resides in Alabama.

The Bruces have been for a long time in Brownsville. Wright Bruce married a widow, Cooper, and two sons, Joseph and Caleb, were given them, both of whom have left families in the vicinity. The Procters, Johnsons and Brigmans have also been upon the ground for many years. At a later date came the Allens, an excellent addition to the population—a mother with two sons and several daughters—from North Carolina. The two sons, Thompson and Joel, by the modest exhibition of real worth, soon took rank with the best citizens, and their sons after them still hold it.

Thomas J. J. DuPre came about 1830, bringing a family of young children, whose descendants are yet upon the ground. Simon Emanuel long lived in the community conducting a mercantile business. Of all these and more much might be penned, but justice to other portions of the county demands space in these pages. The names of two Burkitts, Ephraim and Samuel, must close our sojourn around the spot where our first infant steps were made. These old Burkitts, humble men though they were, wrote their names upon an honor roll with their swords in the days that tried men's souls, and, although the name is no more answered to in Marlboro, yet it is fit that it have mention here. Fifty years ago there were two or three families living in this old neighborhood bearing the name, but, like hundreds more, they have been swept westward by the tide of emigration, and have gone to people other States toward the setting sun. Let this chapter be closed with the record that, for the first fifty years of the present century, there was no place in Marlboro where the educational advantages were any better, if so good, as in Brownsville. The old men whose names have been given in these sketches sought the best talent to teach their children, and, for a time, young people from other and distant portions of the country crowded the academy. Peter Stuart Ney, said to have been the French marshal, was teaching here when Napoleon I. died on Helena. Here Sinclair, the first husband of Mrs. Nancy Cook, did faithful work. Kenneth Black, another noted teacher, here swayed the birch. Brown and McNab, young men "apt to teach," served their patrons well, and here it was that Donald Matheson was first introduced to the people of Marlboro, and introduced as an instructor of youth. Fair-faced, ruddy young Scotchman he was, but an intelligent, cultured gentleman. The elements of his character were of the robust, stern, muscular kind, rather than of the gentle and winning. For wrong-doing, meanness and vice he could have no patience, but loved truth, justice and right. His manner, to some, appeared distant, stern; even cold: Still he had a heart loving, true and warm, ready to respond to the touch of friendship, the cry of distress, the call of his country, and the needs of his church.

CHAPTER VII.

Industrial Affairs of the Early Settlers.

Coming from different parts of the earth, some for the sake of larger religious liberty, some for the love of adventure, and all with a desire to better their financial circumstances, there was everywhere dependence upon individual exertion as well as generous co-operation. The country, wild and uncleared abounding in forests of splendid timber, affording material for building and fencing purposes, a fertile soil, especially upon the banks of the river, with an abundance of fish and game. There was much to do, and much promise of reward to industry and skill. Fortunes were to be made by dint of perseverance and toil; various industries were pursued to meet the necessities of the times, and the sturdy settlers were equal to the situation. Some of those who emigrated from provinces further north are said to have driven their domestic animals across the country to their new homes, where abundant pasturage was found in the lowlands upon which their stock could graze. Large droves of cattle and horses ran wild through the forests and stock raising was at once a profitable business. Entrapping wild cattle and horses was an exciting yet profitable sport. A large, strong pen constructed in the fork of two branches or creeks, into which the frightened beasts were driven and caught, was a simple and favorite plan. Across the public road leading from Bennettsville to Blenheim, and a mile above the latter place, there flows a branch called "Horse Pen," which, according to the statement of the late venerable Daniel John, who was born, lived, and died near its confluence with the Three Creeks, got its name from a pen which was located at the fork and used for the purpose of entrapping wild horses in those early days. In other portions of the country immense herds of cattle were kept; vast numbers of hogs were raised largely upon the mast that fell from the trees, and driven to Charleston and other markets and sold for the best price that could be obtained, and supplies for the family at home brought back. It is not surprising, if exercise and hardship, in the saddle, upon the road, in the woods, amid peril and exposure, should develop the daring, enduring and faithful class of men who shared the dangers and honors of Marion, and such as he, amid the swamps of the Pee Dee and Santee in times a little farther on in the history of the country. It will be remembered, of course, that slavery was an institution of the times, and these early settlers sometimes bought and sold servants. It is told of one of these old stock men that he "gave seventy-seven seven-year-old steers for one woman."

Wheat and corn, especially the latter, was soon raised in abundance, and many a boat laden with corn floated down the Pee Dee to the towns on the coast; and bacon went to the markets by the same means, or was hauled across the country in wagons. Great rafts of timber and boards were floated on the same stream, so that the Pee Dee became a common channel of communication between the people on the coast and those in the interior, long before the age of cotton and steam, many obstructions to safe navigation being removed by private, and some by public enterprise. At an early period indigo became a profitable crop. The rich alluvial bottoms near the banks of the river were especially productive. Indeed, the plant grew wild in the woods, and as there was much demand for the dye in the markets of the world, and the plant a natural growth of the soil, it is not strange that it should soon become a principal article of export to the mother country. Parliament encouraged its cultivation; a bounty was allowed for the indigo raised in the

British American plantations, and tons of the precious stuff found its way to England. Fortunes were made in its cultivation and manufacture. And so by one means and another the settlements on the Pee Dee, almost from the beginning, were prosperous and encouraging, honest labor meeting a rich reward. As in the settlement of all new countries, difficulties and embarrassments had to be overcome, taking time and labor hardly appreciated by the residents in long-settled localities. Highways for travel and transportation, in a land as this was, of dense forests and streams, was a matter of serious concern. But "necessity is the mother of invention," and our fathers were equal to the exigencies of the situation. The first roads they opened were made just wide enough to admit the passage of a rough "sled," simple in construction but answering the purpose when wheels were not at hand. Two side-pieces of oak, with the front ends turned upward to reach the horse's shoulders, fastened together at the lower ends about three and a half or four feet apart, by cross bars, securely tenanted or pinned, it was ready for use. Fence rails were dragged, and fuel was drawn; a box added, and corn could be moved to the barn. Of course, wheels, better conveyances, and better roads had to be, and were provided as soon as concert of action and the necessary means were to be had. And as early as 1747 commissioners were appointed by the authorities of the province "to have the highways and causeways better attended," and the presumption is that about this time the "public road" that has long been known as the "River Road," taking the same general course as the stream, was opened. Then, after a few years, a public ferry was established by law, crossing the river at the mouth of Cedar Creek, a stream flowing in from the west side just above the present Society Hill bridge; and roads were opened out on either side the river, connecting with those running down the country. Thus it will be seen that the public spirited fathers were interested in measures contributing to the public welfare; and as the population increased, conveniences and comforts were also enlarged, and there is evidence that social and religious progress was not neglected. The planters had their meetings for consultation and social intercourse; and the old church at Welsh Neck had its pulpit regularly supplied by able, godly men, who went out after the increasing population, at points as remote as Cheraw, Cashway and elsewhere, as occasion offered, for preaching the Gospel.

From an early date attention began to be given to military affairs; indeed, from the first, some banding together of the people was needed for police regulations, and as a precaution against the raids of unfriendly Indians. So that as early as 1744 we read of the "Craven County Regiment, George Pawley, Colonel." And in 1756, Philip Pledger, a citizen of Marlboro, was "commissioned captain in His Majesty's service," and six years later, George Hicks, another resident of Marlboro, was also commissioned; and it is stated by the same authority (Gregg) that in January 1748, the Craven County regiment consisted of twelve hundred men, and that a general review of militia (the first in Marlboro) took place at Westfields, not far from Cheraw, Oct. 11, 1759. Up to this time very little dissatisfaction was felt in this southern province with the parent government, except the want of courts of justice, that were conveniently accessible. The people were happy in the enjoyment of each other's society on the few occasions when thrown together, and had a little world of their own where their intercourse was neighborly, hospitable and unrestrained. The influence of the sturdy, honest colony that planted itself upon either bank of the Pee Dee, at Welsh Neck, was the ruling element in society, and was felt for many miles around, and for many a year; and had the provincial Governors and Councils and parent government but consulted

the native love of liberty and sense of justice that rests
in the bosom of the true and brave, and fostered rather
than repressed the desire for just and equal rights, in
their subjects, we might have waited till now to set up for
Independence. But the time was coming, and causes
were beginning to operate, which in a few years more
must lead up to open rupture.

Prominent among those causes was the difficulty of
having their grievances and legal wrongs redressed. Except the courts of justices of the peace, which only had
jurisdiction in minor causes, there was no tribunal to which
they could appeal nearer than Charleston. The great
distance, with the expense and inconvenience of travel
made it exceedingly burdensome to jurors, witnesses and
parties to suits who had to attend Court. Consequently
many a man preferred to endure the wrong rather than
seek redress at such cost and trouble; and the evil disposed took liberties and committed crimes, with but little
fear of punishment. As the population increased, causes
of complaint multiplied. The people petitioned the provincial authorities for redress time and again, but all in
vain. They asked for courts to be established at more
accessible points, but no relief came in that way till a few
years before the war began. It was not surprising, therefore, that driven to extremities, the better class of citizens
should take affairs into their own hands, and devise means
of their own for preserving peace and securing their just
and equitable rights. Bands or clubs of men were organized calling themselves "Regulators." At the outset, composed as these bodies were, of conservative, prudent men,
cautious in the exercise of an assumed authority, the effect
may have been good in restraining the lawless and promoting good order and justice, not abusing the powers
they had assumed. But their action received no favor
from the government; on the other hand, they were regarded as prompted by a spirit of rebellion, and instead

of listening to their complaints, and providing redress,
the government sought to repress these disturbances, and
too oft employed instruments of little character—obse-
quious tools of power, who could command no respect,
but rather increased the irritation among the people by
their insolence, and still further weakened their regard
for a government represented so unworthily. But these
contests between the Regulators and the minions of the
government, were preparing the way for that greater contest which was to end in the independence of the Colonies.
If the actions of the Regulators displeased the government, no less were the Regulators exasperated by the
coldness and indifference with which their appeals were
treated, culminating in opposition and reprehension and
commands from the government to disperse. No marvel
if "horse thieves" and harborers of rogues should meet
with more stripes and severer punishment from men, not
only provoked by these crimes, but angered by the opposition of the government that sought to hinder what they
deemed an indispensable remedy. Nor is it strange that,
under such circumstances, another and unlawful party
should be banded in opposition to the Regulators—that
thieves and robbers should unite to resist self-assumed
authority, to arrest and lynch them for their crimes. Such
a state of things could not long exist without ending in
open rupture, and the government appears to have fore-
seen yet greater trouble ahead if some concessions were
not made. Therefore in 1768, by an act of the Assembly
the "Parish of St. David" was organized. It was to embrace a vast extent of country in what was then called
Craven county, on both sides of the Great Pee Dee river.
Of course, this organization was in part designed to be ec-
clesiastical, but civil as well, Church and State united. Commissioners were "appointed for the building of the church
chapel and parsonage house," and to otherwise inaugurate
the affairs of St. David's church. By the same act the

inhabitants of the Parish were entitled to elect one member to the General Assembly, to open and keep in repair the public roads, and the "church wardens and overseers of the poor," were authorized to levy taxes to relieve the poor committed to their charge. And it may be stated that the following citizens of Marlboro had appointments on this first board of commissioners—Claudius Pegues, Philip Pledger, George Hicks, Robert Allison and Charles Bedingfield. This was not all the people asked for; but it was something gained. With a member in the General Assembly, chosen by their own free ballot, they indulged the hope that farther relief might be obtained. On the fourth and fifth days of October, 1768, an election was held and Claudius Pegues, by a vote of 166, was unanimously elected the first representative of St. David's, or of Upper Pee Dee in the General Assembly of South Carolina. He had been but about eight years in the country, and it is greatly to his credit that so brief a residence among his people should have so impressed them with a sense of his worth as that they should commit to his charge interests that were so precious; and yet he is described as "retiring in disposition and habits," He must have been known to be capable, faithful, devoted to the public welfare, and the sacred rights of his countrymen.

But the parochial organization was not adapted to meet the wants of the growing country; the people "were yet without a court easy of access," where justice could be administered. The necessity for some local tribunal was more and more imperative, and after the most urgent and persistent entreaties, a bill was passed July 27, 1769, and signed by Governor Bull, Aug. 2d, organizing "circuit or district courts to be held at Orangeburg, Ninety-Six, the Cheraws, Georgetown, Beaufort and Charleston, to sit six days each, and to be held twice a year, for the trial of causes criminal and civil." This was a large

and satisfactory concession to the people, and quieted for
a time the apprehensions of a general collision, and promoted the prosperity and peace of the country. The
Cheraw District embraced that region included within St.
David's Parish and what subsequently became Darlington,
Chesterfield and Marlboro. "George Hicks, Thomas Lide,
Jonathan Wise, Benjamin Rogers and Eli Kershaw were
appointed commissioners to build a court-house and jail."
This work, however, was delayed by an unfortunate controversy as to the location. Cheraw was growing as a
place of trade; there St. David's, the State church, was
being established; it was at the head of navigation, considered healthy and accessible, and Cheraw very naturally
wanted the court-house of the District of Cheraw. Long
Bluff, on the west side of the river, near Society Hill, was
a contestant. It, too, was a place of trade, near the sacred
spot where the first ancient colony of Welsh first built
their altars surrounded on both sides of the river by a
thrifty, intelligent population, nearer the center of the
district and therefore more convenient to the great body
of the people. Owing to this controversy, the work of
building was hindered until August 1770, when, by an act
of the General Assembly, the commissioners were ordered
to build at Long Bluff. After some delay substantial
buildings were erected, and on Monday, Nov. 16, 1772,
the long-sought privilege of a suffering people was enjoyed of seeing a court open upon their own ground, where
causes criminal and civil were to be settled by judges
"learned in the law," and by "juries of their peers." The
administration of justice was introduced by invoking the
favor of Heaven, and the direction of Infinite wisdom.
Rev. Nicholas Bedgegood, a man long known and honored in Marlboro, the pastor of Welsh Neck church, preached what was termed a "sessions sermon," enforcing the duties and responsibilities of those in authority, as well as
those devolving upon the subjects of law in every con-

dition of society, and directing the thoughts of all to a judgment yet to come, when the Judge of all the earth should fix unalterably the destiny of His creatures. From that day Long Bluff became the resort of lawyers and judges; and a center of influence and interest to an extensive territory. Dark deeds of crime were there to meet due reward; and stern justice be meted out to all classes, and for a time, at least, became a forum for legal lore and contest. Justices Gordon and Murray were the first to preside, and Wm. Henry Mills was the first sheriff in Cheraw District. It is not known if there was a resident lawyer in the district for a number of years, but such men as Powell, Waties and Brevard are supposed to have practiced in the courts at this place. About the close of the war, in consideration, it is presumed, of the efficient services rendered the cause of liberty by Gen. Greene, the name of the little court-house village was changed to Greeneville. But the formation of three judicial districts, Darlington, Chesterfield and Marlboro, out of the old Cheraw district, caused, of course, the removal of the records and all legal business to other localities, and the town gradually went to decay. And the plowshare was ultimately driven through the streets and public ground, upturning the very soil on which the public buildings stood. The long high bluff making the western bank of the Pee Dee yet lifts its front to greet the rising sun, but no longer is the historic ground called Greeneville. Society Hill, a mile or two from the river, a place of considerable trade, the home of a cultivated, intelligent people, has long been the center of influence and resort for the surrounding country.

CHAPTER VIII.

The Family of Col. Kolb and Some of Their Neighbors.

In 1751 the name Kolb first appeared upon the Pee Dee—a name which was destined to become distinguished in after time, and ultimately to become extinct, at least upon the east side of the river. Several men of this name appear in the early records, viz.: Jacob, Henry, Martin and Peter. Whether all brothers, or one a father and the others sons, does not appear. Peter married Ann, the eldest daughter of Rev. Philip James, first pastor of the Welsh Neck church. Col. Abel, who became so distinguished in Revolutionary affairs, and at last sealed his devotion to the cause with his blood, was a son of this marriage. He also married a Miss James and two daughters were given them. Sarah was first married to Benjamin David, and afterwards to Philip Pledger. Ann, the other daughter, became the wife of Maj. James Pouncey. We are to hear of Col. Kolb hereafter, and must be content in this chapter to trace the record of Maj. Pouncey and the noble partner of his life. The father of Maj. Pouncey was named William, and died young, leaving but one other child, a daughter, who married Alex Peterkin. A brother Anthony, was a soldier of the Revolution and held for a time the position of quartermaster in Murphy's regiment, and a sister of these was the mother of the late Daniel John. To Maj. Pouncey and his wife were given four sons and five daughters. William, once the sheriff of Marlboro, married Miss Sarah Sparks. James first married Mary Pledger and afterwards Mary Ferniss. John married Miss Armstrong and Peter Miss Adeline Hodges. The daughters married, Sarah to Daniel M. Crosland and was the honored mother of our fellow citizens, W. A. and

T. L. Crosland. Ann married Mr. Smith of North Carolina. Eliza was the first wife of Dr. Wm. Crosland. Mary was the wife of Dr. R. S. Thomas, and Ellen married C. M. Cochrane, and not long since was yet alive. The name Cochrane, although extinct among us, is nevertheless numerously represented both in Marlboro and Marion. Thomas Cochrane, the first we know of him, lived on Crooked Creek near the site of the old Court House. His first wife was a Miss Council, connected in some way with the Pledgers. The fruit of this marriage was Robt. C., the father of Mrs. Simon Emanuel; Mary, the first wife of John Hamer, Margaret, the wife of James Bethea, and Rachel who married Philip Bethea. And from all these have sprung large families. The second wife of Thomas Cochrane was a Miss Griffin, whose daughter by a former marriage was the wife of John Rogers, and the issue of this second union was Louisa, who married Henry Covington, who lived at Bennettsville in the early years of its history. Martha married Thomas Cargill and had a son who died unmarried. Mr. Cochrane's third wife was a widow Hunter and this marriage was crowned with the birth of Claudius M., mentioned above as the son-in-law of Maj. Pouncey.

From the old family record, from which the above paragraph is taken, another extract will be here made, although it takes us into a locality a little more distant from "the Neck." About 1750 Nathaniel Spears, a native of England, came to Virginia. While there he married Lidia Wise, and soon after came to Carolina and staked down upon the banks of the Three Creeks. Two sons and a daughter were born to this ancient couple, when Mr. Spears died, and his widow married a Mr. Trawick. The daughter, as we have already recorded, married the second Aaron Pearson. One son, David, who is put down as a private in Benton's regiment, 1781-82, raised a family of whom one daughter became the wife of Aaron Coxe, to whom reference has already been made, and a son married a daughter of Robt. Cochrane and went West. The other son, William, married Miss Nancy Breeden, and was the father of a large family. Among his sons two yet remain in the Hebron community, Lewis and Harris. Alfred Parish, Daniel McLeod and Robert Thomas and William Lee married daughters, and William Spears married a Miss Bridges and went to Arkansas. It is alone in this Hebron family that the name Spears, as derived from Nathaniel, is now borne by living men in Marlboro. Nathaniel's other son was James, who married Lidia Meekins. Four sons and five daughters were given this couple. One son, Meekins, died unmarried. Another, David, married Margaret McRae and died childless. James married Deborah Bethea, daughter of James Bethea of Marion and a granddaughter of Thomas Cochrane. To this pair ten children were born. Andrew and Edwin, the only sons, both died young and left no children to bear the name. Ann became the wife of Thomas E. Stubbs. Margaret has been the partner of the writer of these lines for forty-seven years. Martha was the wife of Duncan Moore, Emily became the wife of Isaac Pipkin, and Eliza, first wife of E. C. Pipkin and Rebecca the first wife of Dr. W. J. David. The other two daughters died young. Mrs. Stubbs and Mrs. Thomas alone are living.* Mr. Spears was a man of large brain, great firmness of character, systematic and orderly in all his movements, and Mrs. Spears was every way worthy of his devotion, and if their name has not been transmitted to their posterity, may we not hope that their virtues will live and bear rich harvests of fruit in their numerous seed.

The daughters of James Spears, Sr., became mothers of large families. Two daughters and a son, Nathaniel, married and went West. Ann married Mathew Heustiss

*Both died in 1895.

and lived for a long time where John L. McLaurin lived just across the creek from Bennettsville and their descendants are found among the Heustisses, the Stantons and others with whom they have intermarried. Another daughter, Elizabeth, became Mrs. Jabish Townsend, as already stated in a previous chapter. And a third, Mary, married Daniel John, and has left her impress for good upon a large and highly respected posterity, not only in Marlboro, but in North Carolina and Arkansas as well.

Before leaving the Three Creeks mention is made of the Vinings. The tradition, as obtained from the late John Pearson, whose mother was of this stock, is to the effect that two brothers, Jesse and Jephtha, came from either England or Wales about 1750; that one of them settled in Carolina and the other in Georgia, but whether it was Jesse or Jephtha that became the head of the Marlboro family our informant could not tell. Neither could the Georgia family, which he had visited and found perpetuating both these names and holding like traditions as to their origin. However this may be, the one who came here married a Miss Hilson, according to the tradition, and raised a son and two daughters whose posterity, now bearing other names, abound in the country. The son named Jesse married a Miss Pledger and had three sons— John, who never married; Thomas, who left a son and two daughters among us, and Jesse, who, with a large family of boys, moved to Georgia some forty years ago. Ann Vining became the wife of Aaron Pearson, as we have seen, and the mother of John Pearson, and of course is largely and honorably represented in the county to-day. The other daughter, Elizabeth, first married William Evans, and after his death she married Alexander Peterkin, and became the mother of James and Jesse, from whom the South Carolina family have come. James Peterkin married Barbara McRae. Mrs. Susan Drake at Blenheim, and Mrs. C. D. Easterling, of Bennettsville, are daughters of this marriage. Jessie Peterkin married Sallie McRae, and Mrs. A. B. Henagan and Capt. J. A. Peterkin, now of Orangeburg, were children of this marriage. William Evans, the first husband of Elizabeth Vining, was the son of a young man of the same name who came to Welsh Neck direct from Wales about 1745. He had several sons besides this one. We have heard of Daniel, John and Thomas. From one of these our fellow citizen, the late Thos. A. Evans, of Blenheim vicinity, is descended. William Evans and Bettie Vining were married in 1781 while the war was in progress; and for two years Bettie had frequently to hide their only horse in the swamps of Pee Dee while William was in camp. One son, "Uncle Sandy," as we called him was their first born and after him came Catharine, the grandmother of our fellow citizen, M. D. McLeod. Next Lucy, who married a Mr. Thomson and moved West. Then Elizabeth, who was long known in the Red Hill community as Betsy Huggins; and then Eleanor, who became the second wife of William Thomas, of Brownsville; and the writer was the first born to this marriage.

CHAPTER IX.

Revolution Drawing Nigh.

So much has been written of the causes which led to a rupture and separation of the colonies from the mother country, the story so well told, that but little space need be given it here. It is proper, however, that the part our fathers took in the quarrel and fight should be remembered by their posterity. The concessions which had been made to the people in the back country of South Carolina, as it was then called, in allowing representation in the provincial assembly, and allowing district courts, had allayed excitement, produced a good degree of satisfaction, promoted prosperity and induced the hope that yet other wrongs in the course of time would be redresed and larger liberties secured. But some of the other colonies were not so fortunate in their local governments. Hence, as one encroachment after another was made upon what all considered their just rights as citizens of Great Britain, these local oppressions intensified the opposition to anything like oppression from the parent government, and the common sympathy existing among the various colonies bound them together, so that the sufferings of Massachusetts or Virginia were felt in Carolina or Georgia. An insult offered these they were ready to resent, and long before the first blood shed upon the heights of Lexington fired the American heart and summoned the whole Atlantic slope to arms, there was a general feeling of unrest, grevious complaints and remonstrances throughout the country. As early as 1765 the passage of the memorable Stamp Act aroused the colonies and when it was proposed to hold a "congress of deputies from the several colonies" to protest against usurpation,

South Carolina was among the first outside of New England to respond to the proposition, and was behind no province in manifesting an intelligent spirit of resistance to every other measure of oppression which followed in portentous succession. And when the taxed tea was thrown over board in Boston Harbor the whole country felt the alarm. A public meeting in Boston appealed to the other colonies to stop importing from Britain. Charleston heard the summons and appealed to the people to assemble in that city, the seat of British authority in the province, on the 6th day of July, 1774. This call met a hearty response. The district of Cheraw was ably represented by Col. Powell, who, for several years, had been its honored member in the Provincial Assembly. A large committee was appointed to provide for the public safety, which in the fall issued a call for a "Provincial Congress," which convened January 11, 1775. The proceedings of the Continental Congress were reviewed, delegates appointed to meet those from the other colonies, a new committee of general safety appointed, and all such regulations made as the exigencies of the times demanded. In this revolutionary congress Cheraw district was largely represented, and among the names are several prominent men of Marlboro. These made up the Cheraw delegation: Gabriel Powell, Claudius Pegues, Henry Wm. Harrington, Alex McIntosh, Samuel Wise and George Pawley.

But perhaps the most intelligent expression of sentiment which can be had at this day of the patriotic sentiments of the people of this region is found in the presentments of the grand juries of the day. The population was sparse, and scattered over a wide territory—few public meetings could be held, none largely attended, but these juries, composed of representative men from various sections, put upon oath, might be reasonably expected to voice the general sentiment and feeling of the people.

The liberty is taken, therefore, to quote largely from the charge of his honor, Judge Wm. Henry Drayton, at Long Bluff, at the November term of court, 1774. Judge Drayton had but lately received his appointment. He was born in South Carolina in 1742, was but little past thirty-two, but gifted and learned, was destined to fill a distinguished place in the annals of his struggling country; now upon the Bench and later in the councils of the Continental Congress, he adorned every position which he was called to fill, and when his brief life ended in Philadelphia, while attending the Congress of 1779, South Carolina grieved as a mother for her son. Let us imagine this splendid son of Carolina in the glow of his young manhood, appearing for the first time upon the bench at Long Bluff, addressing his countrymen upon the interests of the hour. After a concise statement of their general duties, he said: "By as much as you prefer freedom to slavery, by so much ought you to prefer a glorious death to servitude, and to hazard everything to endeavor to maintain that rank which is so gloriously pre-eminent above all other nations, you ought to endeavor to preserve it, not only for its inestimable value, and from a reverence to our ancestry from whom we received it, but from a love to our children to whom we are bound by every consideration to deliver down this legacy, the most valuable that ever was or ever can be delivered to posterity—and such are the distinguishing characteristics of this legacy, which may God, of His infinite goodness and mercy long preserve to us, and graciously continue to our posterity. But without our pious and unwearied endeavors to preserve these blessings it is folly and presumption to hope for a continuance of them. Hence, in order to stimulate your exertions in favor of your civil liberties, which protect your religious rights, instead of discoursing to you of the laws of other States, and comparing them to our own, allow me to tell you what your civil liberties are, and to charge you, which I do in the most solemn manner, to hold them dearer than your lives; a lesson and charge at all times proper from a Judge, but particularly so at this crisis, when America is in one general and genous commotion touching this truly important point. It is unnecessary for me to draw any other character of their liberties than that great line by which they are distinguished; and happy is it for the subject that those liberties can be marked in so easy and in so distinguishing a manner. And this is the distinguishing character: *English people can not be taxed, nay, they can not be bound by any law, unless by their consent, expressed by themselves, or by their representatives of their own election.* This colony was settled by English subjects; by a people from England herself; a people who brought over with them, who planted in this colony, and who transmitted to their posterity the invaluable rights of Englishmen—rights which no time, no contract, no climate can diminish. Thus possessed of such rights, it is of the most serious concern that you strictly execute those regulations which have arisen from such a parentage, and to which you have given the authority of laws, by having given your constitutional consent that they should operate as laws; for by your not executing what those laws require, you would weaken the force, and would show, I may almost say, a treasonable contempt for those constitutional rights out of which your laws arise, and which you ought to defend and support at the hazard of your lives. Hence, by all the ties which mankind hold most dear and sacred; your tenderness to your posterity; your reverence to your ancestors; your love to your own interests; by the lawful obligations of your oath, I charge you to do your duty; to maintain the laws, the rights, the constitution of your country, even at the hazard of your lives and fortunes. Some courtly Judges style themselves the King's servants —a style which sounds harshly in my ears, inasmuch as the being a servant implies obedience to the orders of the master, and such Judges might possibly think that in the present situation of American affairs this charge is inconsistent with my duty to the King and a trusty officer under the constitution, when I boldly declare the law to the people and instruct them in their civil rights. Indeed, you gentlemen of the grand jury can not properly comprehend your duty and your great obligation to perform it unless you know those civil rights from which those duties spring and. by knowing the value of these rights, thence learn your obligation to perform these duties."

The quotation is lengthy, but it is not all the eloquence and patriotism which rang out in the courtroom. It is enough to show how the love for liberty consumed the judge and kindled a flame in the bosoms of the people. And the final presentment of the jury was a fitting response to the stirring words uttered by the judge. After a brief report of local matters the paper said: "We present as a grievance of the first magnitude the right claimed by the British Parliament to tax us, and by their acts bind us in all cases whatsoever. When we reflect on our other grievances they all appear trifling in comparison with this; for if we may be taxed, imprisoned and deprived of life by the force of edicts to which neither we nor our constitutional representatives have ever assented, no slavery can be more abject than ours. We are, however, sensible that we have a better security for our lives, our liberties and fortunes than the mere will of the Parliament of Great Britain; and are fully convinced that we can not be constitutionally taxed but by representatives of our own election or bound by any laws than those to which they have assented. This right of being exempted from all laws but those enacted with the consent of representatives of our own election we deem so essential to our freedom and so engrafted in our constitution that we are determined to defend it at the hazard of our lives and fortunes;

and we earnestly request that this presentment may be laid before our constitutional representatives, the common House of Assembly of this colony, that it may be known how much we prize our freedom and how resolved we are to preserve it. We recommend that these presentments be published in the gazettes of the Province." The above was signed and sealed by "Alexander McIntosh, the foreman; Henry W. Harrington, Thomas Ayers," and seventeen others. These were bold, manly sentiments, coming from plain honest men, and although largely inspired by the stirring address of the judge, fast coming to be an idol in the hearts of his people, yet these fearless words but voiced the sentiment of a large part of the population, as the proceedings of the next term of court manifested. Instead of a Drayton to fire their hearts, with his eloquent appeals, "to all they held dearest," at this term the ermine was worn by Justice Gregory. He was fresh from England and loyal in the highest degree, and possibly one of the "style," who, as Drayton tersely put it, regarded themselves "servants of the king." The grand jury made the usual presentments. They added these words: "We present as an enormous grievance the power exercised by the British parliament of taxing and making laws binding upon the American Colonies in all cases whatsoever; such power being subversive of the most inestimable rights of British subjects, that of being taxed by their own consent, given by their representatives in General Assembly, and that of trial by jury, both which are evidently inherent in every British-American, and of which no power on earth can legally deprive them. We, well knowing the importance of these rights, in securing to us our liberties, lives and estates, and conceiving it to be every man's indispensable duty to transmit them to his posterity, are fully determined to defend them at the hazard of our lives and fortunes." But this outspoken, resolute declaration, along with more of the same spirit and tenor, which reflected to some extent, by implication at least, upon the integrity of the judge, was ordered to be "quashed"; yet it all came out in the public gazettes of the day, with the signatures of sixteen good men, such as Thomas Lide, foreman; Sam'l Wise, Claudius Pegues, William Pouncey, Benjamin Rogers, Thomas Bingham and others. Few, if any, of the early declarations of rights were bolder than these set forth under the solemnities of law and under oath, by the patriotic fathers who lived upon the Pee Dee. May the sons and daughters in all time be worthy of their relationship to these "Old Cheraws."

CHAPTER X.

SEVERAL OLD FAMILIES.

Another of these first comers to the Pee Dee was William Terrell, or, as the name was first spelled, Tarell. Bishop Gregg says of this old settler, that "he was the grandfather of the late Captain John Terrell, a worthy descendant of the old Welsh stock, and one of the best men of his day and generation." Captain Terrell's father was engaged in the public service before the Revolution, but did not survive that period. The Captain married Ann, a daughter of Major Robert Allison, a lady every way worthy of her excellent husband; and, as the Captain used to tell it, "the Lord greatly enriched them by giving them ten daughters," and among the Rogers, the Douglas and Beatties, this honored pair have a number of descendants in the county to-day, and many more in Darlington and neighboring States. Many a deed of kindness done by this godly pair brings blessings upon their memory, and "though dead, they yet speak, and in example live."

The late Rev. James H. Thornwell, D. D., a native of Marlboro, was a grandson of Samuel Terrell, a brother of Captain John Terrell's father. Miss Martha Terrell, the mother of Dr. Thornwell, first married James Thornwell, an obscure man, and after the birth of two sons he died. The widow was a woman of remarkable intellect, but, left in penury, she was kindly aided in the care of her charge by Captain Terrell, till she became the wife of Mr. Ananias Graham, and the mother of two sons by tha marriage. Young Thornwell began early to manifest a taste for books, and was furnished with the means of attending such schools as the country afforded by the efforts of his mother and Captain Terrell, until the attention of such men as General Gillespie, of Marlboro, and

Mr. Robbins, of Cheraw, became so interested in his behalf, that he was fitted for college, and enabled to complete the course and receive his diploma, and from thence his career was onward and upward, until few men in the State have attained higher position in the field of thought. No son of Marlboro has perhaps been more gifted, and surely no money ever spent has been more worthily bestowed, than that contributed to educate his splendid mind. The whole State of South Carolina and the Presbyterian Church of the United States felt the blow when the fires of his great intellect consumed his feeble frame, and he fell with his armour bright in the zenith of his power and influence, when the troubles of the country seemed most to need the wisdom of his counsel.

A younger brother of the doctor, Charles A., for whom he felt a paternal sort of interest, and whom he aided in educating in the South Carolina College (where he was for a time a professor, and then the president), was also a man of superior intellect. After his graduation he studied law, was admitted to the bar in 1842, located at Bennettsville, married first a daughter of Meekin Townsend, and directly took a prominent stand among such competitor as David, Dudley and McQueen, and seemed destined to eminence in his chosen profession. In 1852 he was elected a member of the House of Representatives, and re-elected in 1854. After the birth of two sons Mrs. Thornwell died, and he married Miss Hood, and seemed to have a brilliant career before him, but stricken down with disease, it was but a few days and all was over. His only surviving son, J. H. Thornwell, lives in the community yet.

In connection with the education of Dr. Thornwell a name was mentioned which has been long and favorably known among the people of Marlboro, that of General Gillespie. The name as it first appears upon the old

records is spelled Galespy. In 1743 James Galespy, a
man of enterprise and energy, from the north of Ireland,
made his "application to the Council for three hundred
acres of land in the Welsh Tract," claiming to have six
persons in his family. It is likely that he had been upon
the Pee Dee for sometime before this, as tradition
makes him the first man who ever brought a boat to
Cheraw; a business which he seems to have followed in
copartnership with General Gadsden, of Charleston, up
to the time of the Revolution. He married a Miss
Young, and had two sons, Francis and James. The
former died young, but the latter lived to bear his full share
in the stormy period of the Revolution; and was active
both as a soldier and civilian. He settled on the east
side of the river, on the place the family have ever since
continued to live. His wife was Miss Wilds, aunt of
Judge Wilds, a woman worthy of her husband. From
this pair was born "Francis, Samuel and James, and two
daughters, Sarah and Mary." Of these three brothers,
James, or Gen. Gillespie, as he was called from the earliest
recollection of our oldest people, attained greatest prominence. Modest and unpretending, never pushing himself forward, he was yet too generous and patriotic to resist when his countrymen called for his leadership; and
would no more decline a place on one of the boards of
commissioners than a seat in the Legislature of the State;
a position to which he was three times elected by his loving people. In Church or in State, at home or abroad, he
was everywhere a pure-minded, consistent, good man.
Splendid specimen of the old style Carolina gentleman.
In ripe old age, reverses came—war, depredation, oppression, bereavement, losses, yet patiently and calmly he
reposed his trust in the Lord. "Mark the perfect man,
and behold the upright, for the end of that man is peace."

About the year 1742 another name which had been
prominent in the affairs of the country first appeared

among the settlers on the Pee Dee. In July of that year, Thomas Ellerby, who came from Virginia five years earlier, obtained a grant of land on the west side of the river, and was soon an extensive planter, and owned many slaves. Another, John Ellerby, settled on the east side of the river, but seems to have remained in the country but a short time. Thomas Ellerby married Obedience Gillespie, had two sons, Thomas and William, from whom the extensive connection is descended. The spelling of the name, it is said, was changed to Ellerbe, by a schoolmaster to whom Thomas and William were sent soon after their father's death. Both of these men became prominent in the affairs of the country, and were ardent Whigs. The family has been more numerous in Chesterfield than in Marlboro. But William E., a son of the William mentioned above, married a Marlboro lady, Miss Ann Robinson; and from that pair, Col. William T. was descended, than whom, for a time, no citizen of the district was held in higher esteem. For six years a member of the lower House, and four years in the State Senate; wealthy, liberal, successful as a planter—the people loved and honored him, and were grieved when in the maturity of his powers he was cut down. Our young fellow citizen, George Hersey, is a grand-nephew of this gifted man.

Another scion of this worthy name, John C. Ellerbe, came from Chesterfield and captured a fair daughter of lower Marlboro, Maria Wickham, and took her to Marion; and the excellent family of that name in Marion came from that union. The present Governor of South Carolina, Wm. H. Ellerbe, is one of the direct descendants, and, like his ancestor, came to lower Marlboro, and captured one of her fair daughters for his wife, Miss Rogers, a sister of Hon. T. I. Rogers, of Bennettsville. In various quarters of the country the descendants of old Thomas Ellerbe may be found; and whether they take the name, or trace the lineage through a daughter's veins, the splendid form, handsome features, high-toned generous impulses of the ancestors yet characterize the descendants. The old men, Thomas and William, were distinguished in the Revolution, the former commanding a company, first in Kolb's regiment, and afterwards in Benton's of Marion's brigade. So, in later times, when war demanded the service of the strong and brave, the descendants of these old heroes were not found wanting.

William Forniss, another of the old settlers, occupied a fine place in the neighborhood of Dyer's Hill. He, too, was a zealous supporter of the cause of Independence, too old to be a soldier, but helping with his influence and means. His son, an active boy, was ready with his fleet steed to carry intelligence from one point to another in time of peril. He afterwards became known as Major James Forniss, and reared a large family at, or, near the old homestead. But all have passed away; or live in the West. The Major married a Miss Irby, and his daughter married M. L. Irby, and Miss Fannie Irby, of Bennettsville, is, so far as the writer is informed, the last of the Forniss blood in Marlboro.

Mention has been made of the Brownsville branch of the Irby family. The first of this name was Charles, who came from Virginia about the middle of the last century, and settled in upper Marlboro, married Mehitabel Kolb, and became a prominent man. A son Charles lived and died in Brownsville. Elizabeth became the wife of Philip Pledger; another daughter became Mrs. Forniss, and yet another Mrs. Annie Lide; while his other son, James, married Miss Wright, of Marlboro, and from this pair has descended the present families found in the township of Smithville. Charles Irby of this branch of the family, represented his native district in the State Senate, about the time the war came on, and lived only a few years after peace was restored. He never married. Elizabeth Irby, a daughter of the first Charles, became the wife of William Pledger, and the mother of the late Mrs. Joel Emanuel, and of Major P. W. Pledger, both of whom sleep at the old family cemetery on the Irby place. The latter left no representative behind, and the name is extinct in the county. But Mrs. Emanuel left a large number of descendants to honor her memory.

The Pledger name first appears in the annals of Welsh Neck as early as 1752; when Philip Pledger came from Amelia County, Va., and settled in what is now Marlboro County. His wife was a Miss Ellis, of Virginia. He had two sons, Joseph and John, who, with their father, were active Whigs. There were also two daughters, one of whom married James Hicks, and the other first married a Mr. Fields, from whom the family of that name is descended through William Fields, who was a Major in the State Troops in the war of 1812. After the death of Fields the widow married William Terrell, father of that good man so long and favorably known as Capt. John Terrell. The Pledger name is no longer known among us, but in the Donaldsons, and others above mentioned, the honorable characteristics of the family are yet perpetuated among us. In this connection it is proper to make brief mention of the Hicks, who, for a number of years, were prominent people in Marlboro. In 1746 George Hicks, a man of English descent, came to Pee Dee and married a daughter of Philip James, the first pastor of Welsh Neck, and from this pair has descended a numerous progeny, among them the Harringtons, Kollocks, Donaldsons, and perhaps others. A part of the plantation long known as the "McFarland Beauty Spot Place," and latterly the property of the late J. B. Breeden, was formerly occupied by the Hicks family. "The high old house," where Mrs. Hicks lived, and where Dr. Jones, one of the first practicing physicians of Bennettsville, got his wife, is yet remembered by the older people as standing not a half mile from where J. F. Breeden now lives.

CHAPTER XI.

PROGRESS OF REVOLUTIONARY SENTIMENT.

If the foregoing expressions, in a previous chapter, from individuals and the courts, indicated a strong attachment to the principles of liberty, they evinced at the same time, a spirit of determination and increasing readiness for the approaching crisis. If among the first to boldly declare opposition to encroachments upon their sacred rights, the fathers seemed to understand and appreciate that they were assuming a position from which they could not recede. And yet they had not gone so far but that reasonable concessions from the Crown, and a show of just consideration to the interests of the colonies, would have stayed the tide of revolution and restored loyalty and love to the parent government. But such pacific measures were hoped in vain from a proud, powerful government. Royalty yields only to necessity, and 1775 witnessed an effort on the part of its representatives to recall the people to a sense of their allegiance, by issuing one order and proclamation after another, asserting the "divine right," and exhorting to obedience, and warning against disloyalty.

The Provincial Congress, a body organized to promote the interest of the people by counsel and remonstrance and petition, had adjourned to meet on June 20. But on the 19th of April the battle of Lexington was fought; and, although the battle-ground was far to the north, yet the tidings that American blood had been shed upon American soil, for American liberty, stirred the American heart in Carolina as surely as in Massachusetts, and the committee invested with such authority called the delegates together on the first day of June. One hundred and seventy-two brave men responded to the call; among them Samuel Wise, Claudius Pegues and William Henry Harrington, and on the second day of the session passed a paper recognizing the "existence of hostilities"—declaring the "causes sufficient to drive all oppressed people to arms"—that they would "be justified before God and man in resisting force by force, and solemnly engaging that whenever our continental or provincial councils shall decree it necessary, we will go forth and be ready to sacrifice our lives and fortunes to secure our freedom and support." It was further "resolved to raise fifteen hundred infantry and four hundred and fifty rangers." Before the end of the year matters had become so warlike that the royal governor fled from the capitol and took refuge upon a "man of war," dissolving for the last time the "common House of Assembly." Before this year ended a detachment of troops was ordered from the Pee Dee, under Maj. Hicks, to the Congaree, but the order was countermanded while they were upon the march. So that war was upon the people before the end of 1775; although there were some who, no doubt, honestly dissented, and were sincere in their professions of loyalty; doubtless others were indifferent as to the result of the struggle, provided they themselves could be let alone, while yet another class dodged the service, only to plunder and spoil. But thousands of the best people in the land threw the whole weight of their influence, property and personal services into the cause of the struggling colonies.

The year destined to be noted in American history as "Independence Year," opened upon this southern land dark and portentous. It looked as if Charleston was to be assailed from the sea. Ships of war were seen upon the bar, and a call was made for "detachments of volunteers in small parties of twenty or fifty as they could be collected." Maj. Hicks and Capt. Wise, with these detachments, promptly responded. Some of the country troops remained for some time, while others were soon discharged; and this seems to have been a common rule of action. It could not be otherwise; there were no arms, no treasury, no supplies to keep an army in the field. It was an infant republic struggling for birth. When some imminent peril threatened one point, help was called in from neighboring regions, and as soon as the danger was past the body of troops went home subject to call. And so it was that the necessary expenses of these volunteers were not always paid; and may have become a source of irritation and a hinderance to a ready response to an after call. It has been said that "certain expenses incurred by this detachment under Maj. Hicks were not paid"; and it is not surprising if some of these ready patriots from the Pee Dee were a little slow to answer when called again. Yet it is amazing that with resources of all sorts so feeble, and troops so few, the war was maintained so long, covering, as it did, a field as wide as the thirteen colonies, and sometimes running over into Canada. It was the spirit of resistance, indomitable energy and love for the cause they had espoused that animated all classes, that sustained and carried them forward. Bishop Gregg, to whom the writer is so largely indebted for many facts bearing upon the history of these stirring times in Carolina and upon the Pee Dee, has given us an interesting correspondence between "Oliver Hart, pastor of the Charleston Baptist church, and Elhanan Winchester, pastor of the Welsh Neck church, in behalf of the Baptist congregation in general," on the one part, and the Hon. Henry Laurens, Vice-President of the Province of South Carolina, on the other part; which is a most beautiful expression of piety, patriotism, trust in God and devotion to the cause of independence on the part of all concerned. The preachers said, among many other like things: "We hope yet to see hunted liberty sit regent on the throne and flourish more than ever under the administration of such worthy patriots; may we not hope that the time is come in which our rulers may be men fearing God, and hating covetousness, a terror to evil-doers, and a praise to them that do well." In his reply Mr. Laurens said, "Let each man among us, whether in the State or in the Church, whether in public or private life, by example, by precept, by every becoming act, preserve and be ready with his life and fortune to defend the just cause in which God has been pleased to engage us. We shall, weak as we are, succeed against those who have assumed to themselves the power of Omnipotence, who trust in fleets and armies to determine the fight. We shall be the happy instruments of establishing liberty, civil and religious, in a wilderness where towns and cities shall grow, whose inhabitants to the latest posterity will look back to this happy epoch, and celebrate and bless the memory of this generation." Eloquent prophecy! "There were giants in those days." Not alone among the leaders, where circumstances place them in the front, but in the rank and file among the humble and unknown, were men and women as true, as brave, as noble and good as they.

We have seen already that troops had gone from the Pee Dee to the neighborhood of Charleston in response to the call of the Governor, but it is not known whether any from this region were active participants in the memorable struggle of June 28th. There is evidence that Captain Wise, who was a Pee Dee man, was on Sullivan's Island, only the day before, and that Captain Harrington with a company of volunteers was at "Haddrell's Point," (now Mount Pleasant), and it is altogether probable that one or both of these Companies had some part in the memorable contest, which terminated so favorably to the American arms. But in the presence of Moultrie, Rutledge and Jasper, where artillery played the most important part in the fight, it is not likely that half drilled

militia should find prominent mention, and yet from the
correspondence of the men of Pee Dee it is clear that
they were under fire, and endured great privations for
some days in expectancy of the battle. And, without
positive proof, no reason is known for saying Marlboro
was not represented in the fierce engagement that saved
Charleston for a time, repulsed the foe, and gave comparative repose to the whole province for a considerable
time.

It was only six days after the brilliant victory at Fort
Moultrie that the Continental Congress, on July 4th, 1776,
adopted the Declaration of Independence. South Carolina heartily approved the Act, and at a court for the
Cheraws held in November following, the Grand Jury said
in their presentment: "It is with the highest pleasure
that the Grand Jury for the District of Cheraws embrace
this first opportunity of congratulating our fellow citizens
and American brethren on the late declaration of the
Continental Congress, constituting the united colonies of
North America free and independent states, and the inhabitants thereof totally absolved from any allegiance to
the British Crown." It was not until the autumn of 1778
that another court was held for the Cheraws, and that
was the last till the war was ended.

After their signal repulse at Moultrie the British directed
their operations against the northern and more populous
colonies, and the people of South Carolina enjoyed a
season of comparative quiet. Now and then a band of
Tories would dash across the border upon a foray of
plunder, but even they appeared to be awed by the successes of the patriots in the first and only considerable
engagement on Carolina ground. To be sure, there was
one here and there so fired with the spirit of resistance,
and so determined to be free, that if not needed within
their own borders, would seek the service and march to
the front, though far from their own hearthstones. Such

an one was Joshua Ammons, now with Marion in the
swamps of Pee Dee, then in the Continental line an orderly sergeant with LaFayette, or with Greene—he seemed to
watch the progress of events and where the bullets flew
thickest, there he was found ready to hurl death and de-
fiance into the ranks of the foe, and, the war over, to settle
down an humble, consistent Christian man.

About the close of 1778 the clouds again grew thick and
lowering. December witnessed the fall of Savannah and,
judging from a note in the journal of Mr. Pugh, the pastor
at Welsh Neck, and an ardent patriot, it is inferred that
troops from the Pee Dee suffered in that catastrophe.
On the 21st he preached a sermon to his people for the
youths lost at Savannah and says, "We lost many youths."
At the siege of Savannah, Samuel Wise, who had risen to
a Major's commission, a gallant son of Pee Dee, "fell
at the post of duty" in the thickest of the fight. He left
no son to bear his name, but his devotion to his country's
cause entitles his name to grateful memory. South Carolina was now to become the theatre of active operations.
General Prevost, with a large force, was marching towards
Charleston. Again the metropolis was threatened with
blood and carnage, and again large drafts of the militia
were called into service. A regiment from the Pee Dee,
under the command of Col. McIntosh, responded to the
call. But unexpectedly Prevost withdrew and the fall
of Charleston was delayed for a time; and the country had
a brief rest from the ravages of war, only as the "sons of
liberty," felt called to chastise some band of lawless Tories,
who, taking advantage of the absence of the men in camp,
would make a dash for plunder, or to murder some noted
Whig who had made himself obnoxious to them by his
bold declarations or zeal for the cause of independence.
And yet, as the year 1779 drew to a close, men felt that
the struggle was yet before them; and that the storm was
gathering. But the Whigs in the Pee Dee region, not less

than their compatriots in other portions of the State, were ready to make good their declarations, to "sacrifice life and fortune," rather than rest under the heel of British oppression.

CHAPTER XII.

Thomas Parker and Others.

The author will be excused for a more extended notice of the name which he has borne for now nearly three score years and ten, inasmuch as the material is more abundant, not only in Gregg's History, but among the records of the family.

In the year 1699 Tristram Thomas emigrated from Wales to the province of Maryland. He was the father of ten children, and died in 1746. His oldest son, Stephen, came to North Carolina about 1750. He too had a large family, nine sons and four daughters. Of the other sons of Tristram, tradition says, some remained in Maryland and others went into Pennsylvania and regions farther west. About 1759 Robert, the first son of Stephen, came to Marlboro with his wife, Mary Sands, of Virginia, and was soon followed by at least three younger brothers, Lewis, Philemon, and Tristram. The two first settled among the colony of Friends in the neighborhood of Pine Grove, now Adamsville. Tristram settled at what is now McCall's Mills, which he is said to have first built. He afterwards became prominent in public affairs, took a leading part in the Revolutionary struggle, rising to a Major's commission. After the war, he was well known as General of Militia, an honored member of the Legisture, and a leader in organizing municipal affairs in the infancy of Marlboro District, as it was first called. He was as prominent in religious affairs as in civil. He reared a large family, most of whom scattered, except that model of a Christian gentleman, and District officer, the late James C. Thomas, who remained and died among us at a ripe old age, the last of his generation. The General died in 1810.

It is said that either Lewis or Philemon, more likely the latter, married a Miss Breeden, and after the birth of a daughter, who became the second wife of Moses Parker, he died, and his widow married Jessie Bethea, the father of the late Jessie Bethea, of Adamsville. The other brother went to Illinois. Robert, the older brother, who settled near where the present town of Tatum is located, was long known as a Baptist preacher. The church at Salem was organized under his labors, also Catfish in our sister county of Marion. He died in Britton's Neck, of that county, while upon a preaching tour in 1817, in the eighty-fourth year of his age. He was the father of three daughters and nine sons. Nathan, John S., Robert W., Eli, and William have their descendants in the county, and a daughter, the grandmother of Colonel and Tristram Covington, is also numerously represented among the good citizens of the land. We sincerely wish that all the old families in the country could have preserved their genealogical tables as well as this one has. The writer is the fifth from Tristram of Wales, and has upon record the names and dates of birth of ten children. Stephen, first son of Tristram, had thirteen children. Robert, his first son, had twelve. William, his son, counted fourteen, and this writer, the son of William, has numbered eleven.

Upon some other lines, the multiplication has been as large. Other families have borne the name in this country, and do now. We have asked them if their descent can go back to the first Tristram. If so, they are entitled to a place among the branches of the old tree first planted upon American soil in 1699, as an importation from the "County Cairmarthen, Principality of Wales."

About the same time that the above family reached Marlboro, or a little later, there seems to have come a number of substantial people whose ancestors from the British Isles had landed in Maryland and Pennsylvania, but

who now sought a warmer clime. Some of them came
direct from Maryland, and others followed after a brief stay
in Virginia and North Carolina. Their good judgment was
shown in selecting the well-watered, finely timbered, fertile plains of Adamsville and Hebron. They at first gave
to this choice region the designation which still cleaves to
a portion of it, "Beauty Spot." Among these settlers
were Moses Parker, a man of substantial worth and firmness of character, and his brother John, a reckless, dash-
ing young fellow who threw his whole soul into the patriotic cause, and of whom the tradition said, "He'd rather shoot a Tory than a snake." Moses was a serious-
minded Christian man, with a family dependent upon him,
yet spent part of the time in the patriot army. He was
twice married, his second wife being Miss Thomas, as
mentioned above. Poor, when the first marriage was
contracted, spending his last five shillings as a marriage
fee, he not only made a living for his twenty-two children, but acquired large possessions of splendid lands,
flocks and herds, that roamed at will over the thousands
of broad acres called his own. One of his daughters by
the first marriage became the wife of that staunch old
Whig, the celebrated Joshua Ammons, a man of great firmness of character and solid worth. He once, when under the
command of the Marquis LaFayette, seeing his General
wounded, took him in his arms and bore him to a place
of safety. Years after, when the Marquis visited the land
he had helped to free, the humble Ammons, with many
others, made a tedious pilgrimage to look into the face
of that grand old Frenchman, who, seeing his former comrade and benefactor, embraced and blessed him for the
unforgotten deed of kindness. The memory of Ammons
is still a sacred legacy to his posterity, some of whom are
yet among us, proud to have their descent from so true
and brave a man, who has not only written his name
upon the annals of his country with the warrior's sword,

but has also left a pure record as a follower of the Prince of Peace upon the pages of the "Old Church Book" at Beaverdam, alongside that of his venerated father-in-law, Moses Parker. From the twenty-two children of the patriarch Parker has come a numerous progeny of the excellent people of this ancient community. The only surviving son, *Mr. Philip Parker, lives near his birthplace, on land inherited from his father, in a vigorous old age, having seen his eightieth Christmas. He is yet brimming full of life and humor, himself a veritable patriarch, living joyously with the wife of his youth, who has honored him with sixteen children, eleven of whom are alive. From his lips the writer has received much valuable material, drawn from the stores of a wonderful memory, still fresh and exact, of the traditions of the past, learned from the old people he knew in his boyhood and earlier years..

Mrs. Parker, like her husband, is also one of twenty-two children of the late Joshua Fletcher. Raiford, the father of Joshua, John, and Mrs. Axey Bundy, came to Marlboro about 1815 and although so much later than the times of which these pages treat, such has been the prominence and growth of the family that it demands some space in these annals.

Mr. Fletcher and wife, Sallie Holliway, came from Wayne county, N. C. The first wife of Joshua was Miss Nancy Smith, his second a daughter of Moses Parker. His sons who came to manhood and reared families were Raiford, Thomas, John S., Nicholas, Joshua, William and Lewis. The daughters married "Branch" Billy Adams, Robert Adams, Jephtha Adams, Philip Parker, Noah Gibson, Shockley Adams, J. M. Gibson and Jno. L. Easterling. Mrs. Jephtha Adams and Mrs. Noah Gibson were twin sisters and so nearly alike in size and features, and dress and voice, that persons not altogether familiar with them found it difficult to dis-

*Since died.

tinguish one from the other, and as the young maidens grew up they sometimes amused themselves by innocently playing "Who Is It?" "Is it Julia or Ann?" Young Jephtha thought that he knew them apart, and likewise thought he loved Julia. Ann suspected that a courtship had begun, and on one occasion, when Jephtha made his appearance at the old Fletcher homestead, she got the start of her sister, placed herself "in the way" and sure enough "Jep drew up beside her," and began to whisper in her ear the soft tones of his tender emotion. Smiling at her success in the discovery of the secret she fled from his presence and sent Julia to his side, who, not long afterwards became Mrs. Jephtha Adams; the mischievous Ann in time became Mrs. Noah Gibson. With only the State line and a mile of intervening space between them, the twin sisters dwelt side by side until Mrs. Gibson went over the line that separates earth from heaven.

To return to the traditions as remembered by Philip Parker it is said that in those dark days, when the party lines were strongly drawn, and "Tories preyed on Whigs, and Whigs chastised Tories," it came to pass that a Whig by the name of Reed came from camp "on leave of absence." His presence at home being discovered, a party of Tories surrounded his house, cutting off his escape before they were seen. The poor man climbed into the loft of his humble dwelling in the vain effort to conceal himself. "He was ordered to descend and surrender, or the house would be burned over his head." In his extremity he consented to come down and surrender as a prisoner of war, if they would spare the house. But as he descended and approached the door they shot him dead. Tidings of the outrage rapidly spread in the neighborhood. A little band of Whigs soon collected, and, pursuing the raiders, came upon them at another home, not far from where the Rev. W. K. Breeden now lives. So intent were the raiders upon their work of plunder, ripping the beds and filling the ticks with booty, that when their pursuers dashed upon them, they broke for the swamp of Beverly Creek, so hotly pursued by the Whigs that the spoil was recovered, and one of the Whigs captured a splendid horse which, of couse, he never returned to the owner.

The Lesters also trace their origin from Maryland, William, their ancestor, coming from that province about this time. He was the father of Thomas, Nimrod, Bright, and Mrs. Charles Manship. Thomas Lester was the grandfather of the present family in Marlboro county. Charles Manship, who was a wild youth until his marriage, became a Christian, went to school for a time, entered the Methodist ministry, and from him has sprung a respectable family.

Tradition tells of a fine colony of Friends who came into this portion of Marlboro before the Revolutionary war; Ways, Mendenhall, and other sober, industrious, honest people who built for themselves a house of worship at Pine Grove. But when the Revolution ended, and the new government reorganized, these men felt that slavery had become a fixture in the South—an institution that they religiously believed a wrong, and that its existence among them must hamper their enterprise, and possibly corrupt the religion of their posterity—they sold their lands and left in a body for what was then called the "Northwest Territory." The house of worship was used in common by Baptists and Methodists for a season, but eventually went into the possession of the latter, where there has long existed one of their most influential communities. The Baptists ultimately staked down at Beaverdam.

Among other elements that entered into the composition of the population in eastern Marlboro the Scottish is worthy of mention. Two old men, natives of Scotland, are remembered by Mr. Parker, the brothers, John, and

James McCoy (sometimes written McKay). John lived at the mill on Bear Creek, just within South Carolina. One of his sons, Daniel, became a Baptist preacher. With a rich, Scotch accent, his hearers were sometimes amused at his quaint way of putting religious truths. Preaching on the evils of pride, how insinuating, and deceptive, he sang out, "Why, brethren, I used to think I was not proud, but when I came to know myself, I found out that I *was* proud because I *wasn't* proud." Some one is said to have asked him why he read out his hymns in such a " sing-song sort of a tone," and he answered " Well, you all sing so badly, that if I don't sing it out, it won't get sung." Good old man, he " went West " in his old age, and took an interesting family with him.

The other brother lived a mile or two lower down, on the banks of the Little Pee Dee. Mr. "Truss" Bethea married one of his daughters, and has left a highly respected posterity.*

It would hardly be doing justice to the information received from Mr. Parker if no mention was to be made of some of the other neighbors of his father.

William Leggett, who "took up" a large territory of land on Beaverdam and Panther Creeks, around the site of McColl, lived at what is now known as McLaurin's Mill, during the Revolution. He was the father of James, the father of Salathiel and Sherrad, from whom the numerous connections in this and neighboring counties are descended.

Isaac Pipkin came into the neighborhood from Wayne county, N. C. in the early years of the present century with his excellent wife, Mary Benton, and from this couple have descended many of the present population of the community. Mrs. Lewis Parker, Mrs. William Lester, and Mrs. N. M. Gibson, were daughters of Squire

---

*T. H. Bethea, his only surviving son, lives on the large estate left by his father.

7

Pipkin, and the name, as borne by several young men among us, has descended from this one North Carolina Scotchman.

Another extensive family in this portion of the country for a century past has been the Easterlings. They have a tradition that the first bearer of the name landed in Baltimore. When, it is not known, but like many others, they drifted southward, and May 24th, 1733, near the mouth of the Neuse river, in North Carolina, Henry Easterling was born. He was bred a Churchman, but embraced Baptist principles in 1760, and two years afterwards entered the ministry, accepting charge of the Hitchcock church in Anson county. His wife was Miss Ellen Bennett, who blessed him with ten children. About 1772 we find him in Marlboro. In that year he aided in organizing the Beaverdam Baptist Church, which was at first called "Beauty Spot" and worshipped not far from "Beauty Spot Bridge." Mr. Easterling was chosen the first pastor and continued in office for a number of years. The probability is that some of his family remained in Anson, and that others came with him to "Beauty Spot." Two of his sons, at least, raised families here. Shadrach, father of the late Capt. Henry, and Mrs. Betsy Odom; and William, for many years "Ordinary" of his district and the father of a large family of sons and daughters. His wife was Miss Covington, of Richmond county, North Carolina. From these two brothers, Shadrach and William Easterling, has descended a very extensive connection. While the late war between the States was going on two or three young men stationed near Charleston instituted an inquiry through the papers of the day, to ascertain how many Easterlings were in the Confederate army. Sixty-three responded, tracing their descent to the old preacher, Henry Easterling. Twelve gallant young men of this name were in a single *one* of the eight companies raised in Marlboro. Brave boys! many sleep in the soldier's grave, but your surviving comrades forget you not. Ye stood amid the pelting lead, daring to do, and to die. Calm be your rest.

William Bennett, ancestor of a family of that name, came originally from Maryland to Anson county, N. C. where he was living during the revolution. He was a Baptist preacher, yet spent some time with the patriot army. He seems to have made himself especially obnoxious to the Tories, who fired a volley into his dwelling in Anson. Whether it was the prayers or the sword of the old man the enemy most hated, the tradition did not say. He soon after made his home on Crooked Creek in Marlboro, about a mile above what is known as the "Burnt Factory," where he raised his family and where his ashes lie in ground still owned by his posterity. William, Joseph and Nevil, his sons, have representatives in this and Marion County. Eli Willis, the progenitor of that family also came from Maryland, and married a daughter of Mr. Bennett, and from this couple Milby, Jas. B. and others sprang. A number of worthy young people promise to perpetuate the name. Sam Edwards, who lived for a time at the Ervin place, also married into the Bennett family.

Old Mr. John Hamer, who has left a numerous family to inherit his name, was also descended from an old Marylander, William Hamer, who settled in Anson, and married a Miss Hicks. John found his wife in Marlboro in 1791, near the old court-house, Miss Nancy Cochran. Daniel H., William, Thos. C., Henry C., Robert, James and Alfred, Mrs. Nicholls, Mrs. Caleb Curtis, Mrs. Jephtha Robinson, the second wife of Eli Thomas, Mrs. J. B. Willis and Mrs. Rowland, were the children of this marriage. After the death of the first Mrs. Hamer, the old gentleman married a daughter of Mr. Nathan Thomas, of Hebron, and the late Philip M. and the Rev. Lewis M.

Hamer were born of that marriage. Nobody can take it amiss if the pen of a comrade should single out one from this worthy group of fifteen, and give to him special mention. It may be because of a closer intimacy and better knowledge of his worth, that the writer puts him down as among the best of men. We slept under the same blanket upon the naked earth, trod step by step the same tented field, knelt side by side at the same camp fire, and ate from the same dish. Under all the trying circumstances of life in camp, we found Philip Hamer the same noble man, the same true friend, and the tribute here left to his memory is prompted by the affectionate remembrance of true worth, It was with sincerest pleasure that we all, as a forlorn hope, cast our ballots for P. M. Hamer for the House of Representatives in 1876. He filled his place in the memorable Wallace House. He was returned, and filled other positions in the gift of his people, and when in 1887 they laid his body to rest beside his kindred dust, Marlboro buried one of her noblest sons.

CHAPTER XIII.

Progress of Revolution.

If hitherto the patriots in Carolina had occasion for rejoicing that they had gained some victories, and generally held their own against superior forces, the year 1780 opened with gloomy prospects for the cause of liberty. The approach of great armies threatened their feeble defenses. Charleston was again to be besieged, and the Pee Dee militia were called to aid in its defense. A portion of the regiment under Lieutenant-Colonel Kolb and another division under Colonel Hicks, with Major Tristram Thomas, all men of Marlboro, were put upon the march to the scene of conflict, while another detachment under Major Benton remained upon the Pee Dee under arms to watch the movements of the Tories, who were always especially active in predatory warfare when any considerable portion of the available men were away from home. Charleston was taken after a heroic defense of about forty days. Tidings of the British success, and surrender of so many of the best men of the land, filled the inhabitants of the whole country with consternation and alarm. The approach of Wemys with his troopers, to reap the fruits of victory, intimidated many into an enforced allegiance to British rule. His progress was marked with blood, destruction and conflagration, and it is not surprising if many submitted, while others yielded in form, with a secret reservation to resist when opportunity offered. Few were bold enough to answer as old Thomas Ayer did when urged by his neighbors to accept the protection tendered: "*It is not a question of property, but of liberty.*" And yet the cruelties perpetrated by the British and Tories inspired a spirit of resistance and revenge that atoned in large measure for their partial temporary demoralization. Wemys did not long remain at Cheraw, but moved down the river to Georgetown, and thence to Broad river, where he was captured by General Sumter, and is said to have experienced unexpected humane treatment from the men he had wronged. The men whom he plundered—whose houses he had fired, had the honor to treat him as a prisoner of war.

In June of this year, 1780, Major McArthur, with his regiment of Highlanders, came from Camden to Cheraw to have a convenient correspondence with the Tories, and strengthen their cause, and forage upon the wealthy planters of the Pee Dee. For a little while he made his headquarters at Long Bluff. There it is said he "offered a reward for the capture of Thomas Ayer," a noted Whig of Marlboro and a terror to the Tories. He had led a band of daring scouts against a nest of Tories, whom he severely punished by hanging a number of them. McArthur's reward was soon won by a company of Ayer's Tory neighbors. They tied their captive with buckskin strings, which of course would stretch when wet. But about the time they reached Hunt's Bluff on their way to "Headquarters," a terrific thunderstorm broke upon them. As the river was to be crossed and several miles traveled before reaching Long Bluff, it was decided to keep their prisoner guarded in an old out-house near the river till the next morning's dawn, and then resume their journey. Thinking that the prisoner was secure, some of the party, including the leader, went off in search of supper, leaving, as they supposed, a sufficient guard. In the meantime Hartwell Ayer, the brother of Thomas, got word of what was going on, and in the darkness of the night dashed up to the door of his brother's prison. In a rage he dispatched most of the guard, and sent Thomas back to his home to relieve the anxieties of his household, while Hartwell and his party went in pursuit of other game

and left bleeding and wounded two more of the party
they had so unceremoniously cheated out of the coveted
reward. McArthur was terribly incensed when he heard
of the fatal miscarriage of his cherished scheme and
crossed the river with a formidable party. Mrs. Ayer
with two sons, Lewis Malone and Zaccheus, had barely
time to escape to a hiding place in the swamps. Foiled
again, the desperate McArthur burned the dwellings,
killed the stock, sparing only a barn filled with corn,
which he probably meant for his own horses, but which
was hastily removed and secured for the family when the
British left. An humble, faithful neighbor by the name
of James Sweat (a kinsman of the family, of that name
now living in the county), in the kindness of his heart, fed
Mrs. Ayer and her boys for several weeks. Mr. Sweat
afterwards became a Baptist preacher of useful life in the
State of Georgia. Nathan Sweat, the brother of James,
was caught about this time by some of McArthur's party
and was held as a prisoner for some days. Discovering
which was the fastest horse in the camp, he managed to
mount him one day and instantly made a dash for liberty.
The friendly swamp received him and stealthily he worked his way to his mother's door for a morsel of food, and
as she hastily reached it to his hand she cried "Nathan,
the enemy is upon you"; quick as thought the spurs were
applied and again he flew, his pursuers at his heels. The
steps lengthened between them, and McArthur was worsted again and Sweat caught no more, but "lived to fight
again."

But in the progress of events, it was thought needful
to withdraw the force under McArthur to a situation less
exposed. Reports of advancing Continentals caused the
advanced posts like Cheraw, where McArthur had returned,
to be drawn in. Accordingly about the last of July, pre-
parations were completed. A portion of the troops,
along with the sick and a number of negroes whom they

had captured and persuaded to leave their masters, were to be sent down to the river on boats to Georgetown. Somehow or other the Whigs in the neighborhood conceived the idea of capturing this flotilla. James Gillespie a man of much influence, has been awarded the praise for this bold idea. As he moved down the river with a few trusted neighbors, the patriotic citizens gathered to give aid. Major Tristram Thomas was given command. Hunt's Bluff was chosen as the point of attack. In a sudden bend of the river, a battery was thrown up immediately upon the bank. Was it armed? Yes, with threatening looking cannon, but wooden, harmless guns. After awhile the silent garrison beheld the floating armada slowly descending the stream. Thomas made as formidable a show of his little command as he could; some of them armed with pieces as harmless as the pole cannon mounted upon the bank. Yet he boldly demanded an unconditional surrender; and it was made, and more than a hundred prisoners were sent to North Carolina. Scarcely had the bloodless action ended before a large boat on its way from Georgetown to Cheraw with supplies for McArthur hove in sight, as it was being pushed up the stream. It too, was turned over to the American army. It were well if all the enterprises of the American army could have been as successful and bloodless. But not so.

A few days after the events just recorded General Gates made his appearance on the Pee Dee at and above Cheraw, with a considerable force, on his way to Camden. His presence revived the hopes of the people wonderfully. He offered "pardon to all who had subscribed paroles imposed upon them by the hand of conquest," excepting, of course, such as had turned their hand against the patriot cause. Hope again came to the despondent. Hope, which alas, was to be tried most sorely by Gates' defeat at Camden and his consequent retreat through the country into North Carolina For a time the warfare on the upper Pee Dee again became desultory and irregular, but of a most distressing nature. Nobody knew when a band of Tories would sweep down upon a quiet neighborhood, drive off the stock, set fire to the buildings and fences, and murder some well-known Whig. But towards the end of the year the coming of General Greene in the State, and to the Pee Dee, inspired confidence again. Although the results of the year's campaign had been, on the whole, against the cause of liberty, it required but a spark to set the people all ablaze with enthusiasm for the cause they had espoused. Their spirits, sometimes disheartened, but never crushed, now revived again. Sufferings chastened but could not extinguish the love of liberty, nor could disaster quench the purpose to defend their rights to the bitter end.

CHAPTER XIV.

Traditions from Col. John Covington.

A chapter of traditions obtained from Colonel John Covington two months before his death. The Colonel was a remarkable man, born in "Hebron, the garden spot of the sacred soil of Marlboro," as he would characterize it, in the year 1801. He lived a quiet, useful life among his own people, and when interrogated could recall the names and deeds of many no longer known on earth. Never stout and strong physically, his cheerful, hopeful spirits, his joyous, fun-loving temperament, gave him a young heart in his old age. Although looking, waiting for the call to join his loved ones gone before to the "shining shore," he was not averse to telling of the men and women whom he knew in the days of his youth as the companions of his sports. He was familiar with many of the traditions of the old people which had been handed down from parent to child—traditions which should be treasured by those now living, and in turn, handed down by them to future generations. The daily newspaper was in those days unknown and the book agent had not found his way to the homes of Hebron, for "Hebron" it was called in the Colonel's boyhood. His old uncle, Nathan Thomas, "Gumfoot," as he was nicknamed from his cork bottom shoe made to lengthen a leg broken by a fall from his wagon, had, in the century past, given the beautiful section this name in memory of the fair inheritance given the patriarch Caleb in reward for his fidelity and valor.

John, the grandfather of the Colonel, had won the affections of Elizabeth, the daughter of Rev. Robert Thomas, and, leaving his five brothers in Richmond county, North Carolina, had settled upon the north side of Little Pee Dee in Robeson, North Carolina, and was building up a comfortable home when the revolution came on. His sympathy with the patriot cause soon made him an object of dislike to his loyalist neighbors, who stripped him of his means of living and left him with nothing but his family. Leaving his wife and babies with her friends, he sought his revenge in the ranks of the patriot army. When the war ended, he settled upon a farm beside his brother-in-law, Nathan Thomas, upon the plains of Hebron. His children were William, "Truss," Robert, Nancy, Polly and Thomas. The last named married Miss Sallie Cook and left a numerous posterity. Robert and Tristram seem to have died childless. Nancy married an Easterling and Polly a Mr. Conner. William married Miss Mary Bridges, who had previously married a Mr. Connor, and was the mother of Ira and Nancy, who became Mrs. Fred McDaniel. The children of William Covington were John, Henry, Tristram, Nellie, first wife of Lewis Spears, and the first wife of Daniel Parham, and the first wife of Wm. Baggett.

All the sons of Wm. Covington, who was a man of excellent character, were men of more than ordinary prominence in the affairs of the country. Tristram, both in his own conduct and in that of his sons, has commanded the respect and confidence of his countrymen. He and his oldest son, James, have held positions of trust and responsibility in county affairs. Henry was for a long time successor to the Colonel in command of the Hebron company during "ante-bellum" times. Harris, the only son of Capt. Henry, arose to a captaincy in the late "war between the States." He was a lawyer of much prominence, and was considered one of the most brilliant young men in the country. His friends ran him for a seat in Congress after "reconstruction," and, while he received a large vote, he was defeated by the solid colored majority. Gifted though he was, he died in the prime of life, and his manly form sleeps in the same cemetery where lies so many of Hebron's sons.

John Bridges, the maternal grandfather of the Covingtons, came to Carolina from the province of Maryland sometime before the Revolution, and was soon followed by others of his family.

Our friend, Col. Covington, remembered hearing Frank Bridges, a kinsman, relate at a dinner party that when a boy he had enlisted in the army. Because of his size and extreme youth General Marion kept him about his own person, sometimes as a courier and sometimes as a cook, and that he it was who roasted the "historic potatoes" that Marion set before the British officer. The family of this Frank Bridges removed to Alabama in after years, and he is supposed to have been the ancestor of the late Judge Bridges, of Alabama, who married a daughter of David Bethea, elsewhere mentioned. John Bridges, tradition says, left his wife and children behind when he started south in search of a better country. When his eyes rested upon the beautiful, well-watered, fertile plains of Hebron, he concluded that "the better land" was found. Being a good mechanic, he went to work to build a house. He hired and sent a messenger back to Maryland for his wife and children. Mrs. B. was, however, afraid to make the pilgrimage with a stranger. How did she know that he was a "true man" and that her husband had sent him? She declined to undertake the journey. The messenger insisted that he was a "true man," and that Bridges had sent him. Finally the doubting wife consented that if the messenger would return to Carolina, and take back to her the horse that her husband had carried from Maryland, that she would know that her husband had sent him and would believe that he was a "true man" and willingly go with him. Back to the goodly land of Hebron the messenger came. Bridges loved his wife and babes and could rely on the promise. The old Maryland steed was saddled, and the messenger furnished with another horse, and across two States he again pursued his way. When Mrs. Bridges saw the sleek old charger, token of her husband's love, her scruples gave way to her devotion to the man she loved, and mounting, she rode on horseback across two States to the husband of her youth, bringing her two children with her to her new southern home. "Heroines in that day"! Yes, and Rebeccas since the age of Abraham and Isaac. Don't ask me why Bridges did not go himself. His grandson did not know. He did say that Mollie, one of those little ones brought on horseback from Maryland, grew up to womanhood and first gave her young affections to John Stubbs, and after his death she became the fifth wife of John David, who had already several children in his house. She carried three more and Eliza was born in the forty-sixth year of her mother's life. Another daughter of Mr. Bridges, Elizabeth, married Lewis Stubbs, the great-grandfather of our fellow citizens, William, and Wyriott, and the late Albert Stubbs. Sallie, another daughter, married Jonathan Cottingham, from whom the Hebron family of that name sprang. Nancy became Mrs. Conner first and then Mrs. Covington, mother of the Colonel. John Bridges, son of William, married a sister of Jonathan Cottingham, and bargains of this sort have been so frequent among the good people of Hebron until it is hard to find families not related to each other, and some of them can scarcely tell what kin they are to each other.

Another old resident of this community was Richard Edens. He was the father of Allen, long known as a Methodist preacher, whose first wife was Miss Fuller, a sister of the Henry Fuller of ginger-cake notoriety. They became the ancestors of several well-known citizens of Marlboro in later years. Asa, Alfred, Henry, who went into the late war as Captain of cavalry; Allen, a lieutenant of the same company, and T. Nelson, Colonel of militia, a member of the Legislature of the celebrated Wallace House. He was re-elected in 1878 and again in 1888. After the death of his first wife, Reverend Edens married Mrs. Ann McDaniel, the daughter of Nathan Thomas, who bore him two daughters, one of whom is the wife of Alex. Heustiss.

Jonathan Meekins was an early resident of this community. He lived and died at the forks of the road, where Capt. J. T. Covington, who married a granddaughter of Mr. Meekins, now resides. It is quite probable that Jonathan's parents lived somewhere in this section, for a sister of his married the elder James Spears, in 1777. Jonathan, like most of his neighbors, raised a large family, and possessing large tracts of land, settled them around him. Their farms were noted for their neat, beautiful buildings and fences. But amid the changes of time no man of the name lives now upon the inheritance, although the blood of old Jonathan yet tells in various families of other names. Philip P., of Bennettsville, bears the marks and some of the characteristics of his worthy ancestry. "A place for everything, and everything in its place." "System, order, the law of life," were prevailing influences in that home from cellar to garret.

CHAPTER XV.

Operations on Pee Dee, 1781. Col. Kolb.

The presence of Gen. Greene upon the Pee Dee opposite Cheraw for several weeks had encouraged the spirits of the people, and awed the disaffected into comparative order.

Col. Kolb was in favor with his countrymen and exercised a commanding influence in all the Cheraw district. Murphy down the river, Benton on the west side and Marion, from Lynch's creek to Georgetown, held in check the marauders and gave some security to the people. The stay of Greene was brief. The movements of Cornwallis in the upper part of the State induced Greene to move in the direction of Guilford court house, and the Whigs of the Pee Dee were again left to their own resources. The Tories, ever ready to seize on any advantage, now made frequent incursions on defenseless persons and property, concealing their plunder and themselves in the swamps. It was a hazardous service that devolved upon the Whigs. It is said that a band of Tories had a hiding place in the "Three Creeks" at no great distance from where Blenheim now stands, and, this fact becoming known to the Whigs, it was determined to break them up. The assaulting party came quietly to the edge of the swamp, but could see no signs of the enemy's presence. They had reason to believe that they were near the camp, but they knew not exactly its location and had no guide. Amongst the Whig party was a daring young man, Harry Sparks, who volunteered to enter the swamp alone, locate the enemy and report the situation to his comrades. He found the camp, but returned not to his friends. The treacherous foe had discovered and captured him. His friends became uneasy at his stay and, following his tracks, they soon reached the deserted camp where hung the lifeless body of their daring comrade. Of course the fleeing Tories were pursued for miles, far into North Carolina. One of the pursuers was wounded and two of the mulatto Tories were killed, and sometimes afterwards another of the party was caught and charged with aiding in the murder of Sparks. He confessed it and was instantly hung. This was the sort of warfare that was common in all this region for months and years.

Not long after returning from his chase of the murderers of Sparks, Col. Kolb made an expedition into what is now Marion county. Some outrages had been perpetrated there—in the neighborhood of Hulin's mill—now Moody's mill. Several Tories, who had made themselves especially obnoxious were caught; some punished, some "discharged on promise of good behaviour", and two or three killed. Kolb returned to his home at Welsh Neck, and dismissed his men in the belief that things would be quiet for a time.

Instead of awing those turbulent spirits into order his retaliatory measures awoke a terrible spirit of revenge, and especially against the leader of the Whigs. No blood but his would slake their thirst; no life but his atone for the lives he had taken. Suspecting that he would dismiss his men for a time his enemies made haste to perfect their plans, collect their forces and set out on the hunt for revenge. It was less than forty miles to the happy home of Col. Kolb. At a late hour of night they surrounded his house. Roused from slumber thus suddenly, the first impulse of a brave spirit was to defend his property and loved ones to the last. Mrs. Kolb and an only daughter, who became the wife of Major Pouncey, and two sisters, one of whom became Mrs. Edwards, and was the great-grandmother of Mrs. Dr. Bonchier, lately of Bennettsville, and another sister who afterwards married

Evander McIver, constituted the family. Two young
men named Evans were also present as guests of the
family. Kolb knew his foe—that they had come for
his life—and he was determined to resist. The house
was strongly built, the party inside well armed, and might
have had some hope, although an overpowering force
surrounded them. But in the darkness the stealthy foe
had fired the house. Resistance was useless. The ladies
saw the peril and entreated the Colonel to surrender himself as a prisoner of war. He made the proposition, it
was accepted, and, accompanied by his wife and her sisters and his daughter, he stepped out ready to surrender
his sword. A traitorous shot was fired by a Tory named
Goings and the gallant Colonel fell at his own door and
at the feet of his loved ones a martyr to his country's
cause. One of the young Evans was mortally wounded.
The dwelling was hastily plundered and the Tories quickly
fled in the direction from whence they came, doubtless
exulting in their successful exploit and wishing for another victim. Nor had they long to wait. On the route
to Catfish was "Brown's Mill," about a mile above the
present crossing at the old Rogers mill.

Here was a military post, at least a point sometimes
guarded. The guards were surprised, and Capt. Joseph
Dabbs, a noted Whig, whose home was in the neighborhood of Evans' Mill, was killed, and Ned Trawick was
wounded, but escaped. On this same eventful day, April
28, 1781, an old military prison near the residence of
Col. Kolb was assaulted, and several prisoners were released. Moving down the river a short distance, two of
the released Bristishers entered the home of Mrs. Wilds,
a widowed lady, whom they supposed had money secreted
about her person, and violently robbed her of her coin.
But it was destined that their ill-gotten gain should serve
them but a few brief hours. Living in the marshes was a
frail old man named Willis. Nobody thought it worth

while to trouble *him*. Silent and solitary he was allowed to occupy the position of a neutral. Making a scanty support upon his little patch, and upon his shoemaker's bench, he had nothing to tempt the cupidity of anybody, his poor little money was not worth stealing. The robber Britons on their way from Mrs. Wilds encountered this singular old man. He had seen the columns of smoke ascending from his neighbor Kolb's house, had heard the firing at early dawn, had, perhaps, seen the fleeing Tories, and his smothered patriotism was kindled. His old long barreled fowling piece was taken from the rack, heavily charged, and as the redcoats drew nigh he pulled the trigger at the instant they doubled before him, and the two lay dead in the road. Hearing a few days later that Mrs. Wilds had been robbed, he called to see her, and put in her hand " the package of coin, 101 guineas," the exact amount which the soldiers had taken. In vain did she nsist upon dividing the precious treasure with him whose needs were as great as her own.

"Nay, nay," said the old man, "the money is yourn, it's reward enough for me to be lucky enough to git it back for ye." The tradition has not told where the ashes of Willis lie, some quaint oak or elm may stand at his head and overshadow his unknown resting place, or the swollen waters of the Pee Dee may long ago have ploughed a deep furrow through his lonely bed, and washed his decaying bones away, never to be found until the voice of the archangel shall awake a slumbering race to life— but let the generous deed of the humble, solitary old man live in the memory of generations yet unborn. "Full nany a gem of purest ray serene," etc.

In this connection Bishop Gregg gives his readers a thrilling narrative from the lips of the venerable Lewis Malone Ayer, of Barnwell. Mr. Ayer was the father of Mrs. Judge A. P. Aldrich, and of Gen. L. M. Ayer, a member of the Confederate Congress. He was quite young when the events occurred which he related, but they were of a character to make a profound impression upon his mind.

Young Ayer was on a visit with his mother at the house of a neighbor, close by Col. Kolb's, on the morning the Colonel was killed. Young Ayer had been sent out on a fleet horse at early dawn by his mother to carry tidings of the death of one of her relatives to Col. Kolb, knowing nothing of the tragedy at Kolb's house. Meeting old Mr. William Forniss, together they rode up to the burning building, having seen smoke and the returning horse tracks of the assassins. They saw the weeping wife and sisters with their dead, whom with their own hands they had dragged to a safe distance from the flames. But young Ayer could not tarry with those whom he pitied, because information had reached him that his brother-in-law Mr. James Magee, was that very day to visit Col. Kolb by appointment. Magee lived in the Brownsville community and must travel for a part of the route over the same road which the Tories would travel on their way to Catfish, from whence they came, and if they met Magee it would be the last of him. To get ahead of the Tories and turn Magee from the track was the exploit before the boy Ayer. Excited by the scenes before his eyes, and impelled by the desire to save his friends life, he tried the well-known mettle of his mare, who had done him good service of the like kind before.

He had not calculated, however, that the Tories would stop on the road for breakfast until he was almost within their power, when he wheeled around and fled for dear life. They fired too high to reach the boy who lay close to the mane of the splendid mare, which they desired to capture unhurt. Fortunately, however, there was a cow trail with which Ayer was familiar, close at hand. Into this he dashed and cross a boggy marsh, into which his pursuers plunged, but, not knowing the track as he did, they were soon floundering in the mud, and were glad to get out again on their own side. Afraid that the youth would dash ahead and warn the party at Brown's Mill of their approach, the Tories, after this incident, increased their speed and fortunately passed Magee's road before he entered theirs, and this excellent citizen escaped their hands, and lived for many years to see his children's children, and died in his old age, sitting in his chair, with the Bible lying open upon his knees. His ashes lie at old Brownsville. The first wife of the writer's father was a daughter of James Magee, and died in 1820, the mother of nine children, all of whom have since followed her to the grave.

That was a sad day to the people of Cheraw District when Abel Kolb fell by the hand of the foe. He was recognized as the leader of the patriot influence. In command of the regiment, in the prime of life, vigilant, active, daring, he commanded the respect and confidence of his countrymen far and near, and men were looking upon his fast-developing abilities with admiration and hope of a bright career, not only upon the field of strife, but in the pursuits of peace as well. Already before the war came on he was accumulating property and exhibiting energy, enterprise, and skill in the management of affairs. It is not surprising, therefore, if his loss produced despondency in the hearts of some, and a burning for revenge in others.

About this time, or a few weeks before the death of Kolb, there was a skirmish of some importance at Cashway Ferry. A short distance from the landing on the Marlboro side there stood a Baptist house of worship where such men as Brown and Edwards had held forth the Word of Life. It seems for a time to have been one of the posts held by Kolb or Benton, his Lieutenant-colonel and successor in command of the regiment. It was also a convenient shelter for Tories when dodging around in that region. Which party held the building at the time, and which it was that made the assault the tradition does not tell. An entry in the journal of Rev. Mr. Pugh, of Welsh Neck, dated April 17, says: "Bad news of the Tories at Cashway." The writer remembers an evening's conversation under his mother's roof, between Col. Ben Rogers and Uncle Nathan Thomas, in which the affair was talked over. One of the old men had been a participant in the fray, and amused the party as he told how the Tories "took to the swamp."

After the war ended portions of the old "meeting house" were moved to ":Brown's Mill" and entered into a like building erected there.

The writer has heard numbers of the old people of the community tell how they had seen the "bullet holes in the doors and shutters as long as the house stood."

It gave way to a better building about the beginning of the present century.

Near this old church site there lived a number of staunch Whigs. Capt. Moses Pearson, the Coxes, Burketts, and others who often made it hot for the Tories on Muddy creek. About this time a party of Tories came over from North Carolina into what was then called "Piney Grove settlement," now Adamsville, and caught a young boy named William Adams and demanded of him information as to the locality of certain treasure and persons. Adams knew but determined that it would be a wrong to the cause of the country and the safety of his friends to tell what the foe desired to know. They tried to frighten him with threats of hanging, but he would not be frightened. Finally a cord was procured, but still Adams was firm. Around his neck they tied it, but no disclosure would he make. The cord was thrown over a limb, and he was drawn up and choked and let down and ordered again to speak. Still not a word of information could they extort from his lips. The second time his feet were drawn from the earth. Again they let him down and told him this was his last chance for life. Speak the word and life was his; refuse, and hang till dead.

Firmly he stood. To die was better than to live under a burden of shame. Once more the cruel gang drew him up, tied the cord, and went off and left him hanging. Fortunately for him and for Marlboro, too, his mother came along in time to let him down before life was extinct, and he lived to raise a large family of excellent people, and to-day a host of young and old people are proud to have descended from him.

On the eighth day of September of that year was fought the battle of Eutaw Springs, and a portion of the Pee Dee militia was engaged. Capt. Claudius Pegues, of Marlboro, with his company, was on the ground. Joshua David, the ancestor of the family among us, was permanently disabled by a wound in the hand, and Capt. Pegues was shot in the leg. Here it was that Thomas Quick, an humble private in the ranks, seeing his officer's failing strength, though he still stood in the line, seized him as he was falling, bore him off, and with the aid of Nero, the Captain's servant, took him to a place of security and then begged to go back and get another shot at the red-coats who had shot so good a man as his Captain. Never will the Pegues forget the Quicks, and never ought they.

On October 19, 1781, Cornwallis surrendered at Yorktown, Virginia. Charleston was still held, but Governor Rutledge, feeling that the time had come for the more formal establishment of civil government in South Carolina, issued a call for the election of members for Senate and House of Representatives. Since the capital of the State was yet under British power, the meeting was held at Jacksonborough, Colleton county. Tristram Thomas, Philip Pledger, William Dewitt and William Pegues were elected from Cheraw and took their seats in January, 1782.

But peace was not yet. It was not until July of that year that the British Parliament passed a bill to enable the King to consent to the independence of the colonies, and not until November, 1782, were the articles signed by the commissioners.

In the meantime many irregularities and lawless deeds were committed doubtless by both Whigs and Tories. Hard it was for the former to forget the insults offered their families and the injury done their property by their Tory neighbors. Hard for a Tory to feel safe in his house in the immediate vicinity of men he had wronged. Hard for men to settle to pursuits of peace and meet each other as friends who for a long time had been enemies in war. It was long after their officers had dismissed them to their homes, and charged them to bury past emnities and go home to forgive and forget. Long after the Legislature had proclaimed amnesty to such as would come in and swear allegiance, and enjoined the observance of civil order, that Whig and Tory watched and feared each other with many heart-burnings and jealousies. Many a poor fellow was whipped or shot and some hung without judge or jury long after the last "red-coat" had gone, and no doubt but that many a cow, hog or horse was stolen in revenge for deeds of war.

The American cause had triumphed, but loyalty died hard. Not until George III. said: "I was the last man in the Kingdom to consent to American independence, but now that it is granted I shall be the last man in the world to sanction any violation of it," could all men recognize it as an accomplished fact.

CHAPTER XVI.

Bishop Gregg.

As has been already intimated, the writer has made free use of the work of the late Bishop Gregg, of Texas, sometimes giving his authority and at other times giving facts contained in the Bishop's "History of the Old Cheraws," in his own language. No one at this day can hope to tell the story of the early settlers on the Pee Dee without drawing largely from this source. Kindly and generously Bishop Gregg has expressed his gratification in several communications to the author that his book has been of service in this "labor of love." Although he was never a citizen of Marlboro, yet in his early life and vigorous manhood Bishop Gregg was a near and much-loved neighbor; and, by his marriage with one of Marlboro's fairest daughters, became almost a citizen and is justly entitled to a more extended notice than can be accorded to many a worthy son of the soil. His great-grandfather, John Gregg, of Scottish origin, came to the Pee Dee in 1752, and was the father of a large family. A brother, Joseph, settled lower down the river, and from him came the large family in Marion and Florence counties. From James, the first son of John, came a goodly group; among them, David, the father of Alexander, the late Bishop of Texas, whose mother was Athalinda Brocky. "Alexander was born at Society Hill, Darlington county, South Carolina, October 8, 1819. From an early age he was a pupil in the St. David's Academy, of famous memory. At fifteen he went to Mt. Zion College at Winnsboro, so celebrated for years, under the charge of Wilson Hudson, Esq. In the latter part of November, in the year 1835, he matriculated at the South Carolina

College, entering the Junior class. At the reorganization of the college in January, 1836, under Hon. R. W. Barnwell as president, and embracing a curriculum with a more extended and thorough course of study, the young student being only sixteen, he was induced to enter the Sophomore class in order to have the advantages of a three years' course. He graduated in December, 1838, taking the first honor in a class of forty. Naturally drawn to the law, he applied himself to its study and entered the office of Robbins & McIver in the fall of 1839 with the late Chancellor Inglis as a fellow student. In December, 1840, they were both admitted to the bar. Returning to Cheraw, he formed a partnership with Gen. Blakeny for two years and after that was alone for a year." On the 21st of April, 1841, he was married to Miss Charlotte Wilson Kollock, of Marlboro, a lady who had enjoyed the advantages of the highest culture and was possessed of unusual attractions of mind and character. This noble helpmeet cheerfully left her charming home in Carolina, and accompanied her husband to the wilds of Texas where duty seemed to call him. After blessing his life for nearly forty years with her presence and moulding influence, she went to her reward May 20, 1880; but not till her heart had been pained and chastened by the death of a precious son.

The career of Mr. Gregg as a lawyer was unexpectedly terminated in the spring of 1844, when he felt called of God to another and higher course of life; the result of deep and serious religious convictions of earlier years. Now he was moved to abandon all else, and joyously gave himself to the ministry. Received into the Episcopal church by the late Bishop Gadsden, he at once became a candidate for holy orders. The influence of the ministrations of Bishop Elliott, who was chaplain of the college during his student life, doubtless contributed to this result. In June, 1846, he was ordained deacon in St.

David's Church, at Cheraw, by Bishop Gadsden, and in January following, he was ordained to the priesthood, and became the rector of St. David's, in which office he continued thirteen years, not only beloved by his own church, but honored and admired by Christians of every name.

In May, 1859, he was elected by the convention of that diocese Bishop of Texas, and, under the circumstances, felt it his duty to accept the call as the work of his life, although sundering many tender relations. His diocese then, and till 1874, embraced the entire State, which now for the first time had a bishop of its own. In October, 1859, he was consecrated to his office in Richmond, Va., where the general convention of his church was then in session, and as soon as practicable, removed his family to Austin, which was to be their future home. In 1857, while yet a clergyman in South Carolina, Mr. Gregg was elected a trustee of the University of the South, located at Sewanee, Tenn. As Bishop of Texas, he was continued a trustee, and after the death of Bishop Green, of Mississippi, the Chancellor of the University, Bishop Gregg was elected to that office in 1887. The published writings of the Bishop consists of sermons, Episcopal charges, and the History of the Old Cheraws, which appeared in 1867. The circumstances which led to the work are given in the introduction. Every available source of information, it is believed, was examined, and, happily, much valuable matter preserved, thus escaping the ravages and losses which would inevitably have followed during the war between the States. This notice of Bishop Gregg is long, but every word is due. No man has done so much—none can do more to preserve the traditions and history of this portion of the State. Bishop Gregg has died since this chapter was prepared. He died at Sewanee, Tenn., a few years ago.

CHAPTER XVII.

A Chapter of Traditions and Recollections of Mr. Alfred Parish.

Mr. Parish* is one upon whose head rests the frosts of four-score winters, and yet he is a man of remarkable vigor, both of body and mind, a man too, who for this long period has maintained amongst his neighbors the standing of one of solid worth. No man can call his word into question or impeach his honesty, he being a lover of good order, and scorning everything tricky or mean.

He has been three times married, and is the father of thirteen children, ten of whom are living. His first wife was the daughter of William Spears, who was the mother of John, Joel and Henry Parish, noted for their successful farming in the Clio and Red Bluff regions. His second wife was Miss Mary McDaniel, and his third wife was Ellen, a daughter of Daniel Parkham. His parents, Noel Parish and Willie Lawrence, came to Marlboro from Granville county, N. C., in the early part of the present century, and lived first at what is now known as the Ervin place, two miles from Bennettsville. This ancient couple had five daughters who became mothers to several Marlboro families. One of them, Nancy, married Conner Cottingham, from whom sprang Andrew, Elkana and David. Mary married William Bolton, a kinsman of Capt. Frank Bolton, who has so efficiently filled the office of County Treasurer and County Commissioner, and was a gallant soldier in the late war, where he lost an arm. Lucy Parish married Mr. Bristow, the father of the well-known family of that name, which has given to

---
*Since died.

Marlboro two Sheriffs and a clerk of long standing, and which is still an extensive family in the country.

A daughter of Mr. Bristow married Mr. Webster, the grandfather of William, Robert and George. Four brothers of Mr. Parish, Milton, Willey, Caleb and David, moved to Alabama many years ago. When Mr. Parish remembers the country first, Toler McDaniel lived on the road leading from Beauty Spot to Cheraw. Near him was Mrs. Parham with four sons, Avery, James, Lemuel and Wesley, and near the Beauty Spot Fork was Joseph McDaniel. On Carter Branch was Col. W. G. Feagan, and there his body rests. He was the son of the old schoolmaster, Neddy Feagan, who is said to have taught three generations of young ideas under the old *regime* of "birch and brawn." There are a number of worthy people in the county who are descended from this old schoolmaster, and many an old land-paper bears the lines made by W. G. Feagan, "District Surveyor,"

On the hill on the east side of the creek, on the road from Bennettsville to Hebron, lived Jonathan Cottingham, a brother to Conner, already mentioned, and the father of a large family. In his house, and cared for by him, was an old man, his father, Charles, whose body was the first interred in the Cottingham graveyard on the west side of the creek. The late Charles Cottingham, the son of Jonathan, an honest man and good citizen, was the father of most of those bearing the name in Marlboro. James, the "old singing-master," and for many years Major of the Lower Battalion of the 30th Regiment of Militia, moved to North Carolina and was kille by Federal soldiers—a helpless old man, but has descendants in Marlboro county.

When Mr. Parish first recollects the Hebron community, the old men William Bridges, William Covington, Nathan Thomas and Jonathan Meekins, were living in quiet contentment upon their little farms—with abundant pasturage in the forest and meadows, fish in the streams and ponds, deer and wild turkeys in the woods. Now, immense fields of cotton and grain occupy the attention, and reward the industry of a dense population of thrifty people. Mr. Parish thinks that the Conners came from Maryland. He remembers a widow Conner who had a daugher, Nancy, that married William Spears, father of Lewis and Harris. After Conner's death the widow married John Breeden, who had a son, Lindsay, by a former marriage, and who was the father of our fellow citizens; Wm. K., James B., Peter L., Joseph L., Thomas, Andrew, and John L., deceased. After the marriage of the widow Conner and the widower Breeden, a son, the late Major Aaron Breeden, was born. Few families have attained to more prominence and thrift in business circles than this one, the progenitor of which is remembered by Mr. Parish as he lived in Adamsville. Nor has he forgotten how, in his boyhood days, he beheld and tasted the sweet cider as it flowed from the press of old Mr. Breeden, an attraction to the boys of the neighborhood. Upon one of the tributaries of "Three Creeks" in the Beauty Spot section was Fuller's old mill, gone to decay before Mr. Parish's time. But he remembered Henry, the husband of "Aunt Betsy," the maker of the historic "Fuller Cakes," which every old man can remember in his boyhood, as sold from her "cart" on the courtyard and muster-field. Nor has Marlboro ever seen any "ginger cake" since, that has equaled "Aunt Betsy's," has been the verdict of the people for years.

Near the old mill lived Shadrach Fuller, from whom Mrs. Crawford Easterling is descended. A sister married John H. David, the father of Dr. W. J. David, and another sister married James Stubbs, from whom D. C. Odom sprang. The mother of Shadrach and his sisters was an aunt of Mr. Parish. She was Miss Lucy Parish before she married.

The McDaniel family seems to have been a numerous one, and to have intermarried with some of their neighbors already mentioned. We find them in different places, about a hundred years ago. In Beauty Spot were Thomas, Joseph, and Mrs. James Cook, mother of the Bennettsville family, from whom descended Mrs. Rachel Thomas and John B. In Hebron was George, with several sons, Wiliam, Fred, and Thomas McDaniel. Some of the Brightsville Stubbs claim a maternal descent from this name. Mr. Parish is connected with one, if not two branches of the family, and if all have sprung from the same original stock, it must have been one of the first upon the ground.

There was one tradition our friend was not averse to telling. That two of his father's brothers were soldiers in the patriot army while the family had their home in North Carolina. Who shall blame him if he is "proud of that fact?"

One other name was remembered by Mr. Parish as contributing a full share toward the peopling and civilization of the country, Mr. John Murdock, living near the Beauty Spot church. He had several sons, John, Andrew, James, David and Alexander. Several were prominent men, but the name is now extinct. A number of good people amongst us descended from the noble old Scotchman who sought to train his children for honor and piety. The old home is yet occupied by his descendants, children of Capt. McIntyre.

CHAPTER XVIII.

After the Revolution.

With the close of the protracted and arduous struggle through which the country had passed, and the return of peace ; came many responsibilities. The material development of the State, the establishment of schools, the payment of debts, the creation of a currency, and the enforcement of order and law, everything in short, essential to the prosperity of a new government, demanded attention. The halls of justice long closed were to be reopened ; a nation just born was to take its initial steps in self-government, and not license, and lawlessness. The State Legislature was called to meet in January, 1783. Major Tristram Thomas was elected Senator for Cheraw District, and Lemuel Benton, Thomas Powe, William Pegues, William Strother, William DeWitt, and Claudius Pegues, members of the House of Representatives. At that session Claudius Pegues was elected Ordinary for the District, and William DeWitt, Sheriff. Both of these offices at that time were especially important. Many deaths had occurred, many estates were unsettled, and there was great need for prudence and skill in the men who were called to these responsible positions, and it was greatly to the credit of these gentlemen to be counted worthy to fill those places, and that they were not found wanting.

The first general court after peace was declared was held at Long Bluff in November, Judge Grimke presiding. The Judge had but lately received his commission. He was a student in England when the war broke out, but hurried to his native shore and threw himself into the struggle upon the side of liberty. He sat upon the bench and saw before him in the courtroom and the "jury box" the forms of men, who, like himself, had passed through the hardships and dangers of the field while their property was exposed to the depredations of the Tories, and could yet rise above emotions of resentment and hatred. He counseled his countrymen no longer to brand their people with this appellation, but to seek for things that make for peace. For thirty-six years he lived to enforce and expound justice and law. Judging from the anecdotes that Judge O'Neal records of him in his "Bench and Bar," we should say of him, "A terror to evil-doers," and a "Spur to plodding lawyers."

In the Edgefield court, 1815, the sessions docket was exceedingly heavy. The "solicitor, Mr. Starke, presented forty bills of indictment for every grade of offense from assault and battery to murder. Thirty-nine were found "true bills." Many convictions followed. One of the Edgefield rowdies of the day, looking on at the arraignment and conviction of so many, swore it 'was no place for him to be,' for said he, 'Starke holds and Grimke skins.'" No doubt the wise words of this Judge, addressed to a Grand Jury composed of such men as George Hicks, Morgan Brown, Moses Pearson, Philip Pledger, Thomas Ellerbe, and others of like spirit, had much effect in restoring peace and order; in encouraging the people in self-reliance, industry and respect of law. It also encouraged the improvement of public highways and river navigation. It was at this term of court that the Grand Jury recommended the opening of a road from Long Bluff to Barnes s bridge, or Gum Swamp, where it was to meet another from Cross Creek, now Fayettville, in North Carolina, the road upon which Bennettsville is located

It was during the session of 1785 that an Act passed the Legislature, establishing inferior courts of justice, like the County Courts of some neighboring States. By this Act the District of Cheraw was divided into three Counties, Darlington, Chesterfield, and Marlboro, the latter embracing the territory on the eastern side of the Great Pee Dee, and which is included in the County of to-day. By this Act justices were to be appointed, with power to build court-houses, lay taxes for this purpose, hold quarterly sessions, have jurisdiction in causes at "common law," when the debt was "liquidated by bond, or note of hand, or where the damages did not exceed fifty pounds," and in minor criminal cases, with the right of appeal to the higher courts. The first Board of Justices appointed for Marlboro consisted of the following: Claudius Pegues, George Hicks, Morgan Brown, Tristram Thomas, Claudius Pegues, Jr., Moses Pearson and Thomas Evans. The position was one of trust, demanding wisdom and integrity. As "gold is purified in the fire," the ordeal through which these men had passed had proven their character before their fellow citizens. They seemed to have organized at once, and tradition has it that they met for a time at Gardner's Bluff, or near there, but the permanent location selected was nearer to Crooked Creek, near by what is now Evans' Mill. Gen. Thomas's conveyance of the ground to the above-named Commissioners is upon record. The building erected was of wood, two stories high—capacious and substantial, but the locality proved unhealthy. The court-house was found to be inconveniently located, and in 1819 steps were taken to change the seat of justice to a more central and healthy spot. So, in 1824, a new court-house was finished at Bennnettsville, the present site.

It is not to be understood that the Circuit courts were abandoned when the County courts were established. The court for Cheraw District of the Northern Circuit seems yet to have been regularly held, but this dual system does not appear to have been satisfactory, and a change in the system was thought to be necessary. So that, at the session of Legislature, 1799, a bill was passed for "instituting District courts in the several Counties of the State." The Counties were, therefore, called Districts until 1868, when the Convention of reconstruction restored the old title.

Let us turn back to the natal day in 1785 when the three divisions formed in Cheraw District had to be named. One of them, Darlington, took the name of a gallant colonel who distinguished himself in the War of Independence. Chesterfield honored the old English Earl whose name has long been the synonym of dignity and grace. Our own division went across the water also in search of a name, and fixed on England's grand old soldier, who never knew defeat in the battles of a life-time, and honored the Duke of Marlborough by taking his heroic name. Before passing entirely from the County court period of our history, it may be well to mention other men who sat upon the bench of justices. In March, 1786, we find William Thomas, Thomas Lide, and William Easterling. The latter is recognized as the ancestor of the Adamsville branch of the family bearing that name. He was afterwards made Ordinary and served until his death in honorable old age.

Mr. Lide ("Colonel," he was called) is said to have been a man of high character, the grandfather of Governor John Lide Wilson, and the father of five sons; John, Thomas, Charles M., Robert and James; also a daughter who first became Mrs. Twitty and afterwards Mrs. Burn. Charles Motte Lide, one of the sons, was considered one of the most remarkable men of his day. Educated, intellectual, a gifted orator, few men could so sway the emotions of an audience; but strangely erratic, and of feeble health and irregular habits, he sank into an early grave. The Colonel and Justice was a pious man, a prominent Baptist, and died greatly lamented, soon after his appointment to a justiceship in Marlboro. In 1787 William Thomas came from Maryland and settled a few miles above Cheraw, on the east side of the river, married a Miss Little, who had some property, to which he largely added. One son, William L., was given to this pair. He married a Miss Benton, who had two sons, Alexander, who died unmarried, and William L., who married Jane McQueen, and died childless. His widow afterwards became the wife of Col. John Campbell, the Congressman, and passed calmly away within the last few months. Thus it is seen that this branch of the Thomas family is extinct.

In 1789 Drury Robertson was made a justice. It is said that this gentleman came to Marlboro after the war. If so he must have been a man of marked influence, for he became prominent in the affairs of the country at once, having been elected to the Legislature the year before he was made a Justice. There is a tradition that he had a command in the revolutionary army, and this may have helped him to positions where there were so many worthy competitors.

Major Robertson made property, and secured a splendid body of land upon both sides of Naked Creek, and built a mill or two upon that stream. He was the maternal grandfather of that noble son of Marlboro, Col. William T. Ellerbe. Samuel Brown, a member of the Brownsville family, and George Cherry, another citizen of Lower Marlboro, and Benjamin Hicks, also were members of this County Court Commission, before it was finally abolished in 1799. It is proper in this connection to place upon record the names of the men who were elected from Marlboro, to the State Legislature, bearing in mind that until 1790 they were chosen to represent Cheraw District, or St. David's Parish, rather than the separate counties. In 1786 William Thomas was elected Senator, and Calvin Spencer, Robert Baxter, Morgan Brown, Andrew Hunter, Lemuel Benton, and William Strother, Representatives Most of the latter resided on the western side of the river, which was altogether fair, since the eastern side had the Senator. In 1788 the same members appear. On May 12th, of that year, a convention assembled for the ratification of the Federal Constitution. The delegates from the Cheraw District were Lemuel Benton, Tristram Thomas, William DeWitt, Calvin Spencer, S. Taylor, R. Brownfield, and Benj. Hicks. This delegation voted for the ratification. In November of that year Morgan Brown was elected Senator, and Robert Ellison, Charles Evans, Thomas Evans, Robert Brownfield, Drury Robertson, and Henry Cannon, Representatives. It was the Legislature of which these were members that issued a call for a State Constitutional Convention, which met in Columbia in May, 1790. For St. David's Parish the following delegates were sent: Calvin Spencer, Benj. Hicks, Lem Benton, Robert Ellison, Charles Evans, Morgan Brown and Rev. Evan Pugh. This Convention adopted a Constitution June 3d, which gave the three counties of Cheraw District, two Representatives each, and two Senators for the three. At the next election Morgan Brown and Robert Allison were chosen Senators, and Thomas Evans, and John Jones James were Representatives from Marlboro. In 1792, Robert Allison, whose term of service had expired, was re-elected Senator, and John J. James and Benj. Hicks Representatives from Marlboro. In 1794 Marlboro elected as Representatives J. J. James and Drury Robertson, and in 1796, they were re-elected, with William and Tristram Thomas as Senators. In 1798, William Whitfield took the place of Mr. James, and John McIver that of General Thomas in the Senate. In 1800, Drury Robertson was succeed by David Stewart in the House, and Alex McIntosh took the place of William Thomas.

The organization of the militia seems to have received the attention of the Legislature at an early period. In the returns of 1787–1788 the Cheraw regiment, Col. Benton commanding, is put down at one thousand men, and in 1789 a cavalry company was organized at Cheraw with Samuel Taylor as captain, Holden Wade and Benny Hicks, lieutenants, and forty privates. By 1794 the militia of the State had so increased that the Cheraw regiment had grown into a brigade of three regiments, the Thirty-seventh or Marlboro, under Col. Thomas Evans. Col. Benton, who, for long years, had been deservedly popular, faithful and true upon the field of war, foremost as a statesman, a leader in every enterprise looking to the country's welfare, was now in Congress as the first representative of the Pee Dee district. He naturally enough aspired to, and expected to be made a brigadier. But Maj. Thomas was also an idol with his people; faithful, true and capable wherever the voice of his country, or duty to his Saviour called him, and he it was whom his countrymen preferred as the commander of the brigade. The sensibilities of the soldier were touched when one that had fought at his side, and since served as a subordinate, should be promoted above him. Benton promptly resigned his commission as Colonel of the Cheraw regiment, and Capt. Spencer was elected in his place. In 1800 the Cheraw brigade numbered 2,224 men, and the total population of the district is set down at 18,015, an increase of nearly 8,000 since 1792, when the total was 10,706. Of this latter number 3,288 were colored, and in 1800 the slaves were 4,877. For Marlboro, in 1800, the white population was 3,880, and the colored 1,393, nearly three to one in favor of the whites. Now, we are largely outnumbered by the sable faces. Has it been that the white people have emigrated and left their servants behind? or has it been that the natural increase of the colored race has so largely exceeded the white?

CHAPTER XIX.

Prominent Men After the Revolution.

So far as this writer now remembers, in all her history Marlboro has furnished the State but two governors. One of these has already been named in these pages; Dr. B. K. Henagan, who filled out the unexpired term of Gov. Noble, who died in office. The other was John Lide Wilson. This man was born in Marlboro, a few miles from Cheraw, in 1784. After his school days were over he was admitted to the bar in 1807 and settled down to his practice in Georgetown. In the next year he was elected a member of the House of Representatives, and subsequently filled a seat in the State Senate. In 1822 he was made president of the Senate, and, before the session was ended, was elected governor. Judge O'Neal, in his "Bench and Bar," gives an estimate of his character, and says: "His intellect was a fine one; his speeches, political and legal, were always compiled with wonderful arrangement and care, and his voice and manner were fine and graceful. If he had cultivated the great talents with which God had endowed him, he must have been among the greatest men of South Carolina." He died in Charleston in 1849 and was buried there with military honors.

It is fit that mention be made of James R. Ervin, a young man when he came to Marlboro as a lawyer in 1809, having been born in Marion county in 1788. He soon rose to popular favor, and was soon elected a member of the House of Representatives, a position he held until he moved to Marion. But upon his return to Marlboro he was elected to the Senate. Subsequently he went to Cheraw, and the Chesterfield people made him their

Senator. Few men have lived in Marlboro of a more handsome and commanding physique—tall, well proportioned, a countenance beaming with intelligence and humor, with captivating, easy manners and charming conversational powers, he was the center and life of every circle. As an orator, cool, fearless, ready and forcible, he seemed born to lead; and had he not relied too much upon his natural gifts, but given himself more to application, he might have climbed to any height in public favor and position. Among the grand men of a past generation, who swayed popular gatherings in the stirring times of nullification in the Pee Dee section, the writer can remember none, who in his boyhood's fancy, towered above Col. Ervin. He had a son, Major E. P. Ervin, who settled at Bennettsville as a lawyer, went to the Legislature, was commissioner in equity, married a daughter of Mr. John McCollum and left a family of several sons and daughters.

Soon after the Revolutionary War was ended Robert Campbell came to the Pee Dee and settled near Hunt's Bluff in Marlboro. He had been a British officer, had large wealth, married Miss Blair and soon became a money-making, prosperous planter. He was careful in the education and culture of his children, Robert B., James, John and Maria. The daughter, Maria, married David G. Coit, and was the mother of Major J. C. Coit, of Cheraw, and others. Her second husband was Major James McQueen. It is said that when the War of 1812 came on between Great Britain and the United States. the elder Capt. Campbell earnestly urged his first born, Robt. B., to accept a commission in the British army which he offered to procure for him. But the son indignantly refused what to him appeared a traitorous temptation. Young Campbell was gifted, of courteous, courtly manners, splendid form and features, and soon rose into prominence. He married into the Lee family, of Virginia, and was elected a member of Congress. Subsequently he sold his splendid plantation (what is now Drake's Mill and Lowden plantation), and went to Alabama, and filled a mission to Havana, and afterwards to England.

Col. John Campbell, after his literary course, studied law, it is thought at Litchfield, Conn., was admitted to the bar in 1822, but seems not to have practiced long, if at all. He married Mrs. Jane Thomas, the widow of W. L. Thomas. She was Miss McQueen before marriage, a most amiable, excellent woman, who died at a great age only a few years ago. Col. Campbell was first elected to the Twenty-first Congress, which met in 1829. In 1837 he appeared again as a member of the Twenty-fifth and was three times elected after this. He died universally lamented soon after his last election. He was a man of great polish, graceful manner, amiable spirit, refined, modest and yet fearless; one of the most fascinating, fluent speakers of his day, capable of charming all circles in society, the favorite alike of all classes of his people. The Messrs. Campbell, of Blenheim, and James P., of Bennettsville, are descended from the first Robert, but not by the first marriage.

Soon after the war for independence there came to the lower part of Marlboro a man, who, if not distinguished for great intellectual force, was yet notable on several accounts, Baron De Poelnitz. It was claimed that the same lofty spirit that impelled his more distinguished countrymen, Kosciusko and Pulaski, to come from Poland here, moved Poelnitz. He purchased a large body of land on the river, below Three Creeks, and, bringing his effects up the Pee Dee from Georgetown by boat, built a store-house, and thought to establish a town, and to this day the place is called "Ragtown." Tradition has it that he brought numerous seeds from the old world to sow in the virgin soil of the new; and among the rest the introduction of "nut grass" is charged to his account. It used to be told that when the old man came to die, he charged his friends that when they thought him dead they must, before burying him, apply heated irons to his feet, and see sure signs of decay; then place his body in a strong double case, bury it upon a certain sand-ridge in "Ragtown," and "plant an oak at his head, that the dust of his body entering into the growing tree might not be found at the general resurrection." The writer remembers a tree pointed out as the majestic sentinel, keeping watch and guard over the dust of the Baron. Whatever the singularities of this old Baron (and, perhaps, the only one Marlboro has ever had to live and die upon her soil), he seems to have accumulated property, and reared a cultured family. A son, Julius, as remembered, married a daughter of Col. Rogers, and when their children were nearly all grown, went with them to Alabama. A bachelor brother to Julius, odd, simple-minded old man, whom the young people used to love to tease, clung to Julius as the vine to its prop. The name is no longer known in the county. A daughter of the Baron, a beautiful accomplished woman, first married a Mr. Stewart, and after his death became the wife of Robeson Carloss. Mr. Carloss was a prominent useful man in his day, who came from Virginia; lived and raised a family in the Brownsville community; was long known as a justice of the peace. The name is extinct on the Pee Dee.

CHAPTER XX.

MEMBERS OF THE LEGISLATURE AND OTHER OFFICERS.

The journals of the State Senate and also of the House of Representatives have been carefully searched, with the desire to obtain a correct list of the men who have represented Marlboro in the Legislature from the Revolutionary War to the year 1890; and it is thought that the following meets the requirement. It is to be remembered that before, and for some years after the formation of the three counties, Chesterfield, Darlington and Marlboro, out of the territory comprising the "Old Cheraw District," the members were elected as from the old district, or "St. David's Parish," and even after the Representatives began to be chosen from the counties separately, for a number of years, till about 1805, the three counties (or districts as they were called) continued to be a single senatorial district. Therefore, it will be observed that in a few instances, men residing outside of Marlboro are put down as representing it in the Senate; but as at almost every election one or more Marlboro men were returned along with others from the other counties to the House, only such as appeared from Marlboro are enrolled in the list of the lower House:

1783	Tristram Thomas.	1802–03	Thomas Powe,
1784–85	William DeWitt.	1804–05	Benjamin Rogers.
1786–87	William Thomas.	1806–09	Hugh Lide.
1788–89	Morgan Brown.	1810–13	William Whitfield.
1790–91	Morgan Brown.	1814–17	Thomas Evans.
1792–93	Robert Ellison.	1818–21	Robeson Carloss.
1794–95	{ Thomas Powe, Tristram Thomas.	1822–25	Robert B. Campbell.
		1826–29	James R. Ervin.
1796–97	{ William Thomas, Tristram Thomas.	1830–33	Robert B. Campbell.
		1834–37	Barnabas K. Henagan.
1798–99	{ William Thomas, John McIver.	1838–41	Daniel C. Murdock.
		1842–45	James E. David.
1800–01	{ Alexander McIntosh, John McIver.	1846–49	William T. Ellerbe.
		1850–57	C. W. Dudley.

1858–61	Charles Irby.	1876–89	C. S. McCall.
1862–65	Wm. D. Johnson.	1890–94	W. D. Evans.
1865–67	T. C. Weatherly.	1894–	H. M. Stackhouse.
1868–76	H. J. Maxwell.		

REPRESENTATIVES.

1783	Claudius Pegues.	1842–43	{ W. J. Cook, E. P. Ervin.
1784–87	Morgan Brown.		
1788–89	{ Drury Robertson, Robert Allison.	1844–45	{ E. P. Ervin, W. T. Ellerbe.
1790–91	{ Thomas Evans. John J. Jones.	1846–47	{ J. W. Harrington, B. B. Rogers.
1792–93	{ John J. Jones, Benjamin Hicks.	1848–49	{ J. W. Harrington, W. J. Cook.
1794–95	{ J. J. Jones, Drury Robertson.	1850–51	{ T. C. Weatherly, Chas. A. Thornwell,
1796–97	{ Drury Robertson, J. J. Jones.	1852–53	{ Chas. A. Thornwell, T. C. Weatherly.
1798–99	{ William Whitfield, D. Robertson.	1854–56	{ C. A. Thornwell, Chas. Irby.
1800–01	{ David Stuart, Tristram Thomas.	1856–57	{ A. G. Johnson, P. B. McLaurin.
1802–03	William Easterling.	1858–59	{ C. P. Townsend, J. H. Hudson.
1804–05	{ William Whitfield, Robert Allison.		
1806–07	Tristram Thomas.	1860–61	{ W. J. Cook, J. W. Henagan,
1808–09	{ Thomas Evans, John Rogers.	1862–63	{ C. P. Townsend, T. C. Weatherly.
1810–11	{ James R. Ervin, Tristram Thomas.	1864–65	S. J. Townsend,
1812–13	{ T. Thomas, Josiah J. Evans.	1866–67	Harris Covington.
1814–15	William Whitfield.	1868–69	{ James Jones, J. G. Grant.
1816–17	{ J. A. Evans, Geo. R. Whitfield.	1870–71	{ T. P. Stubbs, D. P. McLaurin.
1818–19	James Gillespie.	1872–73	{ J. W. Thomas, Sam'l Jackson.
1820–23	James Gillespie,		
1824–25	{ G. R. Whitfield, T. J. Williams.	1874–75	{ Jacob Allman, T. C. Weatherly,
1826–27	{ Thos. J. Williams, Chas. Lide.	1876–77	{ P. M. Hamer, T. N. Edens.
1828–29	{ John Murdock, John M. Rogers.	1878–79	{ P. M. Hamer, T. N. Edens.
1830–31	{ C. J. Lide, John Murdock.	1880–81	{ H. H. Newton, J. R. Parker,
1832–33	{ John Murdock, Chas. J. Lide.	1882–83	{ J. B. McLaurin, Knox Livingston.
1834–35	Wm. T. Ellerbe.	1884–85	{ Simeon Gibson, F. W. Kinney.
1836–37	C. W. Dudley.		
1838–39	James E. David.	1886–87	{ Jno. N. Drake, W. D. Evans.
1840–41	{ C. W. Dudley, W. T. Ellerbe.	1888–89	{ T. N. Edens, W. D. Evans.

1890–92	{ H. M. Stackhouse, { Jno. L. McLaurin,	1894–96	{ C. P. Townsend, { J. P. Bunch,
1892–94	{ H. M. Stackhouse, { Jas. T. Covington, { Dan C. Roper,	1896–	{ J. F. McLaurin, { J. F. McLaurin, { Knox Livingston, { T. I. Rogers.

It is interesting to observe that of these seventy men whom the people have honored with their suffrages, ten have rendered service in both branches of the Legislature. One of them, B. K. Henagan, practiced medicine. Mr. McCall has been a successful merchant, having at the same time an extensive farming interest, which was also true of Dr. Henagan. Fifteen of the seventy were lawyers, three of whom were elevated to the bench. Several of them devoted much attention to their farms. But taking these from the list there are left fifty-two farmers; a little more than three-fourths of the whole; and some of those who served longest were of this class. One of them was six times elected; another five times. Four were four times, and four others three times; while only one lawyer has been able to carry his election the fourth time, and two others reached a third term. So that if Marlboro is and has always been an agricultural county, so has it been in all the years of its history a government of farmers, and yet in most of the members of the bar that have represented her interests in the councils of the State, she has honored herself in honoring them. Time was, indeed, when the voters of Marlboro scarce thought to inquire into the profession or calling in life, of the man that sought their suffrages. Is he worthy? Is he capable? No doubt mistakes were made, but it was not when a lawyer was in the Senate that "poor Marlboro" rang in the corridors of the capitol. That people is in danger, that allows one class to array itself against another. Just as in the world of nature, we need variety, and can only have the grandest perfection of beauty and utility; so in social, political and industrial affairs we need various classes, industries and callings to give strength, order and success to the whole. As the old men of seventy years ago looked upon the manly form of Gillespie or Robert B. Campbell, and heard their stirring words, they may have felt, these are the men to move senates, sway juries, and impress judges; or, as they met the polite, modest youthful Evans, or laughed over the anecdotes and pleasantries of Ervin, they hardly thought or cared to remember that these were young lawyers, destined to impress themselves upon their country; or later on, when Ellerbe and David met upon the stump, who cared whether he voted for the farmer or the lawyer? Both commanded the respect of his friends for what he *was*, in *himself*, and few men cared as to his calling, so he honored himself in its pursuit.

The following is thought to be a full and correct list of the Sheriffs, Clerks and Ordinaries who have held office in Marlboro from the Revolution to date:

	SHERIFFS OF MARLBORO.	Time of Service.		CLERKS OF COURT.	Time of Service.
1	John Andrews	1785	1	John Wilson	1785
2	James Moore	1786	2	Joel Winfield	1787
3	William Pledger	1792	3	William Fields	1788
4	Thomas Evans	1804	4	Drury Robertson	1789
5	Benjamin Rogers	1808	5	Joel Winfield	1790
6	William Bristow	1812	6	Jno. Winfield	1804
7	Chas. S. Strother	1816	7	John Thomas	1808
8	Joshua David	1820	8	John A. Evans	1812
9	Wm. Pouncy	1824	9	James Gillespie, *pro tem*	1816
10	Geo. Bristow	1828	10	Morgan J. Brown	1816
11	E. L. Henagan	1832	11	Wm. Bristow	1820
12	M. Townsend	1838	12	Wm. Pledger, *pro tem*.	1824
13	Geo. Bristow	1842	13	Joshua David	1824
14	T. C. Weatherly	1846	14	James C. Thomas	1828
15	B. F. McGilvray	1850	15	Geo. Bristow	1832
16	Jno. W. Henagan	1854	16	Robt. D. Thomas	1838
17	B. F. McGilvray	1858	17	Robt. D. Thomas	1842
18	J. L. Breeden	1862	18	Peter McCall	1846
19	A. E. Bristow	1866		Held office till his death 1871	
20	J. L. Easterling	1870	19	T. W. Allen, 1871 to	1876

SHERIFFS OF MARLBORO.

		Time of Service.
21	J. H. Jones	1874
22	A. H. Knight	1875 to 1876
23	G. W. Waddill appointed	1876
24	W. P. Emanuel	1876
	Died	1879
25	B. A. Rogers appointed	1879
25	B. A. Rogers elected	1880
	to	1892
26	J. B. Green elected 1892 to 1896	

CLERKS OF COURT.

		Time of Service.
20	C. M. Weatherly	1876
	to	1892
21	Jas. A. Drake, 1892 to	1896

ORDINARIES OF MARLBORO.

Joel Winfield, clerk, served as ordinary till 1803.
William Easterling served from 1803 till his death, 1835.
Lewis E. Stubbs elected in 1835.
Joshua David elected in ———.
A. N. Bristow elected in ———, served till his death 1867.

In 1868 a new constitution was adopted and the office of Ordinary was abolished, and the office of Probate Judge instituted. Jeremiah Grant was elected first to the office in 1868 and served till 1872.

J. Wesley Smith elected 1872, served till 1876.
Knox Livingston elected 1876, served till 1878.
C. T. Munnerlyn elected 1878, but did not qualify.
Milton McLaurin, appointed, served till 1880.
Milton McLaurin elected 1880, served till 1882.
Milton McLaurin elected 1882, resigned 1884.
W. E. Thomas appointed 1884.
W. E. Thomas elected in 1884, served till 1886.
T. I. Rogers elected in 1886, served till 1888.
Milton McLaurin elected in 1888, still serving, 1896.

CHAPTER XXI.

SCOTTISH SETTLERS. McCOLLS AND McLAURINS.

After the battle of Culloden, which occurred in 1746, many Scottish families emigrated to America. The two Carolinas were fortunate in having some of these valuable people to make their homes within their borders.

Among those ranked as rebels in that conflict several came to the Pee Dee who were destined to distinction in after time; of those the McIvers and McIntoshs are worthy of mention. It is likely also that about the same time the McLeans, McLaurins, McRaes, McColls and others who happened to be on the losing side, crossed the waters, in search of liberty and peace; and settled in the country between the Cape Fear and Pee Dee. But the ancestors of the names at the head of this chapter seem to have come at a later date, soon after the Revolutionary War. The writer is largely indebted to his old friend, Mr. John L. McCall, for valuable information. Mr. McColl,* now seventy-eight, is still vigorous and strong, in body and mind, intelligent, thoughtful, accurate, and greatly interested in having the traditions of the old families preserved, has himself been an active participant in the affairs of the country. He was born in Marion, came to Marlboro a boy of twelve, spent the prime of his life in farming and mercantile pursuits, mostly at Clio, and in its vicinity. He was elected Tax Collector for Marlboro in 1862, and assisted Messrs. McRae and Weatherly in the same service in earlier years. His wife was a daughter of Mr. Archie Sinclair, who came from Isly, in Scotland, and a highly respectable family of sons and daughters

---
*Since dead.

honor the training of the excellent couple. Among them are Mrs. H. H. Newton, T. D. and C. S. McCall of Bennettsville.

When volunteers were called for to go to the Seminole War in 1835, Mr. McCall was serving an apprenticeship in a tailor's establishment, but at once enlisted in the company of Capt. Elmore, of Columbia. He remembers how his youthful mind was impressed with the wealth, liberality and patriotism of the elder Wade Hampton, who offered to furnish twenty horses if the company could be mounted and go as cavalry. That brief service fully satisfied the martial ambition of the young aspirant for fame, and made him content to follow ever after the pursuits of peace. May his last days be as calm as the setting sun, and all that bear his name rise up to bless his memory.

John, the father of the above, came from Appin Scotland in 1791, being then in his fourteenth year. With him were several relatives, and they first found shelter under the hospitable roof of a kinsman, David McCall, who had come over earlier, and was living at what has long been known as the Daniel Graham place, near the North Carolina State line. John McColl lived at what was then called Mt. Washington, now Tatum. Subsequently did business at Marlboro Old Court House. He married a Miss Curry, had but one son, besides our friend, to grow to manhood, and he was killed by a horse.

An uncle named Daniel, died in this country. Hugh G. McColl is also remembered as a native Scotchman, who came over about the same time with the others, was related to them, and settled on Little Pee Dee and is represented in this country yet in the descendants of John C. and Nancy McColl. The old people were fond of talking of "Big Solomon," who married a daughter of "David the first." Tradition represents him as a school teacher, a "man of learning." He was the father of "Long Hugh," who is remembered as a soldier of the War of 1812, the father of David, Solomon, John and Christian. This second David is the father of D. D. McColl of Bennettsville "Big Solomon" was also the father of Peter McColl, who for twenty-five years was the Clerk of the Court for Marlboro and died in office in 1871. He also conducted before the war the first branch bank ever established in this county, being part of the Bank of Cheraw. The neatness of pensmanship of the Clerk's office during his occupancy is a monument to his memory.

Another, Hugh, called "Steady Hugh," came about the same time with the others, from whom is descended Mrs. Effie McLaurin, mother of the excellent young men, John F., Hugh L., Luther and W. B. McLaurin, sons of Capt. L. L. McLaurin. D. D. McColl is also a grandson of this "Steady Hugh," on his mother's side. Another Solomon, called "Little Solomon," of about the same age as Big Solomon, was the father of Hugh D., better known as a deaf mute, who also has representatives in the county. The old people will remember that John "Gurly" was a brother to Hugh D., who married a Miss Cameron, and from whom was descended John, Hugh and Malcom McColl, citizens of the Judson community. "Stumpy" Duncan was the father of that excellent old man Lock B. McCall, who, when near four-score years, was drowned in Beaver Dam Creek, near his residence, while bathing. He was honest, inoffensive and kind of heart. He, too, was a soldier of the Seminole War, a private in the company of Capt. Williamson in Harllee's Battalion. A brother of his named John has left descendants behind him.

Major John McColl, a brother of "Stumpy" Duncan, who commanded the Lower Battalion in the Marlboro Regiment for a time, was a man of excellent character, pleasing manners, and was the father of those worthy men of the Judson neighborhood, Lock and Joseph McColl. It is told of the Major that (like a good many other militia officers in olden time) he did not enjoy an extensive knowledge of "tactics," and that on one occasion, when his battalion was on review, he gave a command which either was awkwardly given or not understood, and the left wing doubled upon itself in much confusion. The Major was quite a short, small man, but was well mounted upon a charger richly caparisoned. Seeing that the left flank was in a tangle, he endeavored to put spurs to his horse, but his heels only reached the lower part of the saddle skirts, but by dint of coaxing and spurring he galloped down the broken lines and cried out in his broad Scotch, "What the dickens got you into sich a hickelty-pickelty? Git ye straight again."

Mr. John A. McColl, exemplary man, splendid, useful citizen, who only a few years ago sank into the grave, full of years, and full of the praises and affections of his countrymen, especially of Hebron and Clio, where he lived so long and lived so well, is said to have sprung from a branch of the family that settled upon Mountain Creek, and his relationship to the foregoing was not so close. John A. McColl's grandparents, John and Margaret McColl, and their children, came from Scotland to America in 1775. They landed at Wilmington and settled near Mountain Creek, in Richmond County, North Carolina. His maternal grandparents, John and Mary Cameron, and their children, came from Scotland to America in the ship Mary Ann, and likewise settled at Mountain Creek, North Carolina. Dougald McColl, his father, married Jeannette Cameron and came to Marlboro about 1819. John A. had two brothers, Daniel, who died in Louisiana, on the Red River, an overseer, and Hugh, who was younger. John A. was the father of nine children. Four only are now alive, Wellington, Alex, Mrs. Lewis Spears and Miss Nancy McColl.

But our friend from whom so much of this information was obtained mentioned two other families of McColls of Marlboro, whom he claims as of the same stock with those above named. One of these, in the childhood of the writer, lived in the Brownsville community, a venerable Scotch lady, we all honored as "Granny McColl." A maiden daughter, Miss Katy, and a son, James, lived with her, and close by lived another son, David R., who was the father of that substantial and highly respected gentleman now living a few miles below Society Hill, my old schoolmate, Mr. John S. McColl. The other family lived for many years upon the "Three Creeks," five miles below Bennettsville, but, so far as the writer knows, no member of it bearing the name is left in Marlboro. But the wellknown and much respected late A. C. McInnis married Miss Flora, a handsome granddaughter of the old man ————McColl, a native of Scotland, who lived and died about half a mile from what was long known as "McColl's Cross Roads." S. J. McInnis is the first born of this interesting couple of pure Caledonian blood. By the way, the intermarriage of Scot with Scot has been especially characteristic of the McColls. Attached to the old "clan," proud of their pure blood, they have married and intermarried until they are all kin, more or less. Some of them spell the name with an A, others retain the O, but nearly, if not quite all of the name in Marlboro, in one line or another, may trace their origin back to Appin.

The McLaurins of Marlboro, if not quite so numerous, have, nevertheless, occupied a conspicuous place among its best citizens. They, also, as far as can be ascertained, came to this country soon after the War of Independence and settled on the Little Pee Dee, some on one side, some on the other, so it has been in all these years that both in Richmond and Robeson Counties in North Carolina, and in Marion and Marlboro in South Carolina, men have lived who have contributed their full share to the prosperity and enterprise of the country. The older people in the eastern part of the State fondly remember three brothers of excellent character, Daniel C., John L. and "Little Hugh" McLaurin, all of whom have left large and respectable families. Daniel C., who lived where the late J. W. Roper resided, kind-hearted, hospitable, and ever ready to serve his country in any position with conscientious fidelity, we all mourn his death as the loss of a valuable citizen. John L. McLaurin, who lived where his son, the late John B., lived, was not less useful, less loved, and perhaps more enterprising and successful. He, too, like his brother, served his people quite acceptably upon the district boards. A son of his, P. B. McLaurin, was returned to the Legislature before the war, and another son, John B., has been elected once since. The third brother, Hugh, spent most of his life in North Carolina, a few miles from Laurinburg, but his sons have several of them been for a longer or shorter period citizens of Marlboro. L. B., Jack, Duncan and the late Jas. R. were sons of this old man. He and his brothers were sons of a native of Scotland. His name was Laughlin, and his wife was a Miss McColl, a sister of one of the John McColls mentioned on a previous page. So that it is not alone of late that the young McLaurins and McColls fell in love with each other.

Another honored old man of this name, John McLaurin, who came over in 1784, married a Miss McNair, of Richmond, N. C., and was the grandfather of Capt. Lock and John J. McLaurin*; the former a man of uncommon energy and push, of fine mind, good judgment, and modest worth ; John J. one of the best of men, a universal favorite as a young man, as an old one, cheerful, kindhearted, venerated and loved. The Captain's wife was Miss Effie McColl, and John J. married a daughter of Daniel C. McLaurin. "Hurricane Daniel," another McLaurin of this stock, strayed off to Sumter County,

* Both dead.

and his large and respectable connections are among the best in our sister county.

Daniel, the head of this latter branch of the family, came to America when his son John was about twenty years old and settled at first near Campbellton, now Fayetteville, N. C. After a few years spent in boating on Cape Fear, the old patriarch came to Marlboro and established himself near where his grandson, John J., now lives. And the impression seems to be that Laughlin, the ancestor of the three brothers, Hugh, Daniel C., and John L., came about 1791 and settled at Red Bluff. In all the years since, the descendants of these old Scotchmen have clung to the grounds where their fathers first felled the forests and built their altars—quiet, unobtrusive people, yet valuable members of society they have always been.

CHAPTER XXII.

CLIO.

This village, situated in the eastern portion of the county, has from the first been favored with a large degree of the Scottish element. It is true that it was at first settled by old Mr. Joe Ivey. It is said that the old man left one of the Carolinas in search of a better land, towards the setting sun; that he went as far as the Chattahoochee, then, as it seemed to Ivey, the outer border of civilization, a beautiful stream flowing amid a wild and howling wilderness, with wild and savage Indians upon either bank—he became disgusted and turned his horse's head towards the rising sun, and returned to the spot where Clio now stands, there pitched his tent, and purchased a home in the virgin forest, with no intention or desire that a town should ever rise upon the plain. Tradition has it, that in the process of time, when at "Ivy's Cross Roads," as it was called, stores, shops, houses and dwellings began to rise around him, the old man explained his change of base by saying, "When they begun to build lead houses, glass shetters, and calico chimbleys it was time for Joe Ivy to git away." But Joe Ivy was a good, honest man, who was ready to aid his fellow man, and whom his neighbors all respected. His two sons, Gadi and Levi, both lived to be highly respected citizens, and have left families to honor their memory. Gadi, especially, lived to a great age, and died at Clio, only a few years ago, the oldest man in the community.

The father of Senator Joseph Hawley, of Connecticut, was the first merchant to open a store at the "Cross Roads." It had already become a sort of center in the community, where the militia met for drill; and "muster-day" had become a day of trade. Not only was Henry Fuller on hand with cakes, but sometimes a "covered wagon" with something for the thirsty militiamen to drink, besides an assortment of flour, bacon, tobacco, and leather, and sometimes the candidates would be there, and speeches be made, a shooting-match would come off, maybe a horse-race or two would be run, a ring be described, a bully would step in and challenge the crowd for a fight and at long intervals somebody would "get hurt." The women in the neighborhood dreaded the "muster-day," and the boy who got the chance of going to muster to see the fun, counted himself a "lucky chap." Mr. Hawley, with genuine Yankee instinct, saw that it was a good place for money-making, and he bought a "little spot" of ground and "put up a store." A good farming country all around; honest, unsuspecting farmers, making good crops, liked the advantage of a home market, and traded with the shrewd Yankee, and he made money. It was not long before others began to think that the "Cross Roads" was a "good stand, and Hawleysville a money-making place." William Rogers, another Northern man, came and set up a store, soon won the affections of a Miss McCollum, and they were married. Rogers became popular, not only as a merchant, but as a public-spirited good man. He soon associated with himself John B. McDaniel, an excellent young man, born and raised in the community, who soon added to the strength of the firm by his marriage to a daughter of Mr. Eli Thomas; then they brought in as a salesman a polished young man, D. J. McDonald, quite an addition to the moral and social tone of the place. Mr. McDonald was respected as a partner, and the business increased. But, greatly to the regret of the community, Rogers sold out and went to Bishopville, in Sumter County, where he did well, and reared a fine family. A son of his is at present quite a prominent and useful member of the South Carolina Conference. Not long after Mr. McDaniel sold out to John A. McRae, and went to Arkansas, where, after conducting a large and successful business, he died a few years ago. He was one of those men whose capacity, manners and spirit bring them into prominence in any community, and his removal from it was deemed a calamity.

T. C. Weatherly, so prominent in Marlboro affairs, and for so long one of its most popular citizens, began his business career at Clio as a salesman with Mr. McDaniel, but soon formed a partnership with Mr. J. L. McColl, which continued until he was elected Sheriff of Marlboro, when he sold out to Mr. McColl and moved to Bennettsville, in the vicinity of which place he lived till his death. He served the people in the State Legislature for several terms. A man of quick mind, ready action, public spirit, good judgment and generous impulses, he exercised a large influence. He died at Glenn Springs a number of years ago, where he had gone for the benefit of his health, and his body brought home and laid in the Methodist church yard in Bennettsville.

The Edens family have for many years been prominent in the affairs of Clio. Rev. Allen Edens, who reared a large family of sons and daughters, several of them settling in the neighborhood, and Col. T. N. Edens, not only running a farm near by, but for a time at the head of a mercantile firm. William M. Bristow, W. C. Medlin, and others, for a brief time, sold goods here before the war. Soon after the war there came among the Clio people a young man of handsome appearance, quiet manners, but fine sense and business talent, first in the humble capacity of a "North Carolina wagoner," dealing mainly in tobacco. Somehow young Hinshaw won the heart and hand of the beautiful daughter of Mr. W. M. Bristow, and soon the youthful pair made Clio their home. From that day began a new era in the prosperity and growth of the place; lumber and flour mills run by steam and presently a foundry and extensive shops went up; many operatives were needed and came; houses were erected, and the place put on a real town-like appearance. When the staid old town of Cheraw came upon the stage and made such a flattering bid for Capt. Hinshaw's services in a foundry at that place that his attachment to the little town he had done so much to enlarge and beautify had to yield, and with him went a number of good people to help build up a new Cheraw. With the Sternbergers, Calhouns, Woodleys, Ropers, Welches and the entrance of a railroad, the town has rapidly increased in population and volume of business. The Medlins, Stantons, and those mentioned above, with others, will not allow the grass to grow in her streets or her just proportion of trade to pass into other channels; but, with enterprise and energy, are opening up new streets and constantly adding to and enlarging the town. Commodious church buildings invite the people to worship, Methodist and Baptist; a good school building, occupied by first-class teachers; a Masonic hall, hotel, workshops and mill, are all in place and room being made for others, while all around the town in every direction are thrifty, successful farmers vying with each other and with others elsewhere in skill and profit.

In going out among the fields around the town, we may find, now and then, what was once an impoverished, worn-out old field, where the owner was scarcely able to make a scanty support, now yielding abundant returns to skilled labor; and the low-roofed cottages of the fathers have disappeared and tasteful, comfortable dwellings, neatly furnished, have taken their places. The writer calls to mind a visit to the old Methodist church that used to stand a mile or two below the town, and must beg to mention a few of the humble but good men who were there. And first of all, he would write the name of the preacher, Dougald McPherson. His presence in some of our modern pulpits would be akin to the effect produced of introducing into one of our fashionable congregations some of those old sisters we read of in Hebrews, "arrayed in sheep skins and goat skins." Mr. McPherson was a diminutive person, slightly stooped, dressed in homespun clothes, a blue cotton handkerchief tied closely around his bald head, with a few stray white hairs peeping out behind his ears, minus his eyebrows, with pale, but benevolent face, a feeble, cracked voice, with scarcely ever the slightest gesture. And yet his neighbors and other intelligent people would sit upon the rough, backlesss benches and listen to that old man preach on a cold wintry day, in an open house, for an hour or more. His language was chaste, his thoughts intelligent, his doctrine evangelical, it is true, but not that held the people. It was the character of the man; his humble, consistent, truthful, honest life, this was the preaching that won his countrymen, and gave him a welcome and hearing wherever he went. Precious old man, when of a great age he sent two noble boys to the war never to return. On Gettysburg's bloody heights, on the same day, from the same volley, they both got their discharge, united in life, in death not divided. Mr. ——— Ammons married a daughter of Mr. McPherson, and works the old farm, but lives in a better house than that which sheltered so long the quiet, pious old couple who lived in the field. It is said that Angus McPherson, who came from Scotland, was the father of Dougald.

About half a mile below the old meeting house lived old Mr. Robert Purnell. His wife was a daughter of Jonathan Meekins. Mr. Purnell was a fine specimen of physical manhood, well proportioned, ruddy face, gray locks, weighing, perhaps, two hundred pounds, he would naturally attract the attention of a stranger. His daughters, who married the Messrs. Allen and T. N. Edens, and a fine-looking young son, who died in early life, are favorably remembered.

A mile or more below, at the Cross Roads, lived Simon Smith and wife, an aged pair, with a single daughter. The daughter afterwards married Charles T. McRae, while an older daughter was already Mrs. Henry Covington. A son, John, had long since married a Miss Weatherly and had gone to Alabama; and William R., a scholarly, intellectual man, was, for a time, a member of the South Carolina Conference, but had recently married and located and for sometime taught school at Parnassus. Another old man remembered as being at that old church now nearly fifty years ago, was James Quick, the ancestor of the worthy family of that name who now live a few miles above Clio. It is doubtful if any man of that day, moving in the same sphere in that community, exercised a wider influence; an influence which has told for good upon his posterity from that day to this.

Still another is remembered, old Mr. Matthew Driggers. He, too, has left a large connection behind him. A younger man than those mentioned above was Wright Wilson, who afterwards became a Methodist preacher, and has a son in the ministry now. Daniel Dunbar is also remembered as living near Clio at the time. He was as the father of the late J. C. Dunbar.

May we not linger yet around this little town to make mention of the Calhouns and others? Would that our space permitted a more extended notice. Within less than two miles Mr. Alexander Calhoun has lived to rear a family and yet lingers upon the shores of time, a pure-minded, consistent Christian gentleman. Of pure Scottish descent, honest, truthful, always modest and retiring, yet commanding the sincere respect of his neighbors, he is among the oldest men in the community. His brothers, John and Dougald, have gone before him to the tomb, but have left their impress upon sons and daughters they have left behind as valuable members of society. Perhaps no man was longer seen around Clio than John Cork. Humble and unpretending, ready to take the road on errands for the merchants, or to enter the shops of the mechanics or the fields of the farmers; wherever he could make himself useful, even to old age, he still trod the streets of Clio, till he died the oldest citizen of the town.

The Stantons, too, have a record in this community older than the town. Handy and Thomas both have left large families of useful citizens and excellent farmers. On the one side of Clio, and now, perhaps, within the limits of the town, may be seen the snowy locks of John, a son of Handy, and the partner of his life's pilgrimage, Sarah Heustiss. Denied, in the providence of Heaven, children of their own, yet seldom without the children of other people, to care for, and to love. Their reward is in Heaven, their record on high. W. Godfrey Stanton, another son of Handy, who married a daughter of Major Aaron Breeden, has long lived near the little town, and sometimes within it, is growing to be an old citizen; bu has sons and daughters to remember him when gone to his long home. On the other side of the town there is Peter and Evander, sons of Thomas Stanton, both with silver locks, but not as old as they look. The former in his bachelor loneliness; the other with a flock around him to honor his memory when gone. Good men both; may they yet be spared the reaper's sickle for many days. Others of this name and family are as worthy of mention but we hurry on to mention other families. Recollection next brings up the gray head of Mr. James Woodley, who died several years ago. He married the daughter of Jonathan Cottingham, who has been mentioned in another chapter. Wr. Woodley lived in Hebron township, but on the Clio side. He was a man of integrity and industry, and taught it to his sons, John C. and Jonathan. John C., his oldest son, married Miss Mary John, and near the village of Clio they have reared a fine family, sons and daughters of character and worth, who know how to appreciate the advantages that have come from a father's energy and thrift, a mother's prudence and piety. Mr. Woodley died a few years ago. Jonathan, living between his own father and Col. Covington, the father of his wife, could hardly be excused, if he had failed to make of himself a comfortable home, and of himself a useful, worthy citizen of the County.

CHAPTER XXIII.

Scottish Settlers—Continued.

About the beginning of the struggle between the Colonies and the mother country there left the Isle of Skye, (as tradition says) an old man with nine sons. Whether Ian McRae foresaw the strife, and wished to be a witness and participant, or whether he thought the king would soon quiet the little "family fray," does not appear. But the six months voyage upon the deep buried old Ian, amid the seaweeds; but from the nine ruddy boys who landed upon the North Carolina coast there has come, it is supposed most, if not all, of the name in Marlboro, and many in Marion and the adjacent counties in North Carolina. "A little silver cup of peculiar shape," with an inscription in Gaelic, with the name "Ian," is yet sacredly preserved as a relic of one of the progenitors of the family. One of the nine brothers, Christopher, lived and reared a large family of sons and daughters, where Mr. Charles Crosland now resides.

John L. Alexander and Colon, Mrs. Sallie Weatherly, Polly McRae, Katie Battle, Barbara Peterkin and Christian Bristow are remembered among them, several of whom have many representatives in the country to-day.

Another brother of the nine was that good old man, Roderic, who settled in the woods, opposite where Mr. James Wright now lives. It is said that when he first "pitched his tent" there the country was so wild and sparsely settled that he "had to build a strong house of heavy logs for his sheep, and fasten it securely to keep them from destruction by the wolves." Of this old man's family, John D., and Duncan D., who was a popular Tax Collector, are remembered with the sisters, Mrs. Alford, the mother of our fellow citizen, Jacob, and his sisters, Mrs. W. C. McLeod, Mrs. John Meekins, Mrs. Hugh Mc-Lucas, Mrs. Margaret Spears, and the first Mrs. Jessie Peterkin, all of them ladies of fine character who have left their impress upon their children, or others placed under their care.

Another of the nine was a grandfather of the brothers, Alex. and Murdoch, of the Red Bluff community—men well known for their worth and honorable position in society. Still another was the father of the late John T. McRae, who lived just across the line in Marion; a few miles below Donohoe. He was the father of Mrs. Philip McRae, Mrs. Duncan Carmichael, and has descendants among us to honor his memory. A daughter, Miss Katie, leaves with those that surround her interesting traditions of the family. Among these it is told that in the absence of Christopher, named previously, who was the grandfather of our late fellow citizen, Jno. A. McRae, "A band of Tories was seen approaching the house, and Mrs. McRae, with an infant three weeks old, seized her baby, and with young Roderic, but fourteen years old, ran off and spent the night in the woods." Another story is that as a band came stealthily to the McRae house, they were too near for the inmates to flee, or to conceal their valuables. "But one of the women placed the silver spoons in her dress bosom, and conscious that she was observed, seized a hank of thread and stuffed that in after the spoons, and when the intruders demanded what she had thus hidden away, she drew out the yarn, and hurled it into the face of one them, saying 'I think you might allow a poor woman to keep her own thread,' and the Tory threw it back, saying 'You are so smart you may keep it.' The beds were ripped open and the feathers scattered in the search for treasure. The excellent Mrs. M. C. McLeod remembers some of those spoons. Mrs. McLucas and Mrs. Spears each inherited a spoon, and she thinks that Mrs. Bristow and Mrs. Sallie Peterkin have one each."

Another of the original nine brothers died a young man at the house of Roderic. Where the others settled is not known, but it is very clear that other McRaes came early to this region of the country. Upon the banks of Three Creeks there lived and died one named James McRae, whose wife, an excellent lady, was also a McRae, aunt to General McQueen. Mrs. Thompson now lives at the old place where Duncan, Philip, James, Colon, Jno. R. Katy, and Mrs. Murchison, if no more, were reared to maturity. A mile or two distant lived another old Scotchman, Charles McRae, generally called "Squire," a local Methodist preacher. The older people may remember him as an old man nearly if not quite as old as Roderic. Our excellent fellow citizen, Hugh McCollum, is a grandson of this old man. His sons, Farquar and Charles T., have their representatives also in the country. What was the relationship between these, or to the large family, it is not known. But like other Scottish people, they seem to have brought their native prejudices with them to the New World. If a marriageable young woman could be found in their own or some kindred clan, who was not too close kin, she was preferred to a stranger in whose veins might flow the blood of foe or alien; and hence from the earliest day of their landing upon American soil, they have married and intermarried until almost every McRae is kin to every other McRae. Yet many another name has been enamored with the charms of Scottish daughters, and managed by art and solemn promises to win them to other names and homes, where yet they have never failed to leave their own Scottish characteristics.

It was a fortunate thing for these pages that a love affair brought together a granddaughter of Roderic McRae and a young scion of a "Laird McLeod of Skye"; and thus traditions of the two families have been united and treasured in one intelligent mind and retentive memory. And from the pen of Mrs. M. C. McLeod there has been culled much of this chapter. She is the loved and honored widow of Major D. M. D. McLeod, who fell upon the bloody field of Gettysburg, the idol of his regiment.

The Isle of Skye used to be under the control of three "Lairds." One of these was a McLeod.

For a time the McLeods and McDonalds lived side by side as loving as brothers, but it came to pass that a McDonald married a Lady McLeod, and afterwards deserted her, a feud arose, war was waged, blood was shed, the McDonalds were worsted and fled to a cave for security. The McLeods built a fire at the cave's mouth, and smoked their enemies to peace, or to death, rather. A son of one of these Laird McLeods married a lady of noble birth, Miss Jane Hunter, and sailed with a brother Alex, his wife and three children, for the ports of America. This Lady Jane Hunter, before her marriage, was some time at Court. She had two brothers, eminent physicians, who took up an unfinished work of Harvey's on blood circulation, and prepared a work which made a sensation in the medical world. One of these brothers is said to have been appointed ship's surgeon under Commodore Anson, on a voyage around the world, and while upon this cruise the specimens and curiosities collected became a nucleus of a splendid museum bearing his name in Glasgow, his native city. While upon this voyage, the vessel touched upon the North Carolina coast, and a party went as far as Anson County, which, it is claimed, received its name in honor of the Commodore.

The McLeod who married Lady Hunter was an adventurer, had a vessel and was called a Commodore. Some years before the Revolutionary War he brought his wife and three children to Wilmington, North Carolina, and while absent on a cruise about 1775, or 1776, his wife died. This sad intelligence reached the Commodore when off

St. Helena and so overwhelmed him with grief that he soon died; whereupon the sorrowing brother, Alex, went to Scotland and induced two maiden sisters, Betsy and Isabella, to come over and take charge of the three children, John, Daniel and Isabella. Sometime after the war the aunt, Isabella, and the three young people came to the neighborhood of Hunt's Bluff, in Marlboro. John, the elder brother, set up a store, and soon died of fever. Daniel married Miss Catharine Evans and reared a large family; John, William, Daniel and Donald McDiarmid were the sons that attained manhood's estate. When the latter was born a Scottish bachelor friend of the family asked to give the child his name, Donald McDiarmid. The parents consented, and when a few years later he made his will he bequeathed a fund to be used in giving the boy a "collegiate education." So it came to pass that D. M. D. McLeod was graduated at the South Carolina College, taught school for a while, loved and married Margaret C. Alford; went to the war in command of a company, became Major, and fell greatly lamented at Gettysburg.

Mr. McDiarmid sleeps in the graveyard at Old Salem. The daughters of Daniel McLeod were the following: Betsy, who married Rev. Wm. R. Smith; Mary, who became the wife of Col. James R. Bethea, of Marion; Isabella, who married Daniel Horn, of Cheraw, and subsequently moved to Georgia; and Ellen, who married a Mr. McIntosh, of Georgia. Sisters and brothers all, except an old friend, Daniel, have passed away. Many pleasant memories crowd the mind of the writer as he pens these lines—memories of Uncle McLeod, Aunt Katie and Aunt Isabella, who had changed her name to Bodiford, who, now in old age, crippled and infirm, had found a home in the house of her brother. Whatever the religion of the McLeods in Scotland they were Methodist here. Prayer and praise ascended from the family altar, and if

"Uncle McLeod was absent, Aunt Isabella led in the prayer." They had built a little log house in the woods not far from where Berry Alford now lives, and called it "McLeod's Meeting House." They had preaching there and a little society which ultimately united with Mossy Bay and formed Parnassus. The writer remembers to have attended service there more than a half a century ago, when the McLeods did most of the singing, and Charles McRae the preaching. On one occasion, when visiting the McLeod boys, other boys of the neighborhood joined us on Saturday afternoon, and somehow we got into the old "meeting house." One of the boys found a window shutter that yielded to his ingenuity and swung open when eight or ten chaps found themselves inside. Some fellow transformed himself into "Uncle Charley McRae," entered the pulpit and began a senseless harangue which he called preaching. The rest of us, seated around the altar, encouraged him with "amens," clapping of hands, and an occasional "hallelujah," when suddenly the door opened and the portly form of Uncle McLeod stepped inside. The reader can imagine how quickly the congregation dispersed without "the benediction." The writer was not so swift in action and was fairly caught and began to weep in earnest, but the laughter of the old man soon reassured him, and we two closed up the house and returned to the dwelling. It was late before some of the boys reported at home.

The McLucases have been a long time in the country. Two brothers, Daniel and John, came with their young families from Scotland. We have no information further as to Daniel. But John has left an excellent family behind him. Two sons, John and Hugh, are both well remembered as good citizens. Hugh married a daughter of that grand old Scotchman, Roderick McRae, who furnished so many wives to the Marlboro men, who have left so salutary an influence upon others than their own children. John D. McLucas, of Marion, and Roderick, of McColl section, of Marlboro, are sons of this worthy pair, and several daughters of fine character are perpetuating the virtues of their descent.

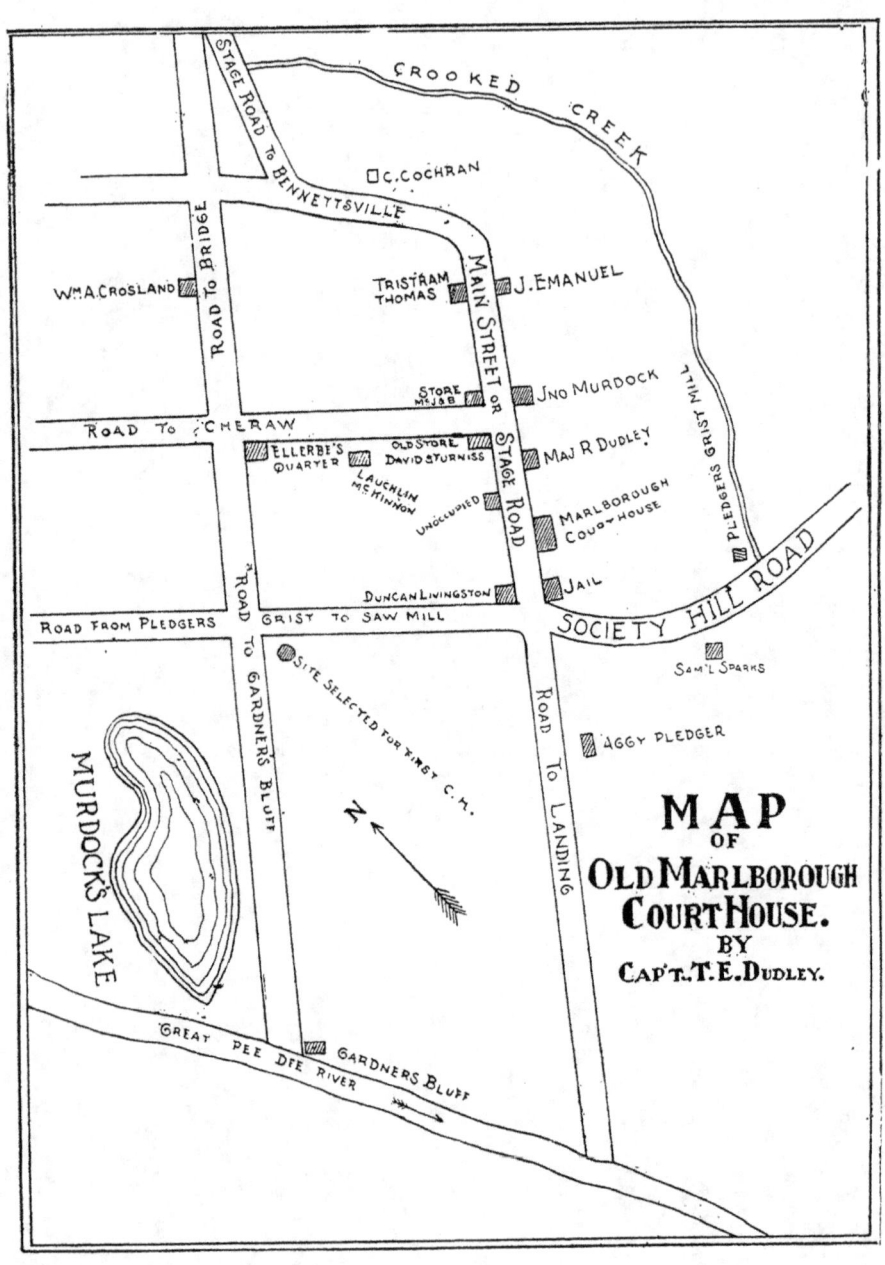

CHAPTER XXIV.

THE OLD COURT HOUSE.

On the 25th of March, 1785, an Act was passed by the General Assembly of South Carolina creating several judicial districts out of the territory of Old Cheraw, including Chesterfield, Liberty (now Marion) and Marlboro. Claudius Pegues, Geo. Hicks, Morgan Brown, Tristram Thomas, Claudius Pegues, Jr., Moses Pearson and Thomas Evans, by the same Act, were appointed to select a site and superintend the erection of a courthouse and jail. The spot chosen was on the north bank of Crooked Creek, about six miles west from Bennettsville, near what has been known as Evans' Mill.* The deed from Gen. Tristram Thomas, conveying the ground to the commissioners above named, is upon record in the Clerk's office. The house erected was a two-story wooden building, convenient in its arrangement, and ample in size for that day. Scarcely any signs of that "old court-house," and the few buildings that arose around it, can now be seen. But the influence of the men to whom the administration of justice was entrusted and upon whom the formation of society and public opinion devolved, lives on, and is felt to-day in all this surrounding country. For the first fourteen years of our judicial history, law was administered by County Courts; and the commissioners to build the court-house

---

*Mr. Aaron Sweat, who is quite an old man, and who is of the same family as the Revolutionary patriot mentioned in a previous chapter, says that Mr. Jesse Pearce, on one occasion, showed him a site that was first selected for the court-house. It was to have been quite near to the Gardner's Bluff road and not far from the present cross-roads leading from Bennettsville to Gardner's Bluff and from Evans' Mill to Cheraw. But the site was finally chosen lower down the river and nearer to Evans' Mill.

were the judges in the first of these courts, and a number of them are represented in some of our most respectable families. Old Judge Moses Pearson's great-grandson, Hon. C. P. Townsend, the senior member of the Bennettsville bar, with credit to himself presided in the courts of the State for several years.

The first Circuit Court held in Marlboro was in the year 1800, Judge Wm. Johnson presiding. This distinguished jurist was elevated to the Supreme Bench of the United States by President Jefferson in 1804. After him such men as Grimke, Waties, Bay, Brevard, Nott, Colcock, and Trezevant held court at the "old court-house." The commission and order of Gov. Drayton requiring the holding of the Court are recorded in one of the old journals in the Clerk's office, presumably because he, Johnson, was sworn in and held his first Court at Marlboro "old court-house." Here, too, such men as Falconer, Witherspoon, Wilds, the Ervins, Robbins, and J. J. Evans "practiced law." And since Evans has been mentioned, who was afterwards made a Circuit Judge and frequently presided in our courts, it is well to name some of the men who have sat upon the bench and are remembered by the writer. J. J. Evans, that grand old Roman, must be mentioned first. His people sent him to the Legislature in 1812 before he was twenty-six years old. Before they could vote for him again he removed to Darlington, and in 1816 was elected to the Legislature from that District. In 1829 he was made a circuit Judge, and in 1850 elected to the United States Senate Marlboro never lost her interest in him, never forgot that he was her own son. And when in 1858 he calmly folded his honors about him and fell asleep, such political opponents as Wilson, of Massachusetts, and Hale, of New Hampshire, vied with each other in weaving garlands for his tomb. Marlboro felt the bereavement not less than Darlington, his adopted home. The humorous, witty Richard Gantt is remembered, who used to pour forth such eloquence and pathos in passing sentence upon criminals as to move the most hardened. Then for thirty-two years the frail form of John S. Richardson was seen upon the bench. When he was seventy a proposition was made in the Legislature to remove him from office "on account of his bodily and mental infirmities," but when he was permitted to speak for himself he utterly demolished the opposition and "all further proceedings were discharged." Daniel Elliott Huger, full six feet high, manly, erect and "firm as granite," the people were always glad for him to preside. Baylis J. Earle, the able, pure, "just judge," was several times on the bench here. Judge O'Neal, who could stand nowhere but in the front rank in statesmanship, agriculture, education, religion not less than as a jurist, he stood among the leaders. Andrew Pickens Butler is remembered on account of his florid face, his snowy locks, his peculiar dancing eyes, his martial bearing, his uncontrollable love of fun, which would sometimes convulse the court-room. In 1846 he was elected to the United States Senate, and for two years honored the position, and died lamented by the whole country. After these came such men as Glover, Withers, Whitner, and Munro. It is a bright array and they have left shining footprints upon the path now trodden by their successors.

After Equity Courts began to be held in Marlboro the bench was graced by the learned William Harper, David Johnson, afterwards Governor of the State; Job Johnson, the dignified, truthful Francis Wardlaw Dunkin, G. W. Dargan, James J. Caldwell, the clear-headed John A. Inglis, Chancellor Carroll and our own W. D. Johnson.

The members of the bar who have illustrated and expounded the principles of law in the courts of Marlboro make an array of talent of which any people might be proud. Reference can only be made to such as have been known and heard. And of these one must be mentioned who was distinguished more in the councils of the nation than at the bar, Col. John Campbell, who succeeded his hardly less notable brother, Gen. Robert B., in the United States Congress in 1836, and where he continued in service to the end of his life in 1844. Polished, amiable, modest and yet fearless, he was one of the most fascinating speakers Marlboro has ever reared. In our boyhood we knew James R. Ervin, of whom it was said "few men were more talented than he." With the settlement of Bennettsville three gifted young men arose as lights in the profession, James E. David, the friend of the people; Col. C. W. Dudley, the astute and successful lawyer, both of whom represented the county in both houses of the General Assembly; and Gen. John McQueen, for a dozen years a member of Congress; and then later on by a few years, three other sons scarcely less brilliant—Chas. A. Thornwell, Samuel J. Townsend and Harris Covington, all of whom were in the Legislature for longer or shorter periods. And then the promising brothers, Daniel White, and Neill D. Johnson, and P. B. McLaurin, all of whom laid down their lives for the "lost cause." Besides all these our courts have been visited by gentlemen from neighboring counties, who have shed light and knowledge upon questions of law and justice; while Withers and Hanna, and the McIvers, father and son, were a terror to evil doers in the office of Circuit Solicitor. W. W. Sellers and J. M. Johnson, of Marion, and G. W. Dargan, of Darlington, have each as solicitor, visited our court from time to time; and Marlboro has been honored in having D. D. McColl and H. H. Newton in the Solicitorship.

It may not be inappropriate to mention the names of members of the Bennettsville bar who are yet alive and shedding luster on their profession. W. D. Johnson, for a number of years prior to the war, sat on the bench as Judge in Chancery; and was also Senator. He was admitted to practice law in 1846, and, though approaching eighty years of age, is still in the active practice of his profession. He removed to Marion a few years after the war, but we have never given up our claim on him. He owns extensive and valuable plantations in the county, and annually makes a visit to his old home. His partner in law, at Marion, J. M. Johnson, lived for some years in the county of Marlboro, first as a successful school teacher, and then as an attorney at law, so that the Bennettsville bar can justly claim them both. Ten years after W. D. Johnson, C. P. Townsend was admitted to the bar. Both before and since the war he has represented the County in the Legislature. For a number of years he filled the office of Commissioner in Equity for the County and after the war was elevated to the bench and filled the place with honor to himself and to the entire satisfaction of the bar and people. As a lawyer in criminal cases or civil suits he stands well to the front. His former partner, John L. McLaurin, the son of P. B. McLaurin, mentioned above, seems to have been born for luck. In a very few years after his admission to the bar he was elected to the State Legislature, and the Attorney-General having been elevated to a seat on the Supreme Bench, he was appointed Attorney-General; soon thereafter the Congressman for this District, Gen. E. T. Stackhouse, having died, McLaurin succeeded him, and has been in Congress ever since. He resigned his seat in Congress to accept the appointment of United States Senator to succeed Senator Earle. He is a fine stump speaker, a shrewd politician, and very popular with the people. H. H. Newton served one or more terms as Solicitor for the Fourth Judicial Circuit. Was a member of the Legislature, and was instrumental in having passed the stock law, for which he was at first roundly abused, but abuse has long since been turned into thanks, and now the people appreciate the fact that he did them a service. D. D. McColl has been a successful lawyer. He was Solicitor for one or more terms, and criminals were justly afraid of him. He has retired from the active practice of law and devotes his time to the interests of the Bank of Marlboro, of which he is the President. T. E. Dudley was admitted to law in 1858 and has always been considered a conscientious, painstaking lawyer, careful and exact in his work, and has held a fair share of practice at the Bennettsville bar. He represented the county in the late Constitutional Convention. J. H. Hudson, a native of Chester, came to Bennettsville in 1853, fresh from the South Carolina College, to take charge of the Male Academy. He taught four years, studied law and was admitted to practice in 1857, and in 1858 was elected to the Legislature. He entered the Confederate service as a private and rose to the rank of Lieutenant-colonel of the Twenty-Sixth Regiment South Carolina Volunteers. He was Circuit Judge of the Fourth Judicial Circuit for four terms, from 14th February, 1878, to 14th February, 1894, and has resumed practice in the courts again. Knox Livingston, a native of Florida, came to Bennettsville in May, 1870, and in that year he and H. H. Newton were admitted to the bar, formed a co-partnership with J. H. Hudson and soon came to the front as successful lawyers. Each has represented the County in the Legislature with marked ability. Other younger men are fast coming to the front as successful practitioners, such as Bouchier, Caston, Rogers (who represented the county in the Constitutional Convention of 1895), H. H. Covington and T. M. Hamer.

CHAPTER XXV.

THE REMOVAL OF THE COURT-HOUSE TO BENNETTSVILLE.

Two causes led to this event: the increase of population in the central and eastern portion of the District, and the unhealthfulness of the "old court-house" locality, on account of the nearness of the Pee Dee swamps. Accordingly, on December 14th, 1819, an Act was passed by the Legislature directing that "a new court-house and jail be immediately erected." Nathan B. Thomas, Gen. Gillespie, Drury Robertson, W. G. Feagan, James Forniss, James R. Ervin and William Brown were appointed commissioners to contract for and supervise the building. The site was selected and John S. Thomas deeded to the authorities three acres of ground since called the "public square." The deed was executed and recorded April 4, 1820. But delays occurred in the erection of the court-house so that when the great storm of 1822 swept over the country the brick walls were approaching completion, but not finished, and the torrents of rain and the force of the wind caused one of the walls to crack from the top to bottom and from that day there were thoughtful men who doubted the security of the building, which was imposing in appearance and convenient in arrrangement. There were people who called it a "man trap," a "dead fall," and were afraid to enter it with a crowd. Hence its brief life, of less than thirty years, for it was not till the beginning of 1824 that it was finished and received, and in 1851 it was torn down. Portions of the "old court-house" near the river and other buildings were removed to the new site. Our fathers began to think "perhaps there will be a village here some of these days," and "it would be well to give the place a name"; and as the Governor of the State at that time was named Bennett, in honor of him they began to call the place Bennettsville. If the thought had once entered their minds that a *town* would grow up around the courthouse, to be governed by a Mayor and Aldermen, with a half dozen churches, fine schools, several dozen stores, great brick blocks and iron horses drawing men and goods to it, upon an iron road, and hauling thousands of cotton bales, weighing five hundred pounds to the bale, and bringing in turn thousands of tons of fertilizers to enrich the soil, they would have given the infant town a more pretentious name. As Monroe was president at the time they might have named it "Monroe." Or if the district of which it was to be the capital must be called after the grand old English Duke and soldier, who never felt the sensation of defeat in a whole lifetime of war, they might have concluded, "we will call the place Marlboro"; and that would have been proper, especially could they have looked forward sixty years, and seen the whole country for miles around, so like a town that you can hardly get out of sight of farm buildings and residences, many of them looking more like a town than ever the "old court-house" and its surroundings did in its palmiest days.

But it is time that something be said of the unique structure that was replaced by the present handsome building. On the 19th of December, 1849, the Legislature appropriated "eight thousand dollars to build a new court-house for Marlboro." M. Townsend, Dr. William Crosland, James Spears and others of like character, had entrusted to them the superintendence of the enterprise. Neil McNeil was the contractor, and after some delays, it was completed and accepted about the beginning of the year 1852. The first court held in it was in March of that year. The people generally, and the courts, were never satisfied with its accommodations and arrangements, and when some years ago, a portion of the plastering and cornicing fell off, it was not difficult to have it condemned as unsafe, and to institute proceedings to build a new one. An act was passed authorizing the measure, and the County Commissioners, P. M. Hamer, J. H. David, and Tristram Covington took charge of the enterprise. The contract was given to Jacob S. Allen, of North Carolina, and in the year 1885 the present building was completed, being the fourth one in a century, and it is devoutly hoped that the men who shall administer law and justice within its walls in the future years, shall never fall below their predecessors in truth, honesty and uprightness.

On the 27th of March, A. D., 1884, the cornerstone of the present handsome and commodious new court-house was laid with due ceremony, and in the spring of 1885 the building was completed and occupied. At a special term of the Court of Common Pleas begun to be holden on the 4th day of May, 1885, Judge J. H. Hudson, presiding, the imposing structure was dedicated. The ceremony was arranged by the Marlboro bar, and was the first of the kind of which we have knowledge. It was unique, original, appropriate, and impressive. The programme was as follows: The proceedings were opened with prayer by Rev. T. J. Clyde, of the Methodist Church followed by the opening address by Rev. J. A. W. Thomas, of the Baptist Church, at the close of which he delivered to the Court the Holy Bible with a solemn charge as to its use. The presiding Judge received the Book and responded to the address. Ex-Judge C. P. Townsend, the senior member of the Bar, on behalf of his brethren, next addressed the Court, and closed by delivering to the Court a pair of scales symbolical of the "Scales of Justice." The presiding Judge, receiving the scales, responded. Next H. H. Newton, Esq., Solicitor of the Fourth Judicial Circuit, addressed the Court, and closed by delivering to the Judge a copy of the General Statutes, on receiving which the Judge responded, and delivered to the Clerk of Court, C. M. Weatherly, the keys of the building, which had been in a few appropriate remarks delivered to him by J. F. Bolton, Chairman of the Board of County Commissioners. The closing prayer was then delivered by Rev. W. B. Corbett, of the Presbyterian Church, and the immense audience of ladies and gentlemen dispersed. Their attention had been held uninterruptedly from the opening to the closing of the impressive exercises, a full record of which may be found in the Journal of Common Pleas, beginning on page 448 of the volume of 1878 to 1886. The record is valuable, and will be interesting to posterity.

CHAPTER XXVI.

BENNETTSVILLE.

On December 14, 1819, an act was passed by the Legislature of South Carolina, Robeson Carlos and James Gillespie representing Marlboro, authorizing the erection of a "new brick court-house and jail." The court-house at that time was situated a mile or so from Pee Dee River, and not many miles from the mouth of Crooked Creek; but on account of the unhealthfulness of the place and its inaccessibility, it was thought best to move nearer to the center of the district; and hence the present site was selected by a State engineer and is said to be very nearly the exact geographical center of the county. The place chosen was "upon the great road leading from Society Hill to Fayetteville in or near an old apple orchard on the land of John S. Thomas." Three acres of land for the court-house and jail and public square was accordingly deeded by John S. Thomas, and the deed was recorded by Wm. Bristow, clerk, April 4, 1820. John S. Thomas lived on the road already mentioned and not more than fifty yards from where the Presbyterian church now stands. He is the maternal great-grandfather of Messrs. L. D., C. T., and John Hamer, at Tatum. James Cook, the grandfather of Misses Olivia and Sallie Cook, and Mrs. J. L. Breeden, and Mrs. Jno. S. Moore was a near neighbor to Thomas, and principally upon land that belonged to them, Bennettsville stands to-day.

Bennettsville was named in honor of the Governor of the State. Governor Bennett was Governor at the time of the passage of the act authorizing the removal of the court-house and doubtless signed the bill. No one knew him, but that made no difference, for men in high places at that day were not only respectable, but respected.

There was some delay in the completion of the court-house and it was not finished till 1824. People at that time did not understand the modern process of "booming new towns," and the town did not grow rapidly. It was before the day of railroads and electricity. Atlanta and Chicago had not been thought of, and the first settlers in Bennettsville doubtless thought it best to go slow. The nearest saw-mill was Vining's, now McDaniel's, and a road had to be opened before they could get there; so that material for building purposes was scarce and hard to get. Circular saws and steam power had not then found a lodgment in the unbroken forests of virgin pine. One or more of the first houses were built of material brought from the "old court-house." The Peter McColl house that was burnt a few years ago was built by Alex. R. Brown, largely from material brought from there. Also the house so long known as the Marlboro Hotel, but popularly called the "Buck Horn," from the pair of large antlers nailed for a long time in the front piazza.

Among the first settlers may be mentioned Wm. Munnerlyn, Joseph D. Massey and Amos A. Galpin. Galpin had a store about where Grace's barber shop stands. Munnerlyn, who was a stepson of John S. Thomas, had a store on the corner now occupied by R. L. Kirkwood. He began on a very small scale, but, by close and judicious attention to business, soon became one of the two leading merchants. He built a large store on the corner now occupied by J. M. Jackson; another where C. M. Weatherly is now doing business, and still another on the corner below the post-office. He was associated in business with his half-brother, Horace B. Thomas, and might have been a very wealthy man, but the seductive and ofttimes treacherous cotton business finally swamped him. He was the father of the late Chas. T. Munnerlyn, who was favorably known here, but moved to Alabama and died a few years ago. Joseph D. Massey had a store on the corner where the

Rowe Bros. are now doing business. Massey came originally from Lancaster, but did not make money. He, in in common with all the storekeepers at that day, sold liquor.

As far back as 1826, besides the names already mentioned, the male population of Bennettsville consisted of Dr. Edward W. Jones, Dr. Wm. Crosland, John McCollum, George Dudley, William Dudley, Horace B. Thomas, Alex. R. Brown. Gen. John McQueen settled in Bennettsville in 1827, and built a law office on the corner now occupied by C. S. McCall's mammoth store. Dr. Jones built the house and lived where Douglas Jennings now lives. He removed to Mississippi in 1834. Dr. Crosland, the father of William, Charles, George, Edward and Throop, had an office about where the building owned by James E. Coxe now stands on Depot street. He built him a bachelor's hall where J. J. Rowe lived, now occupied by Strauss' livery stable, in which he and Mr. Wm. Dudley lived until the Doctor married and settled at the place since occupied by the family. He enjoyed a very lucrative practice and made money.

John McCollum's store stood on the west side of the Public Square, where the post-office now stands. Originally it had a piazza the whole length of the front of the building. Indeed, all of the stores then had them, and benches thereon for the customers to sit upon after coming in from a ride or walk, and after having taken a drink—one or more. His dwelling house stood where Capt. P. L. Breeden now lives. He was an upright, good citizen, and commanded the universal respect of the people. Capt. Joshua David built a house on the east side of the Public Square on the corner. He doubtless lived in it awhile, for he filled the office of Sheriff and Clerk, and for a number of years was Ordinary for the District. The house was afterwards known as the Tavern, and kept for years by Philip Miller. The bakery and candy shop stood immediately on the

corner, and the hotel was a little further back. On the
block where the bank now stands, but on the corner, and
quite near to the street, the Masons erected the Marlboro
Hotel, removing it from the old court-house, it being the
first house erected in Bennettsville. It had, no doubt,
been greatly improved and enlarged since those days, but
like most of the old landmarks, it came to be an eyesore
to the fastidious tastes of the modern Bennettsvillian, and
was removed some years ago, and quite recently has been
entirely demolished and a handsome new hotel built on
the spot.

One of the early settlers, Harvey J. Baldwin, a North-
erner, built a house on the lot formerly occupied by
S. J. Townsend, but now owned by Mrs. Adams, and
known far and wide as the Adams House. Another, Dr.
Benjamin by name, owned the lot and partly completed
a house on the lot now owned by H. W. Carroll. He
sold out to Wm. Munnerlyn and went to Marion. Amos
Galpin, who has already been mentioned, bought land
from John S. Thomas lying on both sides of the street
leading towards Cheraw. The east side of the street, the
block next the Public Square, he sold to Henry Covington,
who in turn sold to Horace Thomas. The west side
was purchased from Galpin by Robeson A. Carloss,
who sold to Gen. McQueen, and Col. C. W. Dudley. The
house now occupied by F. M. Emanuel was built by Rev.
Thomas Cook, who once merchandised in Bennettsville,
on the corner below where the post-office now stands.

This sketch of the first settlers, their homes and places
of business, shows that the little town began gradually to
assume shape and to make its mark upon the geography of
the country. Town lots were laid off, and it is fair to
presume that James Cook and John S. Thomas felt themselves in great luck that the town decided to stake down
at their very doors, and perhaps spread out all around
them. The line dividing their land ran perhaps between

Judge Hudson's law office and the Adams House to the run of the creek, and south towards the Crosland residence. One of the first lots purchased was the Marlboro Hotel lot, which was purchased by Mrs. Dudley, the grandmother of T. E. Dudley. It is perfectly safe to say that not one of the original purchasers are alive to-day. It would be interesting and instructive to note the changes that have taken place in the ownership of the land lying around the Public Square. It would be a revelation to be able to note changes that have taken place in the market value of the land contiguous to the Square since 1826 and up to date.

The land lying to the west of John S. Thomas was owned by Hartwell Ayer, the father of the late Mrs. J. B. Breeden. The dividing line between Thomas and Ayer was about the gully just west of T. E. Dudley's residence. Col. C. W. Dudley purchased two tracts of land from Mr. Ayer, one of seventy acres on the south side of the Society Hill road, and another of one hundred and nine acres to the north of the same road. When the new court-house was being erected, from 1819 to 1824, the land upon which East Bennettsville now stands was doubtless owned by Nathan B. Thomas, the grandfather of the late H. P. Johnson. He was one of the commissioners appointed to supervise the erection of the court-house, and perhaps made the brick for the building.

We have told of the first early years of the history of Bennettsville and something of the early settlers of the town. Those early settlers may have been disappointed at the slow growth of the young town. A few stayed awhile and then moved on to seek their fortunes elsewhere; others remained to aid in the development and growth of the town. At the beginning of the war, say thirty-five years from its birth, Bennettsville was still quite a small place. A few houses were scattered irregularly along the Main street from where Knox Livingston lives down to where T. M. Bolton's residence now stands. Col. Dudley lived still farther on. A little off from the Main street and looking south, could be seen Mrs. Long's and Mr. Alexander Southerland's and the Taylor place; a little further on and looking east was the Presbyterian church, the J. J. Rowe place and Dr. Crosland's, and yet still further eastward was the Methodist parsonage; Judge Hudson's house, and last of all Col. W. J. Cook's, who was living at his father's place, which was there before Bennettsville was founded. This Cook residence is the oldest dwelling in Bennettsville or vicinity. Not long after the Revolution it was erected by William Hodge, a brother-in-law of Loudon Harwell; afterwards he sold the place to James Cook and moved West. Those mentioned, with the residences along the Main street, made up a village of about thirty residences, besides three churches, Methodist, Baptist and Presbyterian; two lodges, Masonic and Temperance; about six stores lying around the Square, several offices and one or more blacksmith and wood shops. The middle-aged people will be able to call to mind Townsend & Douglas, C. S. & M. I. Henagan, John McCollum, and Wm. Murchison as the principal merchants. W. D. Johnson, S. J. Townsend, J. H. Hudson, C. P. Townsend and T. E. Dudley were the attorneys. Alexander Southerland was the postmaster and druggist. J. J. Rowe, the shoemaker; Robt. W. Little, the tailor. J. B. and J. T. Jennings, W. J. David and Wm. D. Wallace did the medical practice for the town and community. Bennettsville then had no barber or undertaker. The men must have known how to shave themselves, and if anybody happened to die the coffin was made of pine-boards at the shop. The town boasted of two good schools, a male and female academy; under the management of first-class teachers.

Then came the war, when merchants, lawyers, teachers and doctors gave up their business and volunteered in

defense of their country and a principle they held dear.
The farmers left their homes and firesides in the care of
their wives and servants, and, side by side with the professional man, bravely battled for a cause they thought
was just. A few old men and the women, children and
servants were left in charge of the town. The war closed,
and brave men came home. Alas! many returned not,
to face demoralization, desolation and poverty. They
courageously took up the burden of life again, and with
no capital save brains and pluck, began the battle against
poverty; and the battle has been successful. To-day Bennettsville bears no resemblance to the town of thirty
years ago. She has lengthened her cords and spread out
east, south and west; new streets have been opened, houses
built, and either east or west Bennettsville has more inhabitants now than the whole town had in 1866. What
changes have taken place in thirty years! There are six
houses in the center of the town that have not changed
location or in appearance since 1866. The jail, Masonic
Hall, Presbyterian church. and the dwellings of Throop
Crosland, Douglas Jennings and J. G. W. Cobb have the
same appearance as they did thirty years ago. The dwellings of F. M. Emanuel, A. E. Bristow, the Cook residence
and the C. W. Dudley place have not changed. Everything else is new or has been so changed and remodeled
as to look new. Where dilapidated stores, shops and
small offices stood around the public square, handsome
brick stores and elegant blocks of brick buildings now
stand. Handsome residences now thickly dot the ground
upon which crops of cotton and corn were cultivated.
Besides the erection of handsome stores and beautiful
residences, other and marked improvements have been
made. The merchants no longer haul freight to and from
Society Hill and Gardner's Bluff. Bennettsville is now
in communication with the outside world. Two railway
lines offer transportation for freight and passage north

and south. Cotton is sold to the local buyer, who ships it by rail, and pays for it with a check on the Bank of Marlboro. Fine graded schools, for both white and colored children, having good buildings and a full corps of experienced teachers, are in full blast, and may be said to be the pride of the town. Good churches, good schools, good stores and dwellings, and good people make a good town; and Bennettsville, having all these good things, is a good town. In Bennettsville fortunes have been made and successes won. What has been may be, and those who are toiling for success in their calling must toil on hoping and working for success.

Since the close of the war in April, 1865, the town of Bennettsville, which was partly burned by Sherman's soldiers, has enjoyed a steady growth. The leading merchants have been James B. Breeden, Wm. Murchison, John D. Murchison, Capt. P. L. Breeden, C. S. McCall, A. J. Rowe, J. N. Weatherly, C. M. Weatherly, J. M. Jackson, Rowe Bros., Simon Strauss, H. W. Carroll and R. Lee Kirkwood. Others are doing business on a smaller scale. All above named have succeeded and most of them remarkably well. Perhaps in no town of its size in South Carolina have so many substantial fortunes, in the space of thirty years, been accumulated by merchants as in Bennettsville; and this not by speculation, but by straightforward methods. In the forefront of those who have amassed property in this line of business are J. B. Breeden, Wm. Murchison, John D. Murchison, who died, leaving large estates, and Capt. P. L. Breeden and C. S. McCall, still living. The first has retired from mercantile life and devotes himself to planting on a large scale, whilst McCall still successfully conducts a large mercantile as well as large planting business with marked success in both. He is the largest holder of real estate in the town. It is a noteworthy fact that all these successful men were farmers' sons and began life with little or no capital. They have been the architects of their own fortunes. The same may be said of D D. McColl, president of the Bank of Marlboro, who, though not a merchant, has, by strict attention to business, professional and financial, kept apace with the foremost of them in the accumulation of wealth. With much satisfaction it is to be remarked that the places of these veterans in mercantile and financial affairs will be taken by worthy young men who are making headway in business, and will maintain the steady and wholesome growth of the town.

Some few family names of the original first settlers of Bennettsville are yet to be found in the town or immediate vicinity. Joel Emanuel, the grandfather of the Messrs. W. P., P. C. and Joel Emanuel and P. A. Hodges lived first at the "old court-house," and when Bennettsville was founded, moved to the new county seat and for a number of years lived in the town and was engaged in the mercantile business, and afterwards lived on his farm north of the town, where he died a number of years ago. He was the brother of Simon Emanuel, of Brownsville, who was the father of Mrs. A. E. Bristow. The grandparents of T. E. Dudley also lived at the "old court-house," and followed on after the new court-house. Mrs. Dudley was the first person to undertake the hotel business in Bennettsville. Samuel Sparks lived at the "old court-house," but never resided in Bennettsville. He was the father of the late Capt. Alex D. Sparks, whose widow lives near Blenheim. Mrs. Keitt, the daughter of Samuel Sparks, married Lawrence M. Keitt, who represented the State in the provisional Confederate Congress which met at Montgomery, Alabama, February 4th, 1861.

The names now found in Bennettsville that were here at, or very soon after the town was founded, are the Emanuels named, the Dudleys, Croslands, Bristows, Cooks and Mrs. Miller. There may be others or descendants of others, but they are not remembered, except in the descendants of Hartwell Ayer, in the children of the late John Harroll, and the descendants of Nathan B. Thomas, in H. P. Johnson and children, and Hope Newton, Jr.

In the preparation of this chapter the writer had access to a file of old papers kindly furnished him by Editor S. A. Brown, containing a "History of Bennettsville," written by the late Col. C. W. Dudley when he was the editor of the paper.

CHAPTER XXVII.

Brightsville.

Brightsville, one of the upper townships in Marlboro, takes its name from Chas. Bright, who was the maternal grandfather of the late E. W. Goodwin. Mr. Bright emigrated to this county from Granville County, North Carolina, in the year 1796. "It is thought he was a Revolutionary soldier. He was filled with the true spirit of patriotism and ardent love of country which characterized the men of his day." Mr. Bright was married when he came to Marlboro, having a wife and five children. He first settled on Crooked Creek, near Bruton's Fork Church, then lived awhile on the stage road, near where Jackson Stubbs now lives, and in 1827 moved to what is now known as Goodwin's Mill. He purchased the mill and a large body of land from Drury Robertson in 1808. He was a man of indomitable energy. When he reached the place now bearing his name he had little or no money. When he died in 1830, at the advanced age of seventy years, he was the owner of thousands of acres of land and more than fifty slaves. Samuel Goodwin, the father of E. W. Goodwin, married the daughter of Chas. Bright. E. W. Goodwin, like his grandfather, was a man of great energy and perseverance. In addition to his mill and large farming interests, he successfully conducted a large mercantile business, and amassed a considerable fortune He died a few years ago lamented, respected and loved by all who knew him. He represented the county in the Secession Convention.

Seventy years ago people did not board a train at their doors and travel at the rate of forty miles per hour. Railroad travel was then unknown and unthought of. Transportation from place to place was by means of stage coaches drawn by horses. The stage line from New Orleans to New York used to pass through this county, and the road from Cheraw to Laurel Hill, by Goodwin's Mill, was a part of the route. About fifty years ago some railroads had been built, but a gap from Camden, South Carolina, to Warsaw, North Carolina, had still to be traveled by stage; and thus it is seen that the "stage road" had some importance attached to it at that day, and doubtless Charles Bright thought himself lucky in making a purchase of land lying alongside the "stage road." The stage road was established here about 1822, having been moved from the road running through Adamsville.

Soon after the Revolutionary War two Odom brothers came to Marlboro from Virginia, James and Sion. The former settled on the place where a grandson, H. K. Odom, now lives, and was the father of a large family. The descendants of this old man are found in various parts of the county, while a goodly number yet remain in the old neighborhood. James, Theophilus, William, Daniel, Abram, Godfrey, Tristram and John, were the sons of the first James, all of whom (Tristram being the last, who died in 1896) have gone to the grave. Chloe, the daughter of James, married Tandy Vance and moved to Missouri; Nancy married Isham Turner, lived first in North Carolina and moved thence to Missouri; Betsy married Allen Wicker, lived first in North Carolina and moved to Marlboro; Jennie first married a man named Smith, and then married Barnabas Wallace, and became the mother of Stephen Wallace, Col. John W., Dr. Murray C., Evander and William. Her daughters, Matilda and Mary, married B. F. and James Parrott, in Darlington; Lizzie married Peter Bowyer; Miranda, Duncan Barentine, and Martha married Cornelius D. Newton. All the Wallace name above mentioned are dead except William, who lives in Camden.

Sion Odom settled near the stage road, not far from where Durant Odom, a grandson, now lives. From him is descended a numerous progeny through Philip, Sion and Sam, as well as others of other names. Many of the respected citizens of the Brightsville and Smithville townships have in their veins the blood of one or the other of these old patriarchs. Another of the name who also came from Virginia, after he was discharged from service in the patriot army, seems to have settled first in Marion County and if he did not come himself to Marlboro, his sons, it is said, did come; and one of these married Miss Dorcas Stubbs and left a daughter, who became the first wife of the late S. J. Strickland.

Another prominent member of these pioneer settlers in Brightsville was Herbert Smith, the father of Dr. T. C. Smith, Frank Smith; Miss Betsy Smith, Mrs. Ann Adams and Mrs. S. J. Adams, of Bennettsville. He first settled on the stage road near where D. D. Stubbs now lives. He was born in 1790, lived at that place only a few years, when he exchanged places with Handy Stanton and moved to the old Telegraph Road, where he resided for sixty-five years. He died in 1883 at the advanced age of 93.

Joel Hall was born in Chesterfield County, South Carolina, in 1807. His father moved from Chesterfield in his latter years, and settled just across the State line not more than two miles from the home of Joel Hall. On December 1, 1833, he married Esther Steen. They had seven children, all are now dead except three sons. His wife died in 1874, and his son, John, was killed the same year by lightning. Mr. Hall died only a year or two ago, approaching 90 years of age. In the year 1836, as told by Mr. Hall, a wagoner from the up-country brought a case of smallpox into that section and died at Bennie Quick's, and was buried near by. The sign of his lonely grave, a few years ago, was yet visible. He was nursed principally by Herbert and William Smith and William Hall, the father of Joel Hall. "The awful disease spread rapidly in the Sand Hills; there were some sixty-five cases, but, strange to say, not more than five or six deaths." Mr. Hall could remember when not more than four or five bales of cotton were made in that entire Sand Hill country: now a public gin turns out four or five hundred bales annually. As a rule the people did not work much in his young days. What a change from the old to the new!

Among the first settlers in the Brightsville section may be mentioned Barney Wallace, who lived and reared a large family on Crooked Creek, near where T. P. Stubbs now lives. Thomas Barrington settled and lived one mile north of Boykin Church, where his son Goodwin lives. Younger Newton, the grandfather of Ira Newton, lived on the same plantation now owned by Ira. John Stubbs, the father of Jackson, Alexander and the late John W., lived where Gus O'Tuall now lives, the home of A. J. Stanton, the old Tax Collector of Marlboro County.

Bishop Gregg, in his "History of the Old Cheraws," mentions the name of John Stubbs, and says of him "that in November, 1753, he took up a grant of land on Catfish Creek in Marion, and was doubtless the ancestor of the large connection of that name in Marlboro." John had a brother named William, for Mr. William F. Stubbs, of Anson County, North Carolina, who is now entering his 92d year, says: "My grandfather informed me that his father, John or William, came from England before the Revolutionary War and settled in Marlboro County," and further says, "He was a small man, a weaver by trade, and married Miss Rebecca Conner, a very large lady, who became the mother of five sons; Lewis, James, Thomas, William, John and doubtless also Peter. Of these, Lewis, the first mentioned, settled where Mrs. Mastin Stubbs now lives, and was the father of Rev. Campbell Stubbs, John J. and Lewis E.; James settled where B. I. Liles now lives and was the father of John, David, Alexander and Silas.

Jackson and the late John W. were the sons of this John and grandsons of James. The daughters of James were Elizabeth, who married Holden Liles, and became the mother of Jas. S., B. I. and Joseph R. Liles; and Mrs. Pearson, Mrs, John M. Miller, and Celia, who married George Bristow, the father of Capt. A. E. Bristow, of Bennettsville; Thomas, the third brother above mentioned, settled where the late Wm. Webster lived. His sons were Benjamin, Thomas, and John. Of his daughters, Lucy married E. W. Goodwin, as elsewhere stated; Rebecca married Peter Hubbard and moved to Mississippi; Feribe married Wm. Hubbard. William, the fourth brother, settled on what has been known as the Brazier place, on the Cheraw road. His sons were James (called "Big Jim"), Peter and William F. This William F. Stubbs, already mentioned as being 92 years of age, says "his mother moved to Marlboro County in 1823, and that he was present at the first term of court that was held at Bennettsville, the spring term of 1824." He was then 19 years of age. He left the county and moved to his present home, McFarland, North Carolina, in 1855. His grandfather was a Revolutionary patriot.

It is proper to follow the Stubbs family with a sketch of the Moore family; for they are descendants on the mother's side, from them. Benjamin Moore, Sr., son of James and Drucilla Moore, was born in Richmond County, North Carolina, in 1769. He was orphaned at an early age, and came to Marlboro in his early manhood. His wife was Francis Stubbs, the daughter of Wm. Stubbs and Elizabeth Hubbard. In the year 1816 he purchased the farm upon which J. Alexander W. Moore lives, paying $1.94 per acre, which he thought was a high price for the land. It was bought of Major Drury Robertson, who owned a territory of land reaching from Goodwin's Mill to Pipkin's Mill. The Major valued the land principally on account of the virgin timber, which was then found in unbroken profusion, and perhaps inserted a timber reservation clause in some of the deeds. The grandsons of Benjamin Moore, Sr., value the land because from it they produce a bale of cotton per acre and provision crops in like proportion.

Benjamin Moore, Sr., died in 1846 and left a large family of sons and daughters. Rebecca Moore, his daughter, married Rev. Pleasant Brazier and moved to Alabama before the late war. Drucilla married Wm. Odom and settled in Tennessee; Nancy Moore married Abram Odom; Catharine was the wife of Theophilus Odom ; Mary Moore married Wm. Easterling and settled in Mississippi, and Parmilia Moore was the wife of the late Stephen Wallace, father of Thos. G. and Barney Wallace.

William Moore, the eldest son of Benjamin, married Mary Adams and settled in Adamsville. The sons of William Moore were Thomas B., John R., B. F., and W. A.; Mrs. Davis an only daughter, who, after Rev. Mr. Davis death, married Capt. E. L. Pearce. James Moore first married Widow Jones, a daughter of the late Henry Easterling, and after her death married Sarah, daughter of Samuel Bethea, of Marion County. James Moore, of Latta, is the fruit of that marriage. Alfred Y. Moore married Mary A. Jones, daughter of Rev. John Jones. His second wife was Elizabeth, the daughter of Philip Odom. Mr. Moore yet lives and is an active man, considering he carries the weight of four-score years. Benjamin Moore married Mintie Easterling, and A. W. Moore, lately deceased, was the son by this marriage. His second wife was Elizabeth Pearson, daughter of the late John Pearson, who is the mother of the Messrs. B. E., P. B. and Carey Moore, and who, after the death of Mr. Moore married Willis Turlington. Duncan W. Moore, youngest son of Benjamin Moore, Sr., was born November 25, 1819. He married Martha Spears, the daughter of James Spears and Deborah Bethea. The four sons,

M. A. J., J. D., C. F., and J. Alex., live at or near by the spot where their father was born and died, and where their grandfather lived and died. Mrs. Frank B. Gibson, of Gibson, North Carolina, and Mrs. E. W. Goodwin, Jr., are daughters of Duncan W. Moore. He was a man of large frame and large heart, and was known far and near as an industrious, successful farmer. Wherever known the Moores are noted as careful, thrifty, money-making farmers, and honest, law-abiding citizens.

North of the "old stage road" and two miles from Goodwin's Mills, lived A. C. McInnis. He was born on the Isle of Jura, Scotland, in 1816. His father, Angus, came to America in 1820; Mr. McInnis was then only four years old, but his recollection of the voyage across the water and the landing on the friendly shores of the New World was perfect and fresh. They intended landing at New York, but adverse winds drove them further north and the landing was made on the coast of Canada. The sail vessels of that day could not successfully buffet the winds and waves, as do the monster iron steamers of the present, and the voyage was long and tedious. Mr. McInnis had been taught to "believe that Satan was black, which he firmly believed." When the vessel anchored and the health officer came aboard, he brought his servant, a negro man, with him Mr. McInnis and a crowd of boys were upon the deck, and when they saw the negro coming on deck they thought he was the devil sure enough, and all hands incontinently cleared the deck and fled below. Mr. McInnis' parents settled in Cumberland County, North Carolina, and he came to Marlboro in 1833 and located at Parnassus, remaining there six years in business with Meekin Townsend, the father of Judge C. P. Townsend, for whom he cherished the most tender feelings of friendship and gratitude. He then moved to Bennettsville, where he lived eighteen years, engaged in the carriage-making business.

As already told in a previous chapter, he married Miss Flora McCall in 1844. S. J., James A., and Archie, now in Mississippi, were of this marriage. After leaving Bennettsville he lived near "the burnt factory," and in 1866 removed to Brightsville. Mr. McInnis was trial justice for a number of years, and, with the exception of a few years, had been a magistrate since 1852 and hence he was entitled to be called "Squire" McInnis. He was an honorable, intelligent Christian gentleman.

We have been writing about Brightsville and some of the Brightsville families, but we will step across the "old stage road," and enter Adamsville township, and not quite a mile south from Boykin Church is where the late Capt. Thomas W. Huckabee lived and died. He died only a very few years ago, having reached four-score years. He died where his father settled soon after the Revolutionary War, having never lived anywhere else. He was the son of Thomas Huckabee, who was a soldier in the Revolutionary War, and served under General Francis Marion. His father was a Virginian by birth, and married Nancy McCall, a native of Scotland, she having come to America in 1790, at the age of eighteen. Captain Huckabee was born in 1811, and had a brother, Allen, who moved West in 1854 and died in Arkansas in 1881. Captain Huckabee was a soldier in the Florida War against the unfriendly Seminole Indians. He served under General W. W. Harllee and Captain James W. Blakeny. He assisted in the erection of Fort Harllee, and was away from home several months. They were disbanded April, 1837. He arrived at home in May, having walked all the way from Charleston. During the first year of the war between the States he was elected Captain of the "Home Guards' and thus obtained the title of Captain.

He was undemonstrative and quiet, yet true as steel. He never sought public notoriety, but might have filled any position acceptably. He taught school for quite a number of years, and spared not the rod to the injury of the student.

Capt. Huckabee first married Penelope Pate, youngest sister of Willis Pate, of Clio. Only one child was born to this marriage, who is the wife of Mr. Tally Huckabee. His second wife was Mrs. Fannie Covington, who was the widow of Noah Covington. A son, Thomas, and two daughters, all grown, are the fruit of this marriage.

A file of papers furnished by J. P. Gibson made it possible for the writer to complete this chapter.

CHAPTER XXVIII.

BLENHEIM.

On August 13, 1704, the celebrated battle of Blenheim was won by the Duke of Marlborough. This signal defeat proved fatal to the plans of Louis XIV. of France, for the French and Bavarian army was almost annihilated in the battle. The Duke of Marlborough, the hero of a hundred battles, was rewarded by his King for the successful issue of the struggle. The manor and honor of Woodstock were conferred on him by the King, and the Queen ordered that a palace should there be built, to be called Blenheim, and there to-day in Blenheim Castle resides the young Duke of Marlborough, who a year or so ago, came to this country and persuaded (?) an American girl to return with him and act in the capacity of Lady Marlborough.

Blenheim, a little town lying seven miles south from Bennettsville, was named in honor of the battle of Blenheim, or more properly speaking of the castle of Blenheim. The late Donald Matheson saw the propriety of so naming it, and suggested the name. He doubtless often wondered why the county seat of Marlboro should have been called Bennettsville, instead of Blenheim, and when the opportunity arose for having a Blenheim in Marlboro, he gladly embraced it. Mr. Matheson was born in Alladale, Ross-shire, Scotland, July 19, 1810, and landed in this country at Charleston, November 29, 1825. He remained there two years or more, spent a year in Sumter, went from there to Marion, and from Marion came to Marlboro. For a while he taught school, both in the Brownsville and Parnassus neighborhoods; and for a few years was employed as a salesman by the Messrs. Townsend near Parnassus, and afterwards by John McCollum at Bennettsville. He married Miss Margaret McLeod, and settled first in Brownsville, but in a few years moved to the place of his late residence near Blenheim. His death occurred a few years ago. He was an intelligent, cultured gentleman, and good blood coursed in his veins.

For fifty years or more there has been a settlement at Blenheim. Several wealthy planters who owned plantations near the river, built summer houses at Mineral Spring, or Spring Hill (called by both names), where they resided during the summer months. It being unhealthy on the river in the summer, they annually moved out to the Spring for the double purpose of finding a healthy locality and good cold water. Gen. John McQueen, Dr. Alexander McLeod, Samuel Sparks, and B. N. Rogers, with their families, during the summer months, together with the people living near by, made quite a pleasant, intelligent little community in the years long gone by. The old people who formed that *ante-bellum* settlement have all passed away, but their descendants and others have come upon the ground, opened streets, built houses, and now have the town of Blenheim upon the maps. The Mineral Spring, the pride of the town, was discovered by James Spears, Sr., in the year 1781.

A. J. Matheson, the merchant prince of the town, is a son of Donald Matheson mentioned above.

By indomitable energy and close attention to business, he has, while yet comparatively a young man, amassed quite a snug fortune. He is the largest owner of real estate in the county, and plants a larger number of acres in cotton, and makes more bales than any man in the county. He also devotes a large share of his time and attention to mercantile pursuits, and has been more largely instrumental in building up the town of Blenheim than any other person. He was the pioneer merchant of the place, and perhaps "builded better than he knew," when he established the first store there at the Cross-roads.

The late F. B. Rogers shrewdly suspected that Blenheim would by a great point for trade, and built a store on another corner of the cross, and bought the farm of Geo. Dudley lying adjacent, as well as quite a number of other farms in the community. Blenheim is a city of parsonages, three being located there, so that preachers sometimes know how to appreciate a good thing when they see it.

Forty years ago, living in the locality of Blenheim, and on both sides of the creek, were a class of honest, honorable, intelligent and industrious men, who did not cringe and beg the world for a living, but by hard and well-directed licks made their own living. The McRaes, Jack and Philip; James Spears, and Light Townsend, the father of John R., Mrs. T. E. Dudley, Mrs. John Irby, and Mrs. W. F. Kinney, knew how to make money by farming. Major Drake, on some of his broad acres, may have given his son, Z. J. Drake, valuable lessons in making corn, which he used to advantage in his successful race against the world a few years ago. The Major may not have thought it possible to make 250 bushels per acre, but he doubtless made enough to keep his mules, sheep, hogs and negroes all fat, and a surplus to sell besides. Daniel John taught his sons the possibilities of the Marlboro soil, and they yet know how to make big crops of big potatoes, heavy corn and heavy hogs, and plenty of cotton as a surplus crop.

CHAPTER XXIX.

The Confederate War.

South Carolina seceded from the union of States by unanimous vote of a convention held in Charleston, December 20, 1860. It is too late to discuss the issues involved or to recount the various causes which led up to such action on the part of the State. It is sufficient to say that heated and partisan discussions in Congress, having a strong sectional flavor, on States' rights and constitutional limitations, aggravated and intensified by the slavery agitation, if not the cause, had much to do with bringing it to pass. Marlboro was represented in that Secession Convention by Wm. D. Johnson, Dr. A. McLeod and E. W. Goodwin, whose actions, with very few exceptions, were endorsed by the people.

Early in the year 1861 the whole Southland was astir with preparation for the inevitable. One thought filled every mind "from rosy morn till dewy eve"; that thought was ever present. The peaceful slumber of the night was disturbed by dreams of that waking thought. That thought was dark, grim-visaged war. Volunteer companies were formed of the flower and strength of the land. From hilltop and valley, from mountain to the sea, men of all classes were enlisting and tendering their services to the State. Our people thought themselves right and fought with as true valor and as pure patriotism as men ever did. The men of Marlboro did their duty nobly in the contest. Before the war Marlboro had an organized regiment of militia of eight small companies, and a voting population of twelve or thirteen hundred, and yet furnished to the Confederate army eight full companies, not including the reserves. After the lapse of more than a quarter of a cen-

tury, the survivors of the war are known from other men
of like age by the empty sleeve or artificial limb or faded
cheek, and not by their abandoned habits and dissipation,
for they have not been less law abiding or more turbulent
or violent than others in like circumstances of trial, nor
have they been outstripped in the struggle for material
prosperity. It is not the smouldering embers of the flame
which so raged in every bosom and made good soldiers of
the men who fought that has sometimes given the pref-
erence in civil affairs to the scarred veteran, but because
the warrior bore himself as a man upon the field, and came
out of the strife unharmed, and with steady aim in peace
as in war, has stood for the right, and shown himself
worthy of the confidence and suffrages of his fellows.
Whether the fighting qualities of the soldiers Marlboro
furnished to the ranks will bear a favorable comparison
with other troops, it may not be proper here to say; but
that their morals, industry, integrity, attention to business and honorable success in life's struggle since the
war, can bear the test of comparison with other classes,
can truthfully be said. The country has honored them,
kind Providence has smiled upon them, their business has
prospered, their plans have succeeded and to-day they
could walk arm in arm over the battlefields with the men
they fought, and breathe no curse and harbor no disloyalty. Let not the character and deeds of those who
fought the battles and endured the hardships of the war,
be misunderstood by the generations yet to come. Let
it be remembered that it was a pure devotion to their
country's call that caused them to buckle their armor on
and take the field. Their convictions of duty were as
honest as were those of our Revolutionary sires, and they
braved danger and death for their country's sake. They
died daring to stand against tremendous odds, because in
their heart of hearts they felt that duty called them there.
Let the children and children's childen of the Confederate

soldiers of Marlboro remember that their sires fought and
died for a principle they held dear. Let not the poets,
orators, and authors of the land of the victors, in recording the glories of the victors, forget to do justice to the
vanquished. Let them not make the impression upon
our posterity that our fathers made a traitorous and dis-
honorable assault upon the principles of free government,
virtue and right.

The following pages will give the names of the officers
and privates who went from Marlboro to the Confederate
War. Through the kindness of officers and men who
wore the gray we are enabled to publish a *full list* of all
the commands that went to the field of strife from Marlboro. A number of men have come into the county from
other States whose names will not appear, but who honorably did their duty in other commands from other States.

Special thanks are due T. E. Dudley, B. A. Rogers, A.
E. Bristow, C. D. Easterling, John A. Calhoun, P. L.
Breeden, T. F. McRae, C. S. McCall, Mrs. Sparks and
others.

COMPANY "G," 8TH REGIMENT, SOUTH CAROLINA VOLUN-
TEERS. ENTERED SERVICE IN APRIL, 1861.

Captain, John W. Harrington. Retired May, 1862.
    Wounded Manassas. Died 1884.
1st Lieutenant, Chas. P. Townsend. Elected captain May,
    1862. Wounded Malvern Hill. Alive.
2d Lieutenant, John R. Parker. Elected 1st lieutenant
    May, 1862. Wounded Fredericksburg, Knoxville, Get-
    tysburg. Captain at close of war. Alive.
2d Brevet, C. M. Weatherly. Elected adjutant May,
    1862. Wounded at Sharpsburg, Berryville, Knoxville.
    Alive.
1st Sergeant, T. E. Dudley. Sergeant-major, November,
    1861. Promoted Captain, October, 1862. Alive.
2d Sergeant, Isaac B. Lester. Died Chancellorsville,
    April, 1862.

3d Sergeant, Jno. T. Murdoch. Sergeant-major May, 1862. Discharged. Died April, 1865.
4th Sergeant, Leggett Odom. Died Richmond, September, 1861.
5th Sergeant, Wm. A. Crosland. Discharged May, 1862. Alive.
1st Corporal, Thos. Easterling. Wounded Savage Station. Died 1878.
2d Corporal, Henry E. Townsend. Died Richmond 1862.
3d Corporal, Jno. R. Cook. Wounded at Williamsburg. Alive.
4th Corporal, R. J. Tatum. Appointed wagonmaster 1862. Alive.
5th Corporal, O. H. Gillespie. Transferred to Medical Corps. Died 1882.
6th Corporal, Hugh J. Douglas. Elected 2d Lieutenant. Killed at Cedar Run.

PRIVATES.

1. Adams, Elijah, appointed color-sergeant, killed Gettysburg.
2. Adams, Harris, appointed second lieutenant, killed Gettysburg.
3. Adams, John Tyler, wounded Williamsburg, died 1871.
4. Andrews, Stephen D., discharged 1861, died 1871.
5. Bristow, Chesley D., assigned to quartermaster department; living.
6. Bristow, Edmund D., discharged April, 1862.
7. Bullard, Henry, living.
8. Bundy, Wm., discharged 1864.
9. Butler, Wm., died 1863.
10. Butler, Elijah, died 1886.
11. Campbell, J., lost sight of.
12. Caulk, Daniel, transferred to cavalry 1862; dead.
13. Cook, Thomas, A. M., wounded Manassas; died 1876.
14. Coward, Louis M., transferred to 4th Cavalry; died in hospital 1862.
15. Crosland, Samuel, died Lynchburg 1861.
16. Connor, Robt. T. D., transferred to 4th Cavalry; died in hospital 1862.
17. Cooper, Wm. C., died since war.
18. Cooper, Vernon H., wounded Fredericksburg; died Richmond.

History of Marlboro County. 197

19 David, Ephraim C., wounded Gettysburg; living.
20 David, Robt. J., wounded Fredericksburg; died at Richmond.
21 David, Joseph H., wounded Chattanooga; living.
22 David, Aiken L., living in Alabama.
23 Dudley, James, promoted second lieutenant 1864; drowned 1868.
24 Driggers, Jesse, killed.
25 Driggers, Jesse G., living.
26 Easterling, Alfred R., died Richmond 1862.
27 Easterling, Robt. C., transferred to 6th Regiment South Carolina Volunteers 1862; alive.
28 Easterling, Josiah K., killed at Gettysburg 1863.
29 Easterling, Wm. T., living.
30 Easterling, Elijah, wounded Gettysburg, Wilderness, Deep Bottom; alive.
31 Edens, Thos. W., discharged 1861; died 1895.
32 Emanuel, Chas. L., transferred 1862; dead.
33 Fletcher, Joshua D., wounded Fredericksburg, transferred to cavalry; alive.
34 Gibson, Wm. L., died Richmond 1861.
35 Gillespie, Samuel, discharged 1861; died at home.
36 Grant, Jno. S., died 1872.
37 Graham, Henry C., died 1862.
38 Harvel, John, wounded Gettysburg, Fredericksburg; killed Chickamauga.
39 Henagan, Jas. M., appointed quartermaster 1862; alive in Alabama.
40 Heyward, Isham, transferred to 21st Regiment South Carolina Volunteers and killed.
41 Hinson, John B., appointed sergeant-major 1863, wounded Sharpsburg and Fredericksburg; alive.
42 Hinson, Philip H., transferred 1863, wounded Chickamauga and Atlanta.
43 Hambrick, Amos, survived the war; lost sight of.
44 Huckabee, John J., wounded Fredericksburg; alive
45 Irby, Wm. W., wounded Williamsburg; alive.
46 Jones, James H., died 1895.
47 Jackson, James A. L., wounded at Fredericksburg; died 1884.
48 Jackson, Enos, wounded Savage Station; died 1864.
49 Johnson, Neill D., died in Virginia 1862.

50 Johnson, Hugh T., transferred to cavalry 1862; lost to sight.
51 Johnson, Daniel, died 1861.
52 Lavinger, Geo. W., wounded Gettysburg; living.
53 Long, Henry A., transferred to 4th Cavalry, wounded Manassas; dead.
54 Liles, Joseph R., discharged; alive.
55 Lavinger, Daniel, discharged.
56 Miller, John M., appointed 1st sergeant, lost leg Chickamauga; alive.
56 Miller, Henry, wounded Knoxville, lost leg; dead.
58 Munnerlyn, Chas. T., elected lieutenant 1862, wounded Fredericksburg; dead.
59 McCollum, Jno. H., appointed 2d sergeant 1863, 1st sergeant 1864; alive.
60 McIntosh, Nicholas H., discharged 1861; dead.
61 McIntosh, Alex., wounded Malvern Hill; killed Gettysburg.
62 McQueen, John, wounded Gettysburg; living.
63 McInnis, Simeon J., wounded Cold Harbor; alive.
64 McKenzie, Alex., living.
66 Odom, Josiah, transferred to 6th Regiment South Carolina Volunteers; dead.
66 Odom, Sion W., transferred to 24th Regiment South Carolina Volunteers; dead.
67 Odom, Philip W., transferred to 24th Regiment South Carolina Volunteers; dead.
68 Parker, Harrison, died 1868.
69 Prince, Jno. T., wounded Fredericksburg; living.
70 Potter, Solomon, transferred to cavalry; lost sight of.
71 Privatt, Evander, wounded Malvern Hill; killed Chickamauga.
72 Pearson, Robt. C., died 1863.
73 Roscoe, John, living.
74 Roscoe, Geo. W., living.
75 Rowe, Joseph H., transferred to 24th South Carolina Volunteers; killed.
76 Rountree, Moses, alive.
77 Skipper, Josiah, lost to sight.
78 Sneed, Israel, wounded Maryland Heights; living.
79 Stanton, Noah, transferred to 24th Regiment South Carolina Volunteers; killed Franklin.
80 Stanton, John A., killed Petersburg 1864.

81 Stanton, Milton, transferred to 24th Regiment, living.
82 Southerland, Thos. A., transferred to medical department; dead.
83 Thomas, Carey J., discharged 1861; alive.
84 Thomas, Joseph M., wounded twice at Petersburg; living.
85 Thomas, Robt. D., died 1882.
86 Thornwell, Chas. A., killed at Deep Bottom.
87 Williams, David, wounded Williamsburg; alive.
88 Wright, Daniel G., died Richmond 1863.
89 Wright, Ellerbe, died Lynchburg 1863.
90 Wright, Geo. W., living.
91 Webster, Henry D., wounded Knoxville; alive.
92 Webster, Thos. M., alive.
93 Webster, Chas. T., wounded Petersburg; alive.
94 Webster, Hartwell, wounded Maryland Heights; died 1863.

Killed in battle, 13; died during war, 22; wounded, 37; discharged, 11; transferred, 17; retired, 3; died since war, 17; lost sight of, 6; living 49.

COMPANY "K," 8TH REGIMENT, SOUTH CAROLINA VOLUNTEERS. ENTERED THE SERVICE IN APRIL, 1861.

John W. Henagan, major 8th Regiment, promoted colonel; killed in battle.
D. M. D. McLeod, captain, promoted major 8th Regiment May, 1862, wounded Gettysburg; died, July, 1863.
Frank Manning, captain, promoted from 2d sergeant to lieutenant 1861; captain 1862, wounded and lost an arm Maryland Heights; alive.
B. A. Rogers, captain; promoted from ranks to lieutenant, 1862; captain, 1864; wounded Gettysburg and Deep Bottom; alive.
F. Sarius McQueen, 1st lieutenant; promoted to captain in regular service in 1861; dead.
John D. McLucas, 1st lieutenant, promoted from ranks to lieutenant 1862; alive.
George R. Hearsey, 2d lieutenant; resigned June, 1861; dead.
Wm. T. Rogers, 2d lieutenant; promoted lieutenant May, 1862; wounded at Gettysburg and Fredericksburg; dead.

200   *History of Marlboro County.*

John A. Peterkin, 3d lieutenant, died of disease in Virginia.
Jas. M. Alford, 3d lieutenant; promoted lieutenant 1861; resigned 1861; dead.
John J. McQuage, 1st sergeant; promoted regimental color-bearer 1861; alive.
John W. Smith, 1st sergeant; detached service Winder hospital; alive.
M. M. Alford, 1st sergeant; wounded Knoxville, captured and died in prison.
Hugh B. McCall, 1st sergeant; wounded at Maryland Heights, captured and died.
Eli Willis, 1st sergeant; severely wounded Cold Harbor; alive.
Frank McRae, sergeant, wounded Cedar Mountain; died in Virginia.
Hugh McLucas, 2d sergeant; wounded Gettysburg, 1863, and died.
Cameron McKinnon, 2d sergeant; living.
John Gunter, 3d sergeant; wounded Knoxville; alive.
John C. Calhoun, 3d sergeant; dead.
Lauchlin A. McLaurin, 4th sergeant; died since war.
Crawford McCall, 1st corporal; killed Gettysburg July, 1863.
Nathan T. Alford, 2d corporal; wounded Wilderness; alive.
Daniel Hargrove, 3d corporal; wounded Gettysburg 1863; living.
Joseph D. Bruce, 4th corporal; living.

PRIVATES.

1 Allen, Elmore, discharged 1861; living.
2 Barrington, Harris, discharged 1861; died since war.
3 Bruce, Thomas, dead.
4 Beverly, W. R., discharged 1861; dead.
5 Cottingham, Chas, died at home 1861.
6 Crowley, Robt. C., discharged 1862; dead.
7 Cope, Thomas, discharged 1862; living.
8 Covington, Eli T., joined company 1865; living.
9 Curtin, ——, dead.
10 Clark, Joseph, dead.
11 Crowley, Wm., substitute for C. M. McRae; dead.
12 Covington, Jas. T., discharged 1861; living.

13 Drake, Ancil, died Warrenton, Virginia, during war.
14 Davis, Columbus, died in prison, Camp Chase..
15 Driggers, Robt. S., discharged in 1861; dead.
16 DuPree, Thos. J., discharged 1861; dead.
17 English, Wm., died disease, Culpeper, Virginia.
18 Edens, Joseph, living.
19 Edens, Thos. H., killed Bean Station, Virginia.
20 Emanuel, James M., dead.
21 Easterling, Lewis R., joined company 1865; living.
22 Easterling, David, joined company, 1865; living.
23 Freeman, L. D., substituted for Thos. Bruce.
24 Freeman, Benj., discharged, 1862; dead.
25 Fletcher, W. R., living.
26 Guzzard, John W., died Rome, Georgia, 1863.
27 Graham, E., died Culpeper, Virginia, 1863.
28 Grooms, E., died Culpeper, Virginia, 1861.
29 Hargroves, James, transferred to quartermaster department 1861; dead.
30 Harril, Tristram, wounded Chattanooga; living.
31 Haitchcock, Thos., wounded Chattanooga; dead.
32 Hays, J. J., captured Gettysburg; living.
33 Hays, Robt. W., living.
34 Haskew, John W., wounded Gettysburg; dead.
35 Huckabe, John, captured; living.
36 Hodge, T. C., living.
37 Ivy, H. W., discharged 1862; living.
38 Ivy, Levi, wounded Malvern Hill; living.
39 Jones, John C., discharged, 1861; dead.
40 Jones, Martin, lost arm first Manassas; discharged; dead.
41 Jacobs, Robt., substitute T. Edens; dead.
42 Jackson, John C., died in prison, Camp Chase.
43 Jacobs, J. Frost, living.
44 John, Daniel C., transferred to cavalry; living.
45 Kirby, H.
46 McCall, Cameron, died Warrenton, Virginia.
47 McCall, Alex., wounded Sharpsburg; living.
48 McRae, A. D., died in 1862.
49 McRae, John D., discharged 1862; dead.
50 McRae, Jno. C., wounded Maryland Heights; died of disease, Virginia.
51 McDaniel, Jas. R., died disease, Knoxville.
52 McLucas, Archie, died at home, 1863.

53 McLaurin, John F., living.
54 McLeod, Murdock, discharged 1861; dead.
55 McPherson, Malcom, killed Gettysburg, 1863.
56 McPherson, Angus, killed Gettysburg 1863.
57 Matheson, Hugh, died in 1861.
58 Manship, John, joined company 1864, died 1864.
59 Rogers, Frank A., living.
60 Rascoe, Daniel, died Virginia 1861.
62 Smith, W. D.
63 Stubbs, Lucius, died Richmond, Virginia, 1861; body buried Bennettsville Baptist church.
64 Sport, George, discharged 1861.
65 Sarris, A. L., died Gordonsville, Virginia.
66 Stanton, A. A., substitute Levi Ivy; dead.
67 Webster, W. R., wounded Seven Pines, Virginia; dead.
68 Williams, Lazarus, wounded first Manassas; discharged 1861; living.
69 Woodley, Alex., died disease, Culpeper, Virginia.
70 Weatherly, A. W., wounded Malvern Hill; living.

Killed in battle, 7; wounded, 22; captured, 6; died in prison, 3; discharged, 14; unknown, 3; died of disease in war, 21; dead, 29; alive, 33.

Company "G," 23d Regiment South Carolina Volunteers.

Captain, R. C. Emanuel, died since war.
1st Lieutenant, Elisha C. Pipkin, died during war.
2d Lieutenant, A. L. McRae, elected captain at reorganization; killed Manassas.
3d Lieutenant, Preston Drake, died since war.
1st Sergeant, Salathiel Leggett, elected 1st lieutenant at reorganization; dead.
2d Sergeant, Wm. W. Covington, elected 3d Lieutenant at reorganization; promoted captain; died since war.
3d Lieutenant, D. S. John, lost leg at Second Manassas; died 1893.
4th Sergeant, Silas Spears, elected 3d lieutenant 1862; wounded Jackson, Mississippi; died.
5th Sergeant, Moses P. Galloway, elected 3d lieutenant 1863; died 1894.
1st Corporal, T. M. J. Summerford; died since war.

History of Marlboro County. 203

2d Corporal, T. W. Allen: killed at battle of the Rappahannock.
3d Corporal, John A. Calhoun, elected 2d lieutenant 1863; wounded South Mountain and Fort Steadman;. alive.
4th Corporal, James Taylor; killed Second Mannassas.

PRIVATES.

1 Ammons, Silas, lost leg at Second Mannassas; still living.
2 Bristow, E. H., alive.
3 Bruce, T. R., transferred to 8th Regiment South Carolina Volunteers.
4 Boan, B. F., still living.
5 Brigman, B. F., still living.
6 Bristow, J. M., transferred; still living.
7 Breeden, R. J., survived the war, but murdered since.
8 Bethea, P. W., alive.
9 Brigman, Frank, alive.
10 Brigman, Madison, still living.
11 Carribo, Henry, killed at Petersburg.
12 Cottingham, Jonathan, transferred; still living.
13 Carter, W. J., transferred; alive.
14 Cope, Elijah, transferred; alive.
15 Calder, Boswell, alive.
16 Calder, W. J., transferred; still living.
17 Calder, Arthur, alive.
18 Cole, James, died since war.
19 Cox, M. C., died since war.
20 Cox, Ely, died during war.
21 Cox, W. E., wounded in foot near Goldsboro, North Carolina; alive.
22 Cox, Elvin, died since war.
23 Cox, C. A., wounded in shoulder at Rappahannock.
24 Carlisle. T. F., wounded at Fort Sumter and Petersburg; alive.
25 Cully, C. W., transferred; died since war.
26 Crowly, W., killed Second Mannassas.
27 Clark, ———, wounded Petersburg; still living.
28 Clark, Daniel, alive.
29 Clark, Elsey, killed Second Manassas.
30 Calhoun, A. L., still living.

31 Calhoun, J. C., killed Petersburg.
32 Calhoun, H. H., still living.
33 Covington, J. A., killed Petersburg, Virginia.
34 Dew, H. C., still living.
35 Driggers, J. H., still living.
36 DuPre, T. J., died since war.
37 Dunford, John, died at Richmond, Virginia.
38 Driggers, Alex., discharged; died since war.
39 Emanuel, Columbus, died since war.
40 Emanuel, Frank, died since war.
41 Earl, Jesse, lost.
42 English, James, died since war.
43 English, John, transferred and died since war.
44 English, Chas., still alive.
45 Freeman, Lorenzo, killed Second Manassas.
46 Graham, J. J., wounded Rappahannock, transferred; alive.
47 Graham, Windsor, transferred; died since war.
48 Gray, William, alive.
49 Gray, Robt., wounded Kinston and Petersburg; alive.
50 Gray, Calvin, dead.
51 Garner, Wm., transferred; alive.
52 Gilbert, Robt., alive.
53 Galloway, Jos. S., wounded Petersburg; alive.
54 Galloway, W. A., wounded Jackson, Mississippi; alive.
55 Galloway, Jno. C., wounded Petersburg; alive.
56 Heustiss, James, discharged, over age.
57 Heustiss, A. J., discharged, under age; alive.
58 Hood, John, died during war.
59 Hood, Wellington, killed Second Manassas.
60 Hood, Wiley, alive.
61 Hubbard, S. G., wounded Second Manassas; still living.
62 Hubbard, E. G., died in Mississippi during war, of fever.
63 Hersey, G. R., transferred; died since war.
64 Haithcock, R. F., wounded Petersburg; alive.
65 Haithcock, R., discharged; died since war.
66 Haithcock, Samuel, wounded Fort Steadman; alive.
67 Hamer, Daniel H., alive.
68 Ivy, H. M., killed Second Manassas.
69 Jackson, Abner, died since war.

70 Jackson, John, transferred; died since war.
 71 Johnson, W. D., lost sight of.
 72 Jackson, A. W., wounded, transferred; alive.
 73 Jackson, Wm., died since war.
 74 Lochlier, John, died in hospital in North Carolina.
 75 Meekins, P. J., wounded Petersburg; alive.
 76 Munford, Wm., transferred; alive.
 77 Moody, Geo., transferred; died since war.
 78 McLaurin, J. B., elected 2d lieutenant at reorganization, resigned; dead.
 79 McLaurin, D. McQ., died during war.
 80 McLaurin, N. D., alive.
 81 McLaurin, Geo., alive.
 82 McLaurin, J. J., died in 1892.
 83 McLaurin, H. L., wounded Petersburg; alive.
 84 McLaurin, D. W., wounded Petersburg; alive.
 85 McLaurin, Hugh, died Jackson, Mississippi.
 86 McEachern, Niell, alive.
 87 McEachern, John, died Richmond, Virginia.
 88 McKenzie, R. H., killed South Mountain, Maryland.
 89 McRae, John T., transferred; killed.
 90 McRae, Chas., alive.
 91 McColl, Silas, wounded Jackson, Mississippi; alive.
 92 McColl, Duncan, transferred; alive.
 93 McColl, Jno. S., wounded Second Manassas, disabled,
 94 McAlister, John, transferred; alive.
 95 McAlister, Chas., transferred; alive.
 96 McColl, Daniel, died Jackson, Mississippi, of fever.
 97 McGilvray, B. F., killed Five Forks, Virginia.
 98 Napier, Joel E., wounded Petersburg; still living.
 99 Parish, Henry, still living.
100 Parham, Henry, transferred; alive.
101 Polson, Alex, wounded and died.
102 Polson, David, alive.
103 Proctor, Frederick, alive.
104 Proctor, Aaron, killed Petersburg.
105 Parham, Robt., alive.
106 Quick, Alfred, died since war.
107 Quick, Giles, died since war.
108 Quick, Philip, died Savannah, Georgia, fever.
109 Quick, Daniel, died at home of fever.
110 Quick, Jas. H., wounded Five Forks; alive.
111 Quick, Henry, killed Second Manassas,

112 Quick, Pleasant, killed Petersburg, Virginia.
113 Quick, E. B., alive.
114 Quick, A. W., alive.
115 Rae, A. P., transferred to North Carolina Regiment; dead.
116 Rascoe, Wm., transferred; died since war.
117 Spears, Harris N., alive.
118 Spears, Wm., alive.
119 Seals, James, wounded Five Forks; died since war.
120 Stubbs, Jas., wounded Petersburg; alive.
121 Stubbs, John, killed Antietam, Maryland.
122 Stubbs, Joel, died during war.
123 Sawyer, Levi, killed Second Manassas.
124 Stergis, John, lost an arm at Second Manassas.
125 Stergis, Joseph, discharged.
126 Sawyer, Joel, alive.
127 Stanton, W. G., alive.
128 Stanton, W. H., died since war.
129 Stanton, J. H., killed Five Forks, Virginia.
130 Stanton, Peter, alive.
131 Steed, W. H., wounded Petersburg; alive.
132 Stogner, John, wounded Jackson, Mississippi; alive
133 Stogner, Wm., wounded Five Forks, Virginia; alive.
134 Sports, John, discharged; bad health.
135 Sports, W. B., died during war.
136 Thomas, Philip, alive.
137 Wallace, Washington, wounded Second Manassas; died since war.
138 Wilkins, J. T., transferred; died since war.
139 Wiloughby, J. P., transferred; died since war.
140 Wiggins, Ham, died during war.
141 Webb, David, died since war.
142 Webb, Alex., wounded Petersburg; died since war.
143 Weatherly, E. A., transferred; still living.
144 Warden, Eli, lost.
145 Welch, Richard, transferred; died since war.
146 Sinclair, D. C., transferred, died since war.
147 McColl, W. M., alive.
Killed in battle, 19; wounded, 33; died during war, 17; transferred, 26; discharged, 6; lost, 3; died since war, 40; alive, 72.

Muster Roll Company "D," 26th Regiment South Carolina Volunteers.

Commissioned and Non-Commissioned Officers.

A. D. Smith, Colonel.
J. H. Hudson, Lt. Colonel.

Smith, A. D., captain; elected colonel 26th Regiment, 1862; wounded Petersburg; died at home.
Davis, Washington W., 1st lieutenant; promoted captain 1862; killed Clay's Farm, Virginia.
Wallace, John W., 2d lieutenant; promoted 1st lieutenant 1862; dead.
Davis, James M., 3d lieutenant; promoted 2d lieutenant 1862; died at home.
Bristow, Alexander E., 1st sergeant; promoted 3d and 2d lieutenant 1862; captain 1864; alive.
Hall, Alexander, 2d sergeant; elected 3d lieutenant 1863; alive.
Hammond, Haynes L., 3d sergeant; transferred to North Carolina Regiment; killed Wilderness.
Quick, Robert, 4th sergeant; promoted 1st sergeant 1864; killed Petersburg, 1864.
Quick, Thomas, P., 5th sergeant; killed Petersburg 1864.
Parker, Peter, 1st corporal; promoted sergeant 1862; died at home.
Brigman, J. Curtis, 2d corporal; alive.
Hayes, James M., 3d corporal; alive.
Roller, John, 4th corporal; killed Secessionville, 1862.
Brigman, Eli, 5th corporal; killed Petersburg, 1864.
Covington, Harris, 2d lieutenant 1861; promoted 1st lieutenant, 1864; captain, 1865; died 1876.
Malone, John C., elected 1st sergeant 1862; transferred; living.
Parham, Alex. K., elected 1st sergeant 1863; alive.
Emanuel, Frank W., elected sergeant-major 1862; ordinance sergeant 1861; died in Texas.

Privates.

1 Bittle, James, H., killed Petersburg 1864.
2 Bolton, Britton, died at home.
3 Brigman, Henry.

4   Brigman, Moses.
5   Brigman, William, killed at Petersburg, 1864.
6   Brigman, Henry.
7   Brigman, Jacob C.
8   Barrington, Goodwin, living.
9   Barrington, Sion R., living.
10 Barrington, Ebby W., living.
11 Barrington, Alex. H., living.
12 Bealancua, Augustus.
13 Calder, Henry, transferred to 8th Regiment.
14 Calder, Stamford.
15 Calder, Daniel, died at home.
16 Covington, Henry, killed Petersburg 1864.
17 Clayton, John, died at home of disease.
18 Cole, William.
19 Chavis, Eliab, alive.
20 Chavis, James, alive.
21 Chavis, Bytha J., died at home.
22 Chavis, Willis J., living.
23 Chavis, John, died June, 1862, at Charleston.
24 Chavis, Nelson, living.
25 Chavis, Eli, living.
26 Chavis, Calvin, living.
27 Chavis, Levi, killed Clay's Farm, near Petersburg, 1864.
28 Chavis, William, killed near Petersburg, 1864.
29 Chavis, Bithel, died at home on furlough, 1864.
30 Chavis, Alfred, killed August 1864, near Petersburg
31 Clark, William.
32 Davis, Younger, died of disease at Secessionville.
33 Dawkins, Elisha A., killed near Petersburg 1864.
34 Driggers, Thomas, killed Secessionville, June, 1862
35 Driggers, Eli, wounded Clay's Farm, Virginia, 1864; alive.
36 Driggers, Gage; alive.
37 Driggers, Peter, alive.
38 English, Alex., wounded Jackson, Mississippi.
39 English, Eli, alive.
40 English, Welcome, killed Petersburg 1864.
41 Fletcher, John S., severely wounded Petersburg, 1864; alive.
42 Griggs, Henry, transferred to Coit's Battery 1864.
43 Gilbert, Simeon.
44 Gibson, Eli, wounded Burgiss Mill, Virginia, 1865; alive.

History of Marlboro County. 209

45 Gibson, Frank B., wounded near Appomatox, Virginia, day Lee's surrender, April 9th, 1865; alive.
46 Gibson, John, killed near Petersburg 1864.
47 Grooms, Evander, killed near Petersburg, 1864.
48 Grant, James T., alive.
49 Guinn, Anderson, alive.
50 Hammond, Stephen, transferred to North Carolina Regiment 1864.
51 Hatcher, Abner, wounded Petersburg 1864; alive
52 Hatcher, Aaron, died at home 1864.
53 Hall, William, alive.
54 Jacobs, Curtis J., alive.
55 Jacobs, Archie, died Petersburg, Virginia.
56 Jones, William.
57 Jones, James H., died 1895.
58 Jacobs, Samuel, alive.
59 Laviner, Hiram.
60 Laviner, Harris, living.
61 Liles, James S., wounded Petersburg 1864; alive.
62 McGee, Wesley M.
63 Mumford, James, killed at Petersburg, Virginia.
64 Morris, Campbell, died since war.
65 McGee, Henry.
66 Mahoney, Thomas, discharged.
67 Oxendine, Manny, alive.
68 Oxendine, Leonard, C., promoted on field, 1864, to sergeant; alive.
69 Odom, Alexander, alive.
70 Odom, Noah, transferred to 4th South Carolina Cavalry; alive.
71 Parks, Alex, died Charleston, 1863.
72 Parker, Andrews.
73 Parham, William, died Church Flats, South Carolina.
74 Perkins, Miles, died in hospital.
75 Perkins, Wm.
76 Prevatt, Evander, died in hospital.
77 Powell, Wm. R., alive.
78 Quick, Aaron T., alive.
79 Quick, Robt. W., died at home.
80 Quick, Evander, alive.
81 Quick, Stephen, wounded Petersburg and Appomatox; dead.
82 Quick, Ebby, wounded Petersburg 1864; alive.

83 Quick, Wyatt, died at home 1863.
84 Quick, Chas. D., alive.
85 Quick, Madison, alive.
86 Roller, Henry T.
87 Roller, Benjamin, alive.
88 Roller, John, killed Secessionville, South Carolina.
89 Rainwaters, Samuel.
90 Rogers, Pinckney, alive.
91 Smith, Stephen.
02 Scott, Benjamin.
93 Sweat, Benjamin, killed 1862.
94 Sweat, Leonard, killed Petersburg 1864.
95 Sweat John, died Secessionville 1862.
96 Steen, Morgan.
97 Strickland, Henry, died Petersburg 1864.
98 Smith, James, discharged.
99 Sweat, William, wounded Jackson, Mississippi; alive.
100 Stanton, John, killed Petersburg 1864.
101 Townsend, Walter S.; alive.
102 Turner, Aaron, alive.
103 Watson, Coleman, died at home.
104 Wilkinson, Gorman, died Charleston.
105 Williams, Chas.

Killed in battle 22; died during war, 21; died since war, 6; alive, 47; wounded, 10; unknown, 23.

On December 25, 1861, Company "F," 21st Regiment, S. C. V., was formally accepted and enrolled for service by the State authorities. On January 6, 1862, orders were received to report at Charleston, but later orders sent the company first to Georgetown, S. C.

Muster Roll Company "F," 21st Regiment, South Carolina Volunteers.

1 Captain, J. A. W. Thomas; twice wounded; died August 2, 1896.
2 1st lieutenant, W. L. Leggett; resigned; died 1892.
3 1st lieutenant, N. A. Easterling; wounded; died in prison.
4 2d lieutenant, R. E. Townsend; alive (1896).

History of Marlboro County. 211

5 3d lieutenant, W. D. Cook; wounded and died in prison.
6 1st sergeant, J. R. Moore; wounded and died in prison.
7 2d sergeant, A. B. Easterling; wounded and afterwards killed at Cold Harbor.
8 3d sergeant, W. H. Adams; wounded, captured and yet alive.
9 4th sergeant, E. J. Feagan; killed at Cold Harbor.
10 1st corporal, H. T. Quick; wounded and died at Cold Harbor.
11 2d corporal, A. W. Moore; captured till close of war; died 1897.
12 3d corporal, J. M. Gibson; killed near Petersburg.
13 4th corporal, T. C. Lester; prisoner at close of war; alive.
14 3d corporal, D. M. Sinclair; killed near Petersburg.
15 3d corporal, W. B. Odom; wounded; captured; alive.
16 2d corporal, D. D. Weaton; prisoner when war closed; alive.
17 Adams, Joshua, wounded; alive.
18 Adams, J. R., killed at Cold Harbor.
19 Adams, W. L., died in hospital
20 Anderson, J. G., (corp.) killed at Petersburg.
21 Anderson, W. T., died in hospital.
22 Barrington, P. L., died in Charleston in camp.
23 Barrington, W., died in hospital.
24 Barrington, Philip, killed at Petersburg.
25 Bennett, F., captured; released at close of war; alive.
26 Bennett, Thos., captured; released at close of war; alive.
27 Bowen, C., wounded; alive.
28 Bowen, F. C., killed at Drury's Bluff.
29 Bristow, D. M., wounded; captured; died in prison.
30 Bristow, R. W., mortally wounded at Fort Fisher; died.
31 Bristow, W. J., killed by accident.
32 Brigman, Geo., discharged; alive.
33 Bundy, G. W., captured at Fort Fisher; died in prison.
34 Butler, Elijah, discharged; died 1886.
35 Butler, Wm., died in hospital.
36 Butler, W., discharged, under age; alive.
37 Calder, J. D., died in hospital.

38 Calder, Stanford, discharged; died October 27, 1891.
39 Clarke, Archie, died in hospital.
40 Clark, Jno. C., discharged; died 1886.
41 Coward, J. H., transferred.
42 Covington, A. B., discharged; alive.
43 Covington, A. D., captured; released at close of war; alive.
44 Cottingham, F., wounded at Walthall and died.
45 Creech, David, captured at Fort Fisher; died in prison.
46 Cummings, Elijah, captured and returned; alive.
47 Currie, N. R., captured at Fort Fisher; died in prison.
48 David, Dr. W. J., transferred to 18th Regiment; surgeon; died 1895.
49 Dial, Jacob, captured at Fort Fisher; died in prison.
50 Dunn, Thomas, killed at Petersburg.
51 Dunn, Wm., died at home on sick leave.
52 Easterling, A. J., died on sick leave.
53 Easterling, G. W., captured and returned; died 1878.
54 Easterling, H. R., died on sick leave.
55 Easterling, Jesse A., 4th sergeant; killed on Morris Island, July 10, 1863.
56 Easterling, Joel A., died at Georgetown, 1862.
57 Easterling, Jno. L., died since war.
58 Easterling, Jno. A., died in hospital.
59 Easterling, Jas. T., discharged; since died.
60 Easterling, W. L., served short time; alive.
61 Easterling, W. T., captured at Fort Fisher; released; alive.
62 Fletcher, Thos., discharged; alive.
63 Fields, Silas, alive.
64 Gibson, A. H., killed at Drury's Bluff, 1864.
65 Gay, P. W., captured at Fort Fisher; died in prison.
66 Grice, E. G., died 1896.
67 Guinn, Geo., alive.
68 Hamer, A. C., wounded at Petersburg; died in hands of enemy.
69 Hamer, C. H., captured at Fort Fisher; died in prison.
70 Hamer, E. C., discharged; died 1891.
71 Hamer, J. C., captured; died in prison.
72 Hamer, P. M., 1st sergeant; discharged; died May 1885.
73 Hamer, R. H., 4th corporal; discharged; alive.

History of Marlboro County. 213

74 Hamer, T. C., died on sick leave.
75 Haywood, Anderson, discharged; died 1892.
76 Haywood, Isham, killed on Morris Island.
77 Haywood, Wm., died in hospital.
78 Heustiss, G. W., wounded and died at Fort Fisher.
79 Howard, John, alive.
80 Hudson, J. H., transferred to 26th regiment, lieutenant-colonel; alive.
81 Herndon, David, alive.
82 Jacobs, B. L., died in hospital.
83 Jacobs, Snowden, captured and released at close of war.
84 Johnson, W. D., discharged; furnished substitute; alive.
85 Leggett, A. J., captured; released at close of war; since died.
86 Lochlin, A., alive.
87 Locklier, Alex., died in hospital.
88 Manship, A., killed at Petersburg.
89 McKaskill, N. C., 2d sergeant; killed at Petersburg, 1864.
90 McCall, J. N., discharged; furnished substitute; alive.
91 McDaniel, I. W., wounded twice; died 1887.
92 McKenzie, J. C., alive.
93 McQuage, J. R.
94 McIntyre, J. T., sergeant-major; wounded; captured at Fort Fisher; died.
95 Moore, B. J., captured on Morris Island; died in prison.
96 Nelson, Ervin, captured; died in prison.
97 Newton, J. C., killed in battle of Drury's Bluff.
98 Odom, D. A., alive.
99 Odom, Henry, killed in battle at Petersburg.
100 Odom, J. E., died in hospital at Georgetown.
101 Odom S. D., wounded; absent on sick leave at surrender; alive.
102 Odom, J. E., wounded severely; died January 1885.
103 Owens, Jno., captured; died in prison.
104 Pate A. D., wounded at Fort Fisher and died.
105 Pate, Willis, discharged; died 1888.
106 Peel, Eli F., at surrender; alive.
107 Peel, Thos., wounded; alive.
108 Polson, W., died at Georgetown 1862.

15

109 Powers, Ervin, wounded; alive.
110 Quick, Angus, captured at Fisher; died in prison.
111 Quick, Henry, killed in battle.
112 Quick, Jno. B., wounded at Fisher; died.
113 Rascoe, Alex, captured; returned at close of war; alive.
114 Rascoe, Wm., died in hospital.
115 Scott, Wash, alive.
116 Smith, C., captured, returned close of war; alive.
117 Spears, J. A., killed at Petersburg 1864.
118 Steen, A., captured at Fisher; died in prison.
119 Stogner, Tom, died in hospital.
120 Stogner, Wm., died at home on sick leave.
121 Stephens, J. E., captured at Fisher, died in prison.
122 Stephens, Reuben, died in hospital.
123 Stubbs, A. A., discharged; died 1893.
124 Stubbs, D. D. (4th Corporal), captured and returned; alive.
125 Stubbs, C. E., wounded; at surrender; alive.
126 Stubbs, J. B., captured and returned; alive.
127 Stubbs, M. W., wounded mortally; died Petersburg 1864..
128 Stubbs, S. F., captured at Fisher; died in prison.
129 Stubbs, T. E., discharged; died since war.
130 Stubbs, T. P., discharged; alive.
131 Tart, W. J., died Georgetown.
132 Terrell, W. T., killed near Petersburg 1864.
133 Thomas, Joe, died in hospital.
134 Turnage, Luke, captured and returned close war; dead.
135 Usher, M., killed Walthall Junction 1864.
136 Wallace, T. G., transferred to cavalry; alive.
137 Waters, Reuben, killed at Petersburg 1864.
138 Weatherford, Jas., died at home on sick leave 1864.
139 Williams, Henry, captured; returned close of war; alive.
140 Williams, Jno., captured and returned; alive.
141 Williams, Sam, transferred.
142 Willis, Allen, killed at Petersburg.
143 Wise, W. W., wounded severely; alive.
144 Woodle, Ransom, severely wounded; since died.

Recapitulation.

Killed in battle, 31; died in hospital of wounds, 5; died in hospital and at home on sick leave, 20; died in prison, 18; accidentally killed, 1. Total killed 75.

Captured and kept in prison till close of war, 23; discharged for cause, 16; transferred to other commands, 7; wounded and continued to serve, 33. Taking out the discharged and transferred and there were 121 men, rank and file, 131 captures and casualties, of the whole number enlisted now living 57, and unknown as to whereabouts, 12. Total number enlisted, 144.

Company "B," 24th South Carolina Regiment Infantry

Was organized in the summer of 1861 for State service. In December the company was received into the service, and assigned to duty at Charleston, South Carolina. In June, 1862, the company was mustered into the Confederate service and assigned to the Army of Tennessee May 6th, 1862.

Commissioned and Non-Commissioned Officers.

J. Edwin Spears, captain; resigned May, 1863; died at home 1865.
R. Johnson, 1st lieutenant; promoted captain 1863; lost arm 1863; resigned 1863; died 1884.
Wm. Griffin, 2d lieutenant; resigned 1862; died at home.
C. D. Easterling, 3d lieutenant; promoted 2d lieutenant 1862; 1st lieutenant in 1863; captain 1863; alive.
J. D. Reese, 1st sergeant; died 1862.
F. P. Tatum, 2d sergeant; promoted 1st sergeant 1862; 1st lieutenant 1863; alive.
W. J. Green, 3d sergeant; promoted 3d lieutenant 1863; killed in battle 1863.
T. B. Moore, 4th sergeant; promoted 2d lieutenant 1863; died 1873.
J. L. Barrow, 5th sergeant; captured 1863; alive.
J. C. Mallonie, 1st corporal, transferred to 26th Regiment South Carolina Volunteers.

216 *History of Marlboro County.*

J. L. Stubbs, 3d corporal; promoted 2d sergeant 1863; alive.
J. P. Hinson, 2d corporal; promoted 1st sergeant 1863.
W. S. Townsend, 4th sergeant; transferred to 26th Regiment.

Privates.

1. Ammons, Allen, dead.
2. Ammons, Alpheus, alive.
3. Ammons, Thos., still living.
4. Arnett, Benj., discharged 1863.
5. Brigman, L., died 1875.
6. Bristow, T. C., alive.
7. Bennett, G. W., still living.
8. Bass, Richard, alive.
9. Bowyer, T. M., transferred 1862; dead.
10. Bethea, A. J., detailed as hospital steward; dead.
11. Bethea, T. T., killed Franklin 1864.
12. Beverly, Robert, promoted corporal 1863; killed 1863.
13. Barrentine, G.
14. Bennett, J. J., camp cook.
15. Calder, H., killed Atlanta 1864.
16. Cope, John, died in hospital, 1864.
17. Cope, E., still living.
18. Calder, R., transferred to Sharpshooters' Regiment 1862.
19. Chavis, J., died at home 1868.
20. Chavis, Wm., discharged 1862.
21. Chavis, Geo., died in hospital 1862.
22. Caulk, James, died in hospital 1862.
23. Caulk, J. C.
24. Crawford, W. H.
25. Crawford, H. B.
26. Crawford, G. G.
27. Covington, H., transferred to 26th Regiment; died 1876.
28. Day, Wm., killed battle Chickamauga 1863.
29. Dunn, Alexander, died in camp 1863.
30. Driggers, M. C., died at home 1878.
31. Driggers, Whit, dead.
32. Driggers, C. O.
33. Driggers, ——, died at home 1862.
34. Ellen, W. B., died at home.

35 Easterling, W. B., promoted sergeant 1863; lost right arm Franklin 1864.
36 Easterling, J. T., color-sergeant; killed Franklin, Tenn., 1864.
37 Easterling, J. N., prisoner 1863.
38 Easterling, W. L., alive.
39 Fields, P., died at home 1863.
40 Fletcher, N., died in camp 1862.
41 Green, J. B., promoted 3d lieutenant 1863; alive.
42 Green, Geo., died 1865.
43 Griffin, John, died 1863.
44 Gaddy, J. W.
45 Gaddy, Wm., transferred 1862.
46 Hinson, H. P., alive.
47 Hinson, E. D., died 1863.
48 Hodges, R., alive.
49 Hodges, J. H., died in hospital 1863.
50 Hall, James.
51 Haithcock R., died in hospital 1863.
52 Hubbard, Martin, lost thumb in battle.
53 Jacobs, Asbury.
54 Jones, J. A., color-sergeant; killed Franklin, 1864.
55 Johnson, J., corporal; killed 1863.
56 Jones, W. W., died at home.
57 Jacobs, J. P., camp cook.
58 Lewis, W. S., appointed sergeant 1863; died 1896.
59 Liles, S. H., corporal; killed 1863 Kennesaw Mountain.
60 McRae, W. J., captured 1863; died at home.
61 Miller, H., transferred to 8th Regiment; lost leg; dead.
62 McCollum, H., still living.
63 Meekins, W. E., corporal; killed 1863.
64 Meekins, P. P., still living.
65 Meekins, Oscar, killed Jonesboro, Georgia 1863.
66 McQuaig H., company courier; alive.
67 Medlin, John, discharged 1862.
68 Medlin, Jas., discharged 1862.
69 Medlin, Jonathan, discharged 1862.
70 Norton, Elias.
71 Norton, Samuel, killed Franklin, 1864.
72 Norton, Jas., died 1862.
73 Odom, S. W., killed Chickamauga 1863.
74 Odom, H. E., killed Jackson 1863.
75 Odom, J. G., died in hospital, 1863.

76 Odom, D. A., transferred to sharpshooters 1862
77 Odom, L.
78 Odom, P. E.
79 Peel, Freeman, captured, 1864; died 1881.
80 Parham A., alive.
81 Parham, Samuel, killed Peachtree creek, 1863.
82 Parker, Wm., killed Peachtree creek 1863.
83 Quick M., alive.
84 Quick, A.
85 Quick, James, died at home.
86 Rowe, W. D., died 1896.
87 Rowe, J. H., died in hospital 1861.
88 Rascoe, H., died in hospital 1862.
89 Stubbs, Thos.
90 Stubbs, Daniel, wounded and discharged 1863
91 Sanders, J., died in camp 1863.
92 Sweat, Jas., died 1869.
93 Sweat, J. W., died at home.
94 Sweat, Simeon, killed 1863.
95 Sweat, Harris, discharged 1863
96 Stanton, N., killed at Franklin, Tennessee, 1864.
97 Stanton, E. G., wounded and discharged 1863.
98 Stanton, M., killed Franklin 1864.
99 Sweat, Sam, died from wounds 1863.
100 Thompson, T. J., discharged 1862.
101 Trawick, Peter, killed Franklin, 1864.
102 Turner, L., died at home.
103 Turner, Jas.
104 Turner, D.
105 Turner, Jack, died 1895.
106 Usher, Chas. died at home 1863.
107 Wallace, J. B., in Texas; alive.
108 Willoughby, R., discharged 1862.
109 Williams, Thos., died 1864.
110 Williams, L.
111 Williams, Joseph, died in hospital 1863.
112 Wright, Daniel, died 1862.
113 Woodley, Jonathan, alive.
114 Woodle, E., wounded 1863.
115 Woodle, Hinson, killed in battle 1863.
116 Waters, J.
Killed in battle, 20; died during war, 23; wounded, 10 died at home, 22; captured, 5.

COMPANY "E," 4TH SOUTH CAROLINA CAVALRY,

Was originally organized in Marlboro County in the latter part of the year 1861. The Company left Marlboro for Georgetown, South Carolina, January 22, 1862, and in the spring of 1864 were transferred to Virginia and became a part of Butler's Brigade of Hampton's Division. The following is a list of the officers and privates:

CAPTAINS.

Wm. P. Emanuel, elected Major May 1862; captured Trevilian Station, Virginia, 1864; died about 1879.

Henry Edens, promoted captain from 3d lieutenant 1862; honorably discharged 1863; died since war.

Peter L. Breeden, promoted from 1st lieutenant 1863; wounded Haw's Shop 1864.

1ST LIEUTENANTS.

B. F. McGilvray, transferred 1862; killed Petersburg, Virginia.

P. L. Breeden, promoted from 2d lieutenant 1861.

Allen Edens, promoted from 2d lieutenant 1863; died at home.

2D LIEUTENANTS.

P. L. Breeden, elected at organization.

Allen Edens, promoted from 2d sergeant 1862.

J. N. Weatherly, promoted from 3d lieutenant 1863; wounded at Lee's Mill 1864; died March 3, 1893.

3D LIEUTENANTS.

Sion H. Alford, elected at organization; dead.

Wm. M. Bristow, elected 1862; resigned 1863; died at home.

Henry A. Long, promoted 1863; died at home 1864.

1ST SERGEANTS.

John J. Herndon, elected at organization; furnished substitute in 1862; dead.

Nevil Bennett, elected 1862; honorably discharged.
Henry A. Long, elected 1862.
Nicholas P. Bone, elected 1863; died since war.

2D Sergeants.

Allen Edens, elected 1863.
Jonathan Adams, chosen 1862.

3D Sergeant.

John S. McColl, died since war.

4TH Sergeants.

C. A. Weatherly.
James C. McRae, 1st corporal; wounded Haw's Shop.
John Parish, 2d corporal.
Joseph Newton, 3d corporal.
Robt. T. Weatherly, 4th corporal; died at Pocotaligo, South Carolina 1863.
Wm. Benjamin Smith, 5th corporal; died since war.

Privates.

1 Adams, Andrew J., died since war.
2 Adams, Peter L., died Camp Waccamaw 1862.
3 Anderson, George, lost sight of.
4 Bone, Nicholas P., elected sergeant; dead.
5 Bone, Leonard D.
6 Bass, Wade, H., wounded Trevilian Station, Virginia.
7 Breeden, John L., killed in 1864.
8 Brigman, Wm., killed at home 1864.
9 Brigman, John, transferred to 26th Regiment South Carolina Volunteers.
10 Brigman, Alex.
11 Brigman, Evander, transferred to 26th Regiment.
12 Britt, James.
13 Britt, Thos. P., dead.
14 Bundy, Wm., dead.
15 Byrd, Levi.
16 Calder, Peter, lost foot at Haw's Shop; dead.
17 Cope, Daniel, captured at Haw's Shop; died in Savannah.

18 Cottingham, Thos., alive.
19 Cottingham, Ucal, wounded Trevilian, died in hospital.
20 Coward, Lewis, went West after war.
21 Cork, James, died since war.
22 Cork, John.
23 Driggers, Aaron T., dead.
24 Driggers, Abner, died since war.
25 Driggers, Philip, killed Lee's Mill 1864.
26 DuPre, Thomas J., transferred, from 8th Regiment to company "E"; wounded; died since war.
27 Earl, Elijah.
28 Easterling, Henry.
29 Edens, Thos. W., died 1895.
30 Emanuel, Chas. L., dead.
31 Evans, C. D.
32 Fraser, John, killed Haw's Shop 1864.
33 Freeman, Benj., killed Haw's Shop, May 28, 1864.
34 Freeman, James, wounded at Reaves' Station; died since war.
35 Gibson, Thos., captured Trevilian; died since war.
36 Grant, Barnabas, captured Trevilian; died Elmira, New York.
37 Grooms, Evander, transferred to 26th Regiment South Carolina Volunteers.
38 Hall, Wm., transferred to company "D," 26th Regiment.
39 Haithcock, Wm.
40 Jackson, Chas., dead.
41 Jackson, Joseph, captured Trevilian Station; died Elmira, New York.
42 Jackson, Laban M.
43 Jacobs, Bethel, dead.
44 Jacobs, David.
45 Jacobs, Samuel, transferred to company "D," 26th Regiment.
46 Jones, John, killed Haw's Shop, May 28, 1864.
47 Lide, William.
48 McLaurin, Alex L., dead.
49 McLaurin, D. P., transferred to company "A," 23d Regiment South Carolina Volunteers.
50 McLaurin, Jas. W., captured Stoney Creek, Virginia; died 1894.
51 McLaurin, Lauchlin A., dead.

52 McLaurin, Loch B.
53 McInnis, James.
54 McInnis, John.
55 McCrimmon, John A.
56 McColl, John S., dead.
57 McColl, Samuel S., dead.
58 McColl, Hugh S., captured Trevilian; died in prison.
59 Morris, Thos. J.
60 Marshall, John.
61 Murdock, John T., dead.
62 Mulligan, James.
63 McRae, Angus, died Pocotaligo, South Carolina.
64 McRae, Daniel C., dead.
65 McRae, John D., dead.
66 McRae, James A., dead.
67 McRae, James.
68 McRae, J. Calvin.
69 Newton, Cornelius D.
70 Newton, Hope Hull, severely wounded, Haw's Shop, May 28, 1864.
71 Newton, Joseph.
72 Newton, Richard D., died Wilson, N. C. 1864.
73 Newton, Peyton V., died 1896.
74 Newton, Thos. B.
75 Odom, Evander W., severely wounded Burgess' Mill 1864.
76 Odom, Noah.
77 Odom, Daniel J.
78 Odom, H. King.
79 Odom, Jas. Thomas; killed Trevilian Station 1864.
80 Odom, John, killed, Haw's Shop, 1864.
81 Odom, Nehemiah.
82 Odom, Robt. H., died since war.
83 Odom, Thos. Q.
84 O'Nails, James.
85 Parker, Andrew, dead.
86 Parker, Elijah, wounded.
87 Parker, Harrison, dead.
88 Powers, Ellison, dead.
89 Parrott, James.
90 Prevatt, Angus, wounded Haw's Shop; died since war.
91 Prevatt, James.
92 Pope, Bennett J., wounded Haw's Shop; died since war.

93 Proctor, Thos. A., died since war.
94 Quick, Leggett.
95 Rainwaters, Joshua, died in prison.
96 Rogers, Wm.
97 Roper, Caswell, wounded Lee's Mill, Va.; died since war.
98 Sanders, Moses P., dead.
99 Sawyer, John H.
100 Sellers, Bryant J., died McPhersonville, S. C., August 13, 1863.
101 Smith, Herbert, captured Trevilian; died in prison.
102 Smith, Joseph R.
103 Stackhouse, H. Milton.
104 Stackhouse, Robt. Boyd, died since war from wound received at Haw's Shop.
105 Stackhouse, John, captured and died Elmira, N. Y.
106 Stuckey, Ben N.
107 Stubbs, Thos. A., dead.
108 Sweat, Henry, died since war.
109 Sweat, Saml., dead.
110 Sweat, Sandford, dead.
111 Sweat, Wm. K , dead.
112 Thomas, James, died Camp Marion, S. C., 1862.
113 Thomas, Nathan S., dead.
114 Weatherly, Isaac, dead.
115 West, William, wounded Haw's Shop; died since war.
116 Young, Jackson, lost sight of.

Where not marked "dead," supposed to be alive.

Wounded, 16; killed in battle, 8; captured, 9; died during war, 29; died since war, 39; alive, 55.

MUSTER ROLL OF COMPANY "I," 20TH REGIMENT, SOUTH CAROLINA VOLUNTEERS.

1 A. D. Sparks, Capt.
2 James A. Peterkin, 1st Lieut.
3 F. W. Kinney, 2d Lieut.
4 J. F. Bolton, 3d Lieut.
5 — Hodges, 1st Serg't.
6 — Emanuel, 2d Serg't.
7 — Walsh, 3d Serg't.
8 — Covington, 4th Serg't.
9 John Manning, 5th Serg't
10 — Ware, Corp'l.
11 — Strickland, Corp'l.
12 — Rowe, Corp'l.
13 Elmore Allen, Corp'l.
1 Allen, J.
2 Barton, J.
3 Barry, D. F.
4 Bristow, J. W.

5 Brigman, J. A.
6 Clark, B.
7 Cope, J. F.
8 Coxe, R. A.
9 Crabb, H. S.
10 Crowley, Robert.
11 David, J.
12 Doty, A.
13 Driggers, J. H.
14 Fowler. W. D.
15 Finlayson, A. E.
16 Frasier, Chas.
17 Frasier, Sam.
18 Graham, J. J.
19 Grice, J. D.
20 Hinds, J. D.
21 Hodges, T. C.
22 Ivey, W. H.
23 Kennedy, J. E.
24 Manning, E.
25 Manning, J.
26 Miles, G. W.
27 Moody, G. W.
28 McColl, L. H.
29 McCaskill, R.
30 McDaniel, J. R.
31 McDaniel, W. H.
32 McLeod, M.
33 McLeod, J. C.
34 McLeod, B. F.
35 McRae, J.
36 Parham, J. H.
37 Parham, H.
38 Parish, Joel.
39 Parker, Sam.
40 Polson, Chas.
41 Polson, Wm.
42 Quick, A. W.
43 Polson, Jerry.
44 Rascoe, Wm.
45 Smith, H.
46 Spencer, T. D.
47 Stanton, J.
48 Tomlinson, Jas.
49 Turner, John.
50 Wallace, S.
51 Wallace, W. T.
52 Thomlinson, L.
53 Wallace, Thos. G.
54 Weatherly.
55 Webster, J.
56 Webster, Jas.
57 Wiloughby, R.
58 Williams, S. V.
59 McLean.
60 Lipscomb.
61 Timmons.
62 Thomas.
63 Lowe.
64 King.
65 Linder.
66 Watson, Sam.
67 Watson.
68 Cowan.

A list of Marlboro men who enlisted in Captain James A. Peterkin's cavalry company, but when the company was disbanded, they united with the Hampton Legion.

Co. "C."

1 Alford, J. M., dead.
2 Bullard, Charles.
3 Bullard, Geo. W.
4 Calder, Wm.
5 Calder, Robt.

Co. "H."

1 Crosland, T. L., alive.
2 Crosland, Chas., alive.
3 Coxe, Edwin, died in prison.
4 Hamer, P. M., died.

Co. "C."	Co. "H."

6 Calder, Arthur.
7 Calder, Stanford, alive.
8 Fletcher, J. D.
9 Fletcher, John K., alive.
10 McLaurin, J. F., alive.
11 McColl, C. S., alive.
12 Calhoun, D. A.
13 Sinclair, Daniel C.
14 Willoughby, J. P.
15 Sanders, Moses.

5 Heustiss, A. J., alive.
6 John, P. M., alive.
7 John, D. C., alive.
8 John, J. T , alive.
9 Spears J. E., died 1865.
10 Quick, James.

ROLL OF COMPANY "D," 3D REGIMENT, SOUTH CAROLINA STATE TROOPS. JUNIOR RESERVES.

CAPTAIN.

Z. J. Drake.

LIEUTENANTS.

E. H. Kirkwood, 1st lieutenant, dead.
J. T. Rogers, 2d lieutenant.
T. F. McRae, 3d lieutenant.

SERGEANTS.

R. S. McLucas.
Houston Manning, dead.
G. W. Ervin.
Joseph H. Gooch, dead.

CORPORALS.

I. P. Gibson.
J. W. Welch.
John Lewis.
Allen Woodle.
J. N. Edens.

COMMISSARY.

H. L. Edens, died near Raleigh, North Carolina.

PRIVATES.

Adams, T. M.
Adams, J. B.
Barentine, J. M., dead.
Breeden, J. F.
Crosland, W. E.
Carlisle, J. A.

Clark, Jesse, died near Charleston, South Carolina.
Chavis, Murray.
David, Wm. R.
Hodges, John L.
Manning, Holland.
Matheson, A. J.
McPherson, Arch.
McRae, William.
Newton, C. Dudley, dead.
Newton, Smith.
Newton, B. J.
Pegues, J. K., dead.
Parham, Malcom.
Powers, J. F.
Quick, J. W.
Quick, Welcome.
Quick, J. F.
Rogers, C. B.
Stubbs, L. D.
Sweat, Ellis.
Sturgis, Milton.
Taylor, John.
Guinn, Thomas.
Rev. Mr. Ogborne, Chaplain of Regiment, died at Fayetteville.

A careful recapitulation shows as follows:

	Killed in battle	Died during the war.	Died since the war.	Captured.	Wounded.	Alive.	Total enlistment; officers and men.
Co. "G," 18th Regt.	13	22	17	—	37	49	109
Co. "K," 8th Regt.	7	27	29	6	22	33	95
Co. "G," 23d Regt.	19	17	40	—	33	72	160
Co. "D," 26th Regt.	22	21	6	—	10	47	125
Co. "F," 21st Regt.	31	44	17	23	33	57	144
Co. "B," 24th Regt.	20	23	22	5	10	45	132
Co. "E," 4th Cavl.	8	29	39	9	16	55	142
Co. "I,"	—	—	—	—	—	—	93
Totals	120	183	170	43	161	358	1000

The figures above show that 12 per cent. of the whole number of men enlisted in all the commands were killed in battle; 18 per cent. died during the war; 17 per cent. have died since the war; 16 per cent. were wounded, and about one-third of the number yet survive. Valuable assistance has been kindly and freely rendered by the officers and men in the preparation of the foregoing rolls, for which thanks are due and hereby given.

CHAPTER XXX.

Early Ministers.

Since the first permanent settlers that we know of were largely religious men, and organized a church on Marlboro's soil as early as 1738, it is proper that some notice be made of the men who led their worship, and gave direction to thought which resulted in the formation of character. It is altogether likely that some of the early pastors of the Old Welsh Neck church lived on the west side of the Pee Dee and were never citizens of Marlboro. The people were settled on both sides, up and down the river, and rejoiced, whether residents on one side or the other, for many years, to meet upon its eastern bank to worship God. The preachers lived upon their plantations; whether on the one side or the other; to the flock it mattered not. The river could be crossed in their little flat-boats and canoes, and neighborhood and religious intercourse be enjoyed. The first pastor of this church was Philip James, and in a "Historical Sketch," by the late pastor of the present Welsh Neck, Rev. John Stout, it is recorded that lineal descendants of that man are found in the present membership. Mr. James was born near Pennepeck, Pennsylvania, in 1701 and was ordained pastor over this church in 1743 by Messrs. Chandler and Simmons. He died in 1753. Rev. John Brown, of whom mention has been made in a previous chapter, was the successor of Mr. James, but did not continue long with the church, but gave his ministry to a field nearer to his home in the region of Cashway. Mr. Brown was the first Moderator of the Charleston Association, which was formed in 1751, and is the second oldest Baptist Association in America. Joshua Edwards was the next pastor, a native Welshman. He was baptized at Welsh Tract in Pennsylvania and ordained at Welsh Neck. Mr. Edwards "was a man of ardent piety and great purity of character," lived to be fourscore and left a numerous posterity; and from him have descended many good people in our neighboring counties. Rev. Robt. Williams was the fourth pastor of this old church. He was born, it is said, in Northampton, North Carolina, in 1717, came early to Pee Dee, and entered the ministry in 1752 and died in 1788. In a sermon occasioned by his death, Rev. Mr. Pugh said of him: "He was kind to the poor, and remarkably so to the afflicted; a man of excellent natural endowments, and a minister who preached the Gospel to the edification and comfort of souls, as many have testified to me; and to crown all, a sincere Christian." He was the grandfather of General David R. Williams, a member of Congress and Governor of the State. He, too, is represented in several of the best families in the country at the present day.

After Williams came Nicholas Bedgegood, an Englishman by birth, described as a classical scholar and a man of good understanding. He married a Miss Murphy, and Nicholas Bedgegood, of Marlboro, was the only child of this marriage, and in the death of the latter the name became extinct in this region of country. Mr. Bedgegood took charge of the church in 1759, and held it till 1765; and for two years he preached in the vicinity of Charleston. Returning to Welsh Neck in 1767, he again resumed the care of the church and continued in office till his death in 1773 or 1774.

During the absence of Mr. Bedgegood in Charleston the church was supplied by a young man who had but just entered the ministry, but who was destined to exert a powerful influence upon the after history of his country and the cause of religion. Rev. Evan Pugh was born in Pennsylvania, educated a Quaker, came in early life to North Carolina, became a Baptist; studied theology, became a minister, and married a Marlboro lady, Miss Martha Magee. A daughter of this union married Mr. Hugh Lide, of Darlington, and from this pair has sprung a splendid family. The two Baptist pastors of Charleston (1890) R. W. Lide and Dr. E. C. Dargan, are grandsons. Mr. Pugh was an ardent supporter of the American cause during the Revolution, and was ready with his means, his voice, his pen, to encourage and help the struggling cause. When independence and peace came his fellow citizens elected him a member of the Convention that formed the State constitution under which we lived till the days of reconstruction. A man of genuine piety, sound judgment and cheerful disposition, after a ministry of forty years he sank into the tomb lamented by all.

After the death of Mr. Pugh, Rev. Elhanan Winchester was in charge three or four years, but, embracing what the church considered erroneous beliefs, he was promptly discharged and Rev. Edmund Botsford was elected in his stead, who, from 1779 until 1796, was the pastor of this church. Temporarily, during the troublous times, he had to flee for safety from the enemy, and his place was supplied by Rev. Joshua Lewis, who was a Marlboro man. Mr. Lewis has been described to the writer as a large, portly man, an Englishman by birth, and lived at what has been known as "the Spring Hill place" on the Cheraw road a mile or so above Easterling's Mills. A popular man and good preacher, ready to go anywhere, among the rich or poor, to relieve distress. A venerable colored man related an incident that greatly impressed his own youthful, untutored mind. The gin-house of his neighbor, Mr. Bedgegood, caught fire, and Lewis was soon upon the ground, and as the old man told it, "Mr. Lewis worked and toiled and hollered and sweat as hard as any nigger dar, and when the trouble wuz all over, he called us all in the big house piazzer, and kneeled down and prayed." He preached at Cheraw and Saw Mill. His last sermon was at the latter place. On the next Sunday he was to preach at Cheraw, but sent a message to his people that he was too sick to attend, and before night he was dead. His grave may be seen at "Old Saw Mill" church to this day, near where the pulpit stood in which he had so often preached the glad tidings to his neighbors. He died about 1812 and left no children.

CHAPTER XXXI.

Churches— Baptist.

It has been shown in a previous chapter that the Colonial Council of the Province of Carolina, in order to induce the Welsh to settle in the Province, admeasured and had laid off a large body of land for the Welsh settlers. In 1736 or 1737 a colony of Welsh settled along the east bank of the Pee Dee from the mouth of Crooked Creek and extending several miles down the river. These early Welsh settlers first planted Baptist principles upon Marlboro soil. In January, 1738, they met and organized themselves into a Baptist church, calling it Welsh Neck. The spot where the church stood is just to the right of where the public road leading from Bennettsville to Society Hill approaches the banks of the Pee Dee River. It is now covered by majestic trees and a thick undergrowth hides the ground. Here repose the ashes of most of the original colony, with many of their descendants. A monument marks the resting place of Col. Kolb, a Revolutionary patriot and officer, who was slain by Tories in the porch of his mansion a few hundred yards from where the ancient house of prayer then stood. It might be interesting to take our stand at Long Bluff, the site of the old church, and gather up the legends and traditions of the times forty years after its organization, when wolves and hyenas in human form stealthily crept around the homes of the settlers to carry away their stock and property and shoot them in the arms of their loved ones. How, even then, a Pugh, a Williams, a Brown preached the Word while the brethren watched for the approach of armed forces that lurked around. None of these things broke the spirits or damped the zeal of these early Baptists.

This ancient church sent out several colonies organized upon the principles of the mother body. Brownsville, which was first called Cashway and situated nearer to and lower down the river than where it now stands, was an offshoot from the old Welsh Neck. It was organized into a church in 1789. "Old Brownsville church" stood a mile or two east from where the present church now stands. So that the present house of worship, which was built in 1858 or 1859, by H. G. Lucas, is the third one, all occupying different locations, but in the same community. In 1872 Brownsville church dismissed a number of her members to constitute the Mineral Spring church, which was formally dedicated June 30th, 1872.

Beaverdam (now McColl) was formed into a church in the year 1771 by Henry Easterling at or near what is known as Beauty Spot Bridge, and was called Beauty Spot. From there they moved to Pine Grove, where they worshipped in common with other denominations in a house built by the Quakers or Society of Friends, who left the house unoccupied and to be used as a place of worship. It ultimately fell into the hands of the Methodists and the little handful of Baptists worshipped for a while at "Parker's Machine," two miles above, near what is known as Mason's Cross-roads. From there they moved to the old site on Beaverdam Creek, near McColl, and built a small framehouse which was standing as far back as 1840. Soon after or about that time a better building was erected, which was destroyed by the Federal army in 1865. Some years after the war, another and better building took the place of the one destroyed by the army, and in 1891 it was removed without injury from its old site and located in the town of McColl and re-dedicated June 21st of that year.

Clio is mainly an offshoot from Beaverdam. It was organized in 1873 or 1874 with members drawn largely from Beaverdam.

The Baptist church at Tatum was organized a few years ago with members almost exclusively from Beaverdam. Tatum church was dedicated April 3d, 1892.

Salem Baptist church was constituted in part at least of members from the "old Welsh Neck," in 1793. Robert Thomas, the grandfather of J. A. W. Thomas, was instrumental in founding the church. He lived in the Beauty Spot region and was long and favorably known as a Baptist preacher engaged in the holy calling before the Revolutionary War began. He used to travel, generally on horseback, extensively in the Pee Dee region in evangelistic work, and at last died in 1817, while away from home on one of these preaching tours, at the advanced age of 84. From its organization in 1793 to near the time of his death, he ministered to the church at Salem. A new house of worship was built in 1880.

The Bennettsville Baptist church traces her lineage back to the "old Welsh Neck"; but did not spring directly from it, but from Cheraw. Cheraw was dismissed from Welsh Neck and organized in 1782. "A part of the membership of Cheraw Hill church, desiring to become an independent church, were regularly dismissed" and constituted a church called the Saw Mill Baptist church in December 1820. Saw Mill, now a colored church, is in the immediate neighborhood of T. E. Dudley's Mill. When constituted, steps had just been taken looking toward the removal of the court-house to Bennettsville. At that time the population was more dense along the river than elsewhere; the only means of transportation for farm produce was by flatboats down the river to Charleston and Georgetown or by wagons to Fayetteville. It was not strange therefore that the church should be located in that community. The court-house was removed to its present location, and thither the tide of population was moving, and in the course of some years the church wisely determined to remove its location to the county-seat. In

September, 1832, this entry was made upon the minute book: "The church met at new meeting-house in Bennettsville Sermon by our pastor, C. Stubbs. Brethren present: C. Stubbs, Thomas Stubbs, Jno. Thomas, M. Heustiss, L. Harwell, W. Pearce, A. Lamb, J. Goodson, A. N. Bristow, J. O. David, E. David, E. Curtis and Jno. Terrel." It is not known when the pastorate of Rev. C. Stubbs first began. He was in charge in 1829, before the removal to Bennettsville; and here he continued, with but a short interval, until 1837. "He was a man of great energy and decision of character; a prudent counselor, and considering his early education, a good preacher. His ministry here and elsewhere was successful, for he preached more or less at all the churches in Marlboro." He was a prudent man of business, and left a valuable estate to his heirs. He died September, 1844, lamented by his brethren. Mrs. B. A. Capel, and Messrs. W. H. and W. J. Stubbs are his grandchildren.

In October, 1837, an event occurred which weakened the pecuniary and numerical strength of the church. It was the organization of an independent church at Bruton's Fork. A new house was built at Bruton's Fork in 1878.

In 1839 Rev. W. Q. Beattie was called to the pastorate of the Bennettsville church and continued in that relation for fifteen years. He was an educated man, was born in the North, came South, married and settled in the county, here worked for his master and here died. The symmetry of his character and the love of his heart were both beautiful; yea, as beautiful as his snowy head and benignant smile. In 1851 the steeple was built and other improvements added to the church; and again in 1858 side galleries, new seats and other improvements. In 1881 a baptistry was built, the pulpit moved to the opposite end of the house, seats changed, and the church otherwise improved.

In 1888 a parsonage was purchased. The church was enabled to make the purchase mainly on account of a bequest left the church by R. Q. Beattie, a son of Rev. W. Q. Beattie. He willed ten per cent. of his estate to the church, which amounted to nearly eight hundred dollars, and thus the church came into the possession of a parsonage.

The church building was erected on a lot of land deeded for that purpose by Wm. Munnerlyn, and was first occupied in September, 1832. And now, just sixty-four years from that date, and in the same month, the foundation has been laid and the work progressing rapidly towards the erection of a new brick building, which, when completed and furnished, will cost ten thousand dollars. The generations preceding us built churches for us to worship in and it is right that we should build for the generations yet to come.

A Baptist church, called Hickory Grove, was organized October 4, 1890, in the northeast section of the county.

A fond son will be excused for making prominent mention of his father in connection with the Baptist churches of Marlboro. The life of J. A. W. Thomas was so intertwined and interwoven with the life of the churches that a sketch of the Baptist churches would necessarily be incomplete without prominent mention being made of him. The best years of his long life were given to the churches; for them he lived; for them he died. Through summer's burning heat or winter's chilling blast, year in and year out, for forty-seven years he regularly met his appointments. Sickness a few times prevented, but inclement weather was not considered by him a good reason for not meeting an appointment to preach. He reasoned thus, "A few may go and I dislike to disappoint even a few."

J. A. W. Thomas, the son of William Thomas and Eleanor Evans, was born December 31st, 1822, in the Brownsville section of Marlboro County. His father died when he was less than thirteen years old, and being the eldest of five childen, the care and support of the family devolved in large measure upon him. His opportunities for obtaining an education were therefore limited. He, however, did attend irregularly the neighborhood schools and when eighteen went for a part of a year to Wake Forest College, North Carolina, and the balance of the same year he attended school under Rev. W. R. Smith, a Methodist preacher who taught at Parnassus. Two years after his father's death the family left the Brownsville neighborhood and moved to what is now called the Alford place, in the immediate locality of old Pee Dee church. At the age of fifteen he united with the Brownsville Baptist church and was baptized by Rev. Campbell Stubbs. A few months after, uniting with the church, he was elected church clerk. In January 1845 he changed his membership from Brownsville church to Salem, and on the same day was elected church clerk. He also for several years served the Salem church as deacon, taking his turn in leading the prayer-meetings and Sunday-school. In August, 1848, license to preach the Gospel was granted him by the Salem church. On Sunday night, September 10th, 1848, his *first sermon* was preached in the Bennettsville church from John, 9:35. "The Salem church, two months after voting the license to preach, asked him to preach for them twice a month; a call came from Brownsville to preach there once a month, and New Providence church in Darlington County, thirty miles distant, asked for the other Sunday." So, from the first, the young preacher, as he was called, had as much as he could do.

On the memorable snowy Sunday April, 15, 1849, J. A. W. Thomas was ordained to the full work of the gospel ministry in the Salem church, and from that day forward devoted his time to the active work of the gospel ministry. His work has been done in his native county, excepting short periods of service done in counties adjoining Marlboro. It may not be inappropriate to give a summary of the churches he has served and length of

time he served them. His ministerial work began first
with the Salem church, and then very soon after or about
the same time with the Brownsville church. He began
to serve these two churches in 1848, after he was liscensed
to preach, and before his ordination, and preached continuously at Salem till 1862. After an absence of three
and a half years in the army he resumed the pastorate of
Salem in 1867 and continued to serve the church till 1885,
making thirty-one years in all. Beginning in 1848, he
preached three years at Brownsville; and generally his
work there was in connection with Rev. Joel Allen,
who was the pastor of the church. For one year, beginning in 1848, he went thirty miles from his home to New
Providence in Darlington county, and while there would
sometime preach at Hartsville, being perhaps the first to
preach a Baptist sermon at that place. In the autumn of
the year 1849 his services at Bennettsville began and continued without a break (except during the war) till 1882,
making thirty years service with the Bennettsville church.
His work for several years at first was in connection with
Rev. W. Q. Beattie, who was pastor of the church. He
preached thirty-one years, more or less continuously
at Bruton's Fork church, beginning there in 1852. Beginning in 1866 he preached at Cheraw for three years
giving them one Sunday in the month. Before the war
he preached for several years in the Sand Hills, in the
afternoon, going from Bennettsville once a month.

In 1851 he began his work with the Beaverdam church
(now McColl), and there his last days' work on earth was
done. It is likely that he preached more sermons to the
congregation of Beaverdam than to any other. His services
there extended through a period of thirty-six years. During the war, and for two years succeeding, he did not
preach at Beaverdam. For two years the Dargans, father
and son, were the pastors of that church, and for two other years, R. Ford was the pastor. But during all of the

other years, since and including 1851, up to the day of his death, August 2, 1896, J. A. W. Thomas ministered to them in spiritual things. His last sermon there was from the text found in 1 Samuel, 30:24. In the afternoon of the same day he preached his last sermon to the church at Tatum, from John 12:19. Tatum is a new church, which he was instrumental in founding, and to which he preached till his death, about seven years, preaching for about two years in the academy and the Presbyterian church, till the Tatum Baptist church was built.

He served the church at Gibson station in North Carolina for about nine years. For about eight years he preached at Mason's Cross-roads once a month in the afternoon. Before the war he went in the afternoon of one Sunday in every month to the Judson church in Marion for several years. Since the war he preached at Catfish church, in Marion County, for two years. The Clio church he served for five years; and the church at Mineral Springs for perhaps ten or twelve—some of the time in connection with other ministers. Other Baptist preachers have been in the county and have had charge of and acceptably ministered to different churches for longer or shorter periods. The Allens, father and son, of Marion County, Ford, Battle, Pratt, Jordan and Easterling; but J. A. W. Thomas, through a long life, lived for the churches, and worked for them, and with them and was instrumental in the organization of several, and the building and rebuilding of several more. In addition to his work with and for the churches, since the year 1865, he married two hundred and fourteen couples; and from the beginning of the year 1881 to August, 1896, he attended two hundred and fifteen funerals.

In the course of forty-eight (48) years in the ministry he preached about 6,195 times, an average of one hundred and twenty-nine sermons per year for each of the forty-eight years; and an average of two and a half times for every Sunday in the forty-eight years. He preached on texts taken from every book in the Bible, including both the Old and New Testaments; the Psalms furnished the largest number of texts, four hundred and eleven; while the books of Ruth and Obadiah only furnished one each. Five books furnished over two hundred each, six books more than one hundred each, and eight books more than fifty texts each, while twenty-seven books furnished ten and less than fifty each. He always wrote his sermons out in full, and estimated that his "written manuscripts would make seventy volumes of four hundred pages each." He prepared and wrote in full more new sermons during the last years of his life than ever before. His library has never been extensive, and his theology was drawn largely from the Bible. He went into the Confederate army from a sense of duty, and fought for a principle that he thought was right; but was thankful that he was better known in the army as a preacher than as a soldier. He preached constantly and on one occasion baptized about forty in the surf on Sullivan's Island.

CHAPTER XXXII.

Methodist Churches.

A sketch of the Methodist churches of Marlboro properly begins with the Beauty Spot church, the mother of Methodist churches. The first house of worship was built there in 1783 on land given by Turbet Cottingham. It was "built of logs, covered with long boards held in place by weight poles, and the seats were split pine logs." That primitive church may have been inconvenient and uncomfortable, but the day of small things should never be despised. The zeal and devotion there displayed by those early Methodists has perhaps been an inspiration to those coming after them: at all events, zeal and devotion to their church and religion have characterized the Methodists of Marlboro, and to-day they are stronger numerically than all the other denominations combined. They have twenty-two active churches, and all well located and actively at work.

The first itinerant preachers who visited Beauty Spot were Jeremiah Mastin and Hope Hull in the year 1783. They at first preached in the private houses of the neighborhood till the church was finished. The first Quarterly Conference held at Beauty Spot was on 23d February, 1788. Bishop Asbury presided and preached from Isaiah 36: 1-6.

In 1810 the congregation at Beauty Spot erected their second church. It was a neat frame building. During that year the first camp-meeting was held at Beauty Spot and the last one held there was in 1842. Robert Purnell, the first local preacher in Marlboro, was one of the early members of Beauty Spot church. He preached in the county for fifty years, and died in 1830. The name is now extinct in the county, but his descendants are here.

The third church was built in 1839. It was 60x45 feet and cost more than $1,100. It was a large, roomy church for that day and was used by the congregation forty-four years. It was erected by John McCall, of Darlington, under the supervision of Rev. Thomas Cook, Eli Thomas and Thos. S. Covington. In 1883, when the fourth church was built, a new site was selected on the same road, but two miles further east. When it was built the old church was sold at public outcry, and purchased by a gentleman who has not removed it, and there it stands to-day on the sacred spot of ground where repose the ashes of those who in the years gone by worshipped within its walls. The present house of worship was completed and dedicated June 17th, 1883. Rev. T. J. Clyde preached the sermon and Rev. Lewis M. Hamer delivered an historical address. The cost of the building was $2,000. It was erected by Mr. Bounds, under the direction and care of P. M. Hamer, Crawford Easterling, David Easterling and L. D. Hamer.

Among some of the local preachers who have from time to time preached at Beauty Spot may be mentioned A. H. Adams, Wm. K. Breeden, Thomas Cook, Allen Edens, John Jones, Chas. Manship, Cornelius Newton, Richard Welch and Wright Wilson. Some of the prominent male members were Eli Thomas, Robert Bolton, Jas. H. Bolton, John H. Hamer, Thomas Cook, W. J. Cook, and John Murdoch.

Hebron.

Hebron Methodist church is located in the center of one of the garden spots of the county. The farms lying adjacent to the church are very fertile and are cultivated with great care and system. Highly respectable, industrious and intelligent people live on the farms and justly pride themselvvs on being able to make an entire success of farming. The church is about six miles southeast from Bennettsville and was built in the year 1848. Its original membership went out from Beauty Spot, the mother church. The Hebron Academy building stands near the church, and hard by is the cemetery, noted far and near as being the neatest and best cared for cemetery in this whole region of country. A few years ago, 1879, a handsome new church was erected.

About 1760 Ivy's church (now Clio) was situated near what is now Dunbar. It was afterwards moved to a point one mile below the town of Clio, and there they worshiped until 1885, when a church was built in Clio. They have had five churches. One was burned in 1866 by the incendiary's torch.

Parnassus.

In the years prior to 1835 the Methodists in the Parnassus community worshiped at Mossy Bay. The location of the old church is yet well-known on account of the graveyard. The dust of our forefathers buried there has long since mingled with the mother earth. There they worshipped; there they lie buried, and from thence their bodies will arise on the great resurrection morn. The site of the old church is in the immediate neighborhood of J. R. Townsend's residence. In that day there was also a Methodist church called "McLeod's church," located near where Berry Alford lived. It was on the McLeod land, and was doubtless built by or through the instrumentality of Donald McLeod, grand-father of Mrs. W. Z. Donaldson and D. McD. McLeod. During the year 1835 a church was built at Parnassus; the membership of Mossy Bay and "McLeod's" churches united and made the new organization. The church was built by John Sinclair, and the dedicatory sermon was preached by Rev. Nicholas Ware, a local preacher who lived in the Brownsville neighborhood and preached in the lower

section of the county. Our forefathers worshipped at both
of the old churches, and then our parents and grandparents attended the Parnassus church. Some of the prominent members and attendants at Parnassus in the long
ago were Thomas Barnett, James Galloway, John L. McRae, Thomas Kinney, Daniel John, James Spears and W.
R. Smith. The last named was a Methodist preacher and
lived in the neighborhood of the church and frequently
preached. The present church building was erected by
Mr. H. G. Lucas just prior to the late war. It is well located, in a thickly populated community and has a large
membership of substantial, pious and devout people.

Zion church, located a few miles west from Parnassus,
near John C. Townsend's, has been organized and built
since the war, and belongs to the Blenheim Circuit.

BENNETTSVILLE CHURCH.

On the 21st of June, 1834, Col. Wm. J. Cook conveyed
one and a half acres of land to Thomas Cook, John L.
McRae, Wm. Dudley, John McCollum, Alexander J. Miller, Jas. C. Thomas and Alexander R. Brown, as trustees
for the Bennettsville Methodist church. The deed was
not recorded till 1846. It is fair to presume that the
church was built within a year or two after the conveyance
was made. The town of Bennettsville had even then begun to show signs of growth and life, and the Methodists
residing in town up to that time had held their membership at Beauty Spot. The members residing in Bennettsville doubtless experienced some difficulty in reaching
their place of worship, and influenced by the belief that
Bennettsville would some day grow to be a town of some
size and importance, wisely determined to build a church
in the young town. The Baptist congregation had just two
years previously built a new house, and this might have provoked them to good works. Let the causes influencing them
be what they may, just ten years from the completion and

occupancy of the new court-house they took steps towards the building of the *first* Methodist church. It seems strange that the people of Bennettsville should have waited eight or ten years after the completion of the court-house before a church was built in the town. The Baptists living in the town at that time worshiped at Saw Mill and had just built a new church there in 1820; so it was natural that they should wait awhile and be well convinced that Bennettsville was to be a reality before beginning another new house. But the Methodists needed a new house at Beauty Spot when the town was founded, for in 1839 they erected a new building at Beauty Spot.

The first church, built more than sixty years ago, was a plain square building without steeple, portico or other architectural adornments. It was covered on four sides, forming a quadrangular roof, ending in a sharp point at the apex. Two doors opened from the street and led you directly into the body of the church. The house was never painted and the bell was swung to a frame platform outside the church. The singing was done by the congregation without the aid of an organ or cornet. Major Townsend or Judge Hudson, with the aid of a silver tuning fork, could be relied on to "raise the tune." In the "amen corner" of the church devoted to males (for males and females each occupied their own portion of the church) sat Col. Wm. J. Cook, Dr. Crosland, Wm. Dudley, John McCollum, James C. Thomas and Rev. Thomas Cook. In the opposite corner sat Mrs. Fannie Easterling, Mrs. Sarah Cook, Mrs. Jas. C. Thomas, Mrs. Little and Mrs. Rowe. They have all gone to their reward.

About 1871 the present building was erected on the site occupied by the old church. It was made a station in 1883 and has been served by T. E. Wannamaker, J. L. Stokes, J. W. Daniel, W. S. Wightman, E. O. Watson and now (1897) is again under the care of Rev. J. L. Stokes.

BOYKIN.

A preaching place was established about one hundred years ago at Boykin; about the same time a school was established there and was taught by Lemuel Boykin, from whom the place took its name.

A fine spring of freestone water near the church doubtless influenced the establishment of this educational and religious center. The spring has been flowing through all these years without cessation or diminution, yielding from one hundred to two hundred gallons per hour of as pure water as any in the country. It is not definitely known when the first schoolhouse or church was built. The earliest recollection of some of the oldest people indicates a small log schoolhouse in which Barnabas Wallace, afterwards a prominent planter in the vicinity, taught. Many years before the war, a good framed school building was erected, principally through the efforts of Rev. Cornelius Newton, who lived about three miles southeast of the place and always took a lively interest in its educational affairs. About 1845 or before, Robert Fairly taught school for a number of years at this place. He was a famous teacher, and much loved by scholars and patrons. He came from the Scotch settlement of Richmond county, North Carolina. James Stewart also taught here. He was a Scotchman and bachelor and famous for his wit and peculiarities of disposition. Alexander J. Stanton also taught there many years. He was a man of positive disposition and wielded the "rod" with a master hand. He was Tax-collector for two terms and died several years ago, leaving a large and interesting family. Thomas W. Huckabee, who has been mentioned elsewhere, taught there from about 1850 to 1855. And various other men have occupied the teacher's chair in that school, which has done its work in training the best citizens this county has known.

There were three church buildings erected there from the beginning; the first was built of hewn logs dove-tailed at the corners; the second was a frame building about 30x40 feet, and it stood, as did the first, on the south side of the road. This building was erected about 1830. It had the usual high pulpit, and benches made from heavy plank with a six-inch board about high enough to strike the shoulder blades for a back. The last church, which now stands there, was built in 1859 or 1860 by H. G. Lucas, who built several of the churches in the county and died a few years ago at Parnassus, and was followed just two days after by his wife. This church is 40x60 feet, and is one the best church edifices in the county. It has sheltered one of the largest memberships in this section of country. Barnabas Wallace, Samuel Odom, Sr.; Younger Newton, David C. Newton, Tobias Calder, John W. Stubbs, Thomas Barrentine, Needham Ryal and others had their membership here in the generation before the last. Of the last generation were such names as James M. Gibson, Noah Gibson, Robertson Adams, Jephtha Adams, Ebenezer W. Goodwin, Giles Newton, Anderson Newton, William Peel. The last named could neither read nor write at the age of nineteen years, when he married, but began to study, learned to read and write and has read the New Testament through one hundred and fifty-eight times, word for word, since 1844.

James W. Gibson and Noah Gibson were brothers and together with William, Eli, Ziba, Nelson M. and the Rev. Thomas Gibson were the sons of Nathaniel Gibson. They were all reared near the North Carolina line, and were strong men, physically, intellectually and morally, and have made their impress upon the communities in which they have lived. The Rev. Thomas Gibson, who lived over the line in North Carolina a few miles, was a surveyor and a local minister of fine reputation. His labors in and around Boykin church were abundant, and "none named him but to praise." He was a sweet, spiritual, Christian gentleman. All these brothers are dead except Eli, who is seventy-two years of age and has been a member of the Methodist church for fifty years, and Nelson M., of McColl, who has reached his three-score and ten and calmly awaits the summons to go up higher. He has been a close personal friend of the author of this history for fifty years, and has been frequently called "his Methodist deacon at Beaverdam." The Gibson family is of English extraction. Noah was very successful as a merchant, and by his skill in business and his industry amassed a large fortune. He was the father of Francis B. Gibson, who is his worthy successor in the mercantile business at Gibson, North Carolina. Noah left several sons and daughters, all of whom occupy prominent positions in church and society. James M. Gibson lived within about half a mile of Boykin church. He reared a large family and always took a prominent part in church and school matters. These and other prominent laymen among the Odoms and Quicks and other families were reared under the influence of Boykin church, nearly all having crossed over the river prior to this record. Most of them left families and descendants who are worthily sustaining their record for piety and good citizenship.

The traveling preachers who served this church were those who were from time to time assigned to the Bennettsville Circuit, and their names are given elsewhere in this volume. Cornelius Newton, Henry Covington, Aaron Turner, James Turner and James Odom were local preachers who were members here and did their faithful work here and in other parts of Marlboro, and even across the North Carolina line. Cornelius Newton married the daughter of Rev. Robt. Purnell, who is elsewhere named as the pioneer local preacher of the Beauty Spot section. Cornelius Newton was born 25th December, 1797; was a son of Younger Newton and grandson of Giles Newton, Sr., who came to this county from Henrico County, Virginia, in the latter part of the last century, and was the great progenitor of all the Newton family in this country, which has grown to great proportions and intermarried with the Adams, Gibsons, Fletchers, etc., till its relations number in the hundreds, perhaps. Cornelius Newton is the only one of the local preachers whose complete history we have been able to get. He was married, as stated, to a daughter (Dorcas) of Robt. Purnell on 31st December, 1818, and joined the church in the summer of 1820, and embraced religion in October, 1821, appointed class leader in 1822 and licensed to exhort in 1830; licensed to preach in 1834; ordained Deacon in 1838; and was recommended for Elders' Orders in 1842. He reared a large and interesting family, many of whom still survive; among them Cornelius D. Newton, Joseph Newton and Hope Hull Newton. He was a successful planter and a faithful soldier of the cross, and after "having served his own generation, by the will of God fell on sleep" in the summer of 1878. Among those who labored in this vicinity in later years as local preachers were Wm. K. Breeden, who lived in the Smyrna section, and Andrew Adams, who still survives and was born and reared in the vicinity of Boykin church. Who can tell how much the local preacher has had to do with the successful growth of Methodism in this and other sections?

Boykin, sixty years ago or more, was a famous campmeeting place, and during these annual summer convocations, ministers, local and itinerant, went from other sections of country and heartily engaged in the services. Time and space both forbid telling more of the history of this church and community. A chosen people; a chosen land, and the deepest spiritual influences from time immemorial are enough to evolve a superior type of Christian civilization, just such as has long been and doubtless will continue to be in the vicinity of Boykin church.

EBENEZER.

About 1856 or 1857 Rev. P. E. Bishop, the pastor of the Bennettsville Presbyterian church, appreciating the fact that a section a few miles south from Bennettsville was comparatively destitute of Gospel privileges, determined to carry the Gospel to that community. He was assisted in his efforts by Rev. Paul F. Kistler and Rev. J. A. W. Thomas, and a union church was built. It was called Pine Plains and services held alternately by the three preachers named. The Methodist faith largely predominated in the community and Rev. P. F. Kistler was doubtless the first preacher to preach a sermon to the congregation which formed the Ebenezer M. E. Church. His first sermon was preached beneath the spreading branches of a large oak tree, near the spot where the church now stands. About the year 1858 the first church was built, and the dedicatory sermon preached by him. Rev. Mr. Kistler yet lingers on the shores of time, and resides at Bamberg, S. C. He married a sister of Dr. J. T. Jennings, of Bennnettsville. The membership came from Beauty Spot and Hebron. About 1892 the old church was sold to Mr. R. M. Edens and a new house built on the site of the old one. The Ebenezer church belongs to the Blenheim Circuit.

BETHEL.

Bethel M. E. church was built in 1875 or 1876, during the pastorate of Rev. J. M. Carlisle. He gave it the name and told the people how to pronounce it, and impressed upon the people the fact that the accent should be placed on the last syllable, and that a hyphen should be placed between the two. Bethel is really old Level Green with a changed name and location. Level Green church stood where George M. Webster now resides. The land (one acre) upon which it stood was, upon the 28th day of August 1844, deeded to John Jones,

Philip Barrentine, James Moon, H. H. Williams, Benjamin Moon as trustees, by Ananias Graham and wife. The church was therefore built about 1845, and the membership went from Beauty Spot, the mother of Methodist churches, and from Bennettsville, which had been built a few years before. From some cause Level Green languished, and perhaps died, but its successor, Bethel, is destined to be a strong church. It is in a thickly settled community of prosperous young farmers who will be able and willing to give it their support.

Breeden's Chapel.

Not many years ago Mr. Joel Hall and others built a brush arbor, and invited the Rev. Wm. K. Breeden to preach for them. He preached for sometime under the arbor, but Mr. Hall, not being satisfied, determined in his old age to have a church near him; he canvassed the country for subscriptions and donations, was successful, and to-day there stands on the hill, just in front of his late residence, a large, beautiful church bearing the appropriate name of Breeden's Chapel, and long may it stand among the lonely pines, a monument to the efforts of Mr. Hall, and of the piety, Christian character, and Godly labors of the man whose name it bears. The church was built in 1887. They have both gone to their reward; Mr. Hall several years ago, and Mr. Breeden in 1896. From the time Mr. Breeden entered the ministry in the early sixties to the time of his death, his life was full of useful work.

Bethlehem.

The history of Bethlehem M. E. church, in the extreme southern part of the county, is similar to that of other churches. They began with a log house. The date of organization is not known; but it is well known that our fathers attended a camp-meeting held there in their youth, and that would make Bethlehem one of the old churches. They have had at least three houses of worship. The present house was built by H. G. Lucas about 1858 or 1859.

SMYRNA.

Smyrna was first located a few hundred yards from where it now stands, and quite near to J. F. Breeden's place, formerly the Wm. Pearson place. A house was built where the church now stands, about 1846 or 1848 for a gentleman, not now a youth, remembers attending service there the 15th of April, 1849, "the day of the big snow" in April. His recollection is that the church was new and had but recently been completed. The present church was built by Samuel Sparks in 1884. Mr. Sparks, while building it, fell from a scaffold, and was quite badly hurt.

PINE GROVE.

It is safe to say that Pine Grove has been a place of worship for more than a century. The Quakers first worshipped there, but, as has been already told, on account of slavery they moved to the Northwest and the other denominations used their house. Rev. Cornelius Newton remembered attending a revival meeting held jointly by the Baptists and Methodists early in the present century at what is now Pine Grove church. During the progress of the meeting a "young man, riding in a gig, came up to the meeting ground, alighted and made his way into the congregation near the altar, and paid very respectful attention to the services then in progress. After the close of the services, his acquaintance was sought, and it was ascertained that he was a Baptist minister (Rev. W. Q. Beattie) who had just finished his education and journeyed South to preach the Gospel. He was invited to preach at the next service, and he charmed the whole congregation with his graceful speech and melting words, and many were the shouts that were raised as he eloquently portrayed the glories of salvation, and when he would have ceased, cries oi 'go on,' 'go on,' spontaneously arose from the congregation."

It has not been ascertained when the present church or the ones preceding it were built. In 1871 and a few years succeeding, a camp-meeting was held at Pine Grove—the last held in the county but perhaps not the first held at Pine Grove.

A good school has for many years been kept up at Pine Grove. The Academy is just across the road opposite to the church, both being in a beautiful grove of majestic oaks. Under such men as Robert Johnson, J. Monroe Johnson, Hope Newton, Hamilton, Craven and others, along with the unanimous hearty support of the patrons, educational as well as religious interests have been maintained at Pine Grove.

There are a number of other Methodist churches in Marlboro, but the difficulty of obtaining information, and the lack of space, will preclude a more extended notice than a mere mention of their names. Antioch, Hickory Grove, Shiloh, New Hope, Beulah, Manning's Chapel, Pleasant Hill, Oak Grove, and McColl.

In the preparation of the foregoing chapter invaluable assistance has been kindly rendered by Rev. L. M. Hamer, Rev. J. L. Stokes, H. H. Newton and others.

Circuits and Preachers.

The circuit embracing the churches of Marlboro was first called Pee Dee. It embraced territory lying North at least as far as Rockingham, and presumably extended down the Pee Dee river, perhaps to its mouth. The name was changed from Pee Dee to Rockingham Circuit in 1832, and a parsonage established at Rockingham. At the close of the year 1845 the circuit was reduced in size and the name changed to Bennettsville. A parsonage was built in Bennettsville, and H. H. Durant was the first preacher to occupy it in 1846. At that time Bennettsville Circuit doubtless embraced all the churches located in Marlboro. Now the same territory is covered by five circuits and one station; named as follows: Bennettsville Station, and Bennettsville, Brightsville, North Marlboro, Blenheim and Clio Circuits. Bennettsville was made a station in December 1883. The pastors have been T E. Wannamaker, 1884; J. L. Stokes, 1885-6; J. W. Daniel, 1887-90; W. S. Wightman, 1891-2; E. O. Watson, 1893-95; J. L. Stokes, 1896, and now serving. The parsonage originally stood on the same street and and just south from Judge Hudson's, on the lot now belonging to Mrs. Barnes. It was sold and another built on the opposite side of the same street. In a few years it was disposed of, and a handsome two-story structure erected in East Bennettsville.

Bennettsville Circuit is now composed of four churches, Pine Grove, McColl, Beauty Spot and Smyrna. The parsonage is located at McColl.

Brightsville Circuit was set apart from Bennettsville Circuit in 1849, and is composed of Boykin, Bethel, Antioch and Breeden's Chapel. The parsonage is near Gibson Station, North Carolina. This Circuit has been served by G. M. Boyd, R. W. Barber, P. A. Murray and B. M. Grier.

The churches in North Marlboro Circuit are New Hope, Oak Grove, Ebenezer, Shiloh and Pleasant Hill.

Clio Circuit was first known as South Marlboro, and was a part of the Bennettsville Circuit till 1874. The churches now composing it are Clio, Bethlehem, Beulah, and Manning's Chapel. The parsonage is at Clio. The preachers who have had charge are J. T. Kilgo, G. T. Harmon, J. C. Bissell, G. M. Boyd, D. D. Dantzler, F. Auld, R. A. Child, John Owen and J. B. Traywick.

Blenheim Circuit was a part of the Clio Circuit until the close of the year 1887. The churches forming it are

Hebron, Parnassus, Ebenezer and Zion. G. M. Boyd, W. H. Kirton, J. A. Porter, J. W. Ariail, L. F. Beaty, T. G. Herbert, Sr., and P. B. Wells are the preachers who have been in charge. The parsonage is located at Blenheim.

The following list gives the names and date of service of the preachers who have had charge of the Bennettsville Circuit since the year 1821 and up to date.

1821 John Boswell and —— Tradewell.
1822 Jeremiah Norman and Morgan C. Turrentine.
1823 John Boswell and Malcom McPherson.
1824 Nicholas Ware and Elias Sinclair.
1825 Elias Sinclair.
1826 J. L. Jerry and J. Hartley.
1827 Joseph Moon and W. T. Smith.
1828 —— Groover, W. M. Wightman and —— Culverhouse.
1829 John H. Robeson, —— Humbert and Wm. Murrah.
1830 Noah Lany, Samuel W. Capers and John McColl.
1831 Wm. King, Jackey M. Bradley and —— Boseman.
1832 Wm. King, —— Allen and Wm. Whitby.
1833 Joel W. Townsend and John L. Smith.
1834 John Watts and J. W. Welbourn.
1835 Allen McCorquodale and A. W. Walker.
1836 John H. Roberson and Thos. Sumter Daniel.
1837 John H. Roberson and John McMackin.
1838 Chas. S. Walker and Paul A. M. Williams.
1839 Theophilus Huggins and Wm. C. Clark.
1840 Wm. T. Harrison and Wm. A. McSwain.
1841 Abel Hoyle and Miles Pucket.
1842 Ira L. Potter and A. Richardson.
1843 Jacob B. Anthony and John W. Vandiver.
1844 Lark O'Neal.
1845 M. Robbins and Robt. J. Limehouse.
1846 Henry H. Durant.

1847 Marcus A. McKibben.
1848 Dennis J. Simmons.
1849 James W. Wightman.
1850 John A. Porter.
1851 Jackey M. Bradley.
1852 John H. Zimmerman.
1853 Robert P. Franks.
1854 Lewis M. Little.
1855 Lewis M. Little and John W. Crider.
1856 Henry M. Mood and John W. Crider.
1857 Henry M. Mood and J. E. W. Fripp.
1858 Paul F. Kistler and J. M. Cline.
1859 Paul F. Kistler and E. F. Thwing.
1860 R. R. Pegues and A. H. Harmon.
1861 R. R. Pegues and —— Allston.
1862 Tracy R. Walsh and J. B. Campbell.
1863 Tracy R. Walsh and R. R. Pegues.
1864 J. A. Porter and M. C. Davis.
1865 J. A. Porter and M. C. Davis.
1866 T. R. Walsh and A. McCorquodale.
1867 T. R. Walsh and R. R. Pegues.
1868 M. L. Banks.
1869–1870 Claudus H. Prichard.
1871 John A. Porter.
1872 J. A. Porter and J. F. England.
1873 John A. Mood and L. M. Hamer.
1874 John A. Mood and Dove Tiller.
1875 John M. Carlisle and J. L. Stokes.
1876 John M. Carlisle and D. G. Dantzler.
1877 Thomas Mitchell and Thomas E. Gilbert.
1878 Thomas Mitchell and J. W. Tarbox.
1879 T. Mitchell and F. Hauser.
1880 J. W. Murray and —— Graham.
1881 J. W. Murray and P. B. Murray.
1882 J. W. Murray and J. E. Beard.
1883 Thomas J. Clyde and John C. Kilgo

1884 Thomas J. Clyde and J. A. Harmon.
1885 Thomas J. Clyde and E. G. Price.
1886 Thomas J. Clyde and E. O. Watson.
1887 James C. Stoll and John A. Rice.
1888 James C. Stoll.
1889 George M. Boyd.
1890 W. H. Kirton.
1891–1894 W. S. Martin.
1895–1896 J. S. Beaseley.

CHAPTER XXXIII.

Presbyterian Churches.

Great Pee Dee Presbyterian church, now located at Blenheim, is considered the parent church of the Bennettsville Presbyterian church. The old church yet stands five miles from Bennettsville on the public road leading from Bennettsville to Blenheim. The Great Pee Dee church, being inconvenient for the worshippers living at Bennettsville, in 1852 measures were adopted looking towards the erection of a building in Bennettsville. A lot measuring one acre, fronting Marion street, was purchased of Hartwell Ayer, for $150.00, and the deed taken in the name of L. B. Prince and George Dudley, on October 5, 1852. Subscriptions were made by the members in Marlboro, Cheraw, and by others friendly to the object. Messrs. W. D. Johnson, Chas. A. Thornwell, Neil McNeil, Geo. Dudley and J. Beatty Jennings acted as a building committee. Messrs. Jones and Lee, architects of Charleston, S. C., furnished the plan, and the work was let to D. A. Boyd, of Virginia, the lowest bidder, at $2,800.00 On May 12, 1855, the church was dedicated. Rev. Jno. C. Coit conducted the service, being assisted by Rev. A. D. Campbell. The Bennettsville church was placed under the jurisdiction of the Harmony Presbytery of the South Carolina Synod. Through a petition presented by Alexander Southerland and others, and by order of Presbytery a committee composed of G. C. Gregg, J. A. Wallace and A. D. Campbell was appointed to organize the church on the 1st of December, 1855. Dr. James H. Thornwell was present and aided in the service. W. D. Johnson and J. Beatty Jennings were elected ruling elders and obligated by Dr. Thornwell. Rev.

A. D. Campbell acted for a few months as stated supply, and a call having been accepted by Rev. Pierpont E. Bishop, on 19th of April, 1856, he was installed as pastor. Rev. P. E. Bishop served the church acceptably and faithfully till March 5th, 1859, when in the vigor and prime of manhood, and in the zenith of his usefulness he was taken away by pneumonia. His ashes now repose in the churchyard by the side of his wife.

On November 10th, 1860, Rev. Charlton W. Wilson was installed pastor of the church. He died at Petersburg, Va., June 4th, 1864, a chaplain in the Confederate army In 1870, Rev. E. H. Buist was stated supply; and in the early part of 1871 Rev. Joseph Evans became stated supply for the church. On the 21st of November, 1874, Rev. D. S. McAlister was installed pastor, and continued in that relation till December 6, 1881, when he resigned the charge of the church. April 2, 1882, Rev. W. B. Corbett became stated supply, and continued till his death, April, 1894.

From May 12th, 1855, 156 members have been enrolled, including the organization and those admitted on examination and by letter. Baptism has been administered to forty-nine adults and infants. There are fifty-two members in good standing, enrolled and living, of which number thirty-four per cent have been added during the first six months of 1896.

Samuel E. Bishop and W. Beatty Jennings have gone out as ministers of the Gospel from this church.

About the year 1832 Archibald McQueen, a Presbyterian preacher residing in North Carolina, came to this county at stated times and preached at what was known as the "Old Club House." It stood not far distant from Drake's Mill, which then belonged to the Campbells. What the "Club House" was originally erected for we are not advised, but the presumption is that there was a "race track" in the vicinity. At all events Gen. Robert B. Campbell, who owned the land upon which the "Club House" stood, was not averse to having services held there on Sundays, and for a time the arrangement continued. But from some cause, not now known, services were afterwards held near where Hill's store was, in the vicinity of Zion church. But about the year 1834 the great Pee Dee church was built, and the membership to whom Mr. McQueen had been preaching was organized into a church. Mr. McQueen was the first pastor. D. G. Coit, who married Miss Maria Campbell, was ruling elder. The Campbell families, McQueens, B. N. Rogers, McLeods, Sparks, Drakes and Mathesons have been members and supporters of the church. About 1855 the Bennettsville Presbyterian church was organized and the strength of Great Pee Dee weakened by the removal of quite a number to Bennettsville, prominent among whom were W. D. Johnson, Alexander Southerland and Dr. J. B. Jennings. The names of some of the preachers who have supplied the pulpit of Great Pee Dee church for longer or shorter periods are Revs. Archibald McQueen, P. E. Bishop, C. W. Wilson, A. D. Campbell, Martin Brearley, Cousar, McAlister and Richards. About 1882 a new Presbyterian church was built at Blenheim and the old Pee Dee church sold to the colored people.

The Presbyterian church at Tatum was organized in the Academy building June 15th, 1890, and for about a year they worshipped in the Academy. In the spring of 1891 the church was completed and dedicated, Rev. H. G. Hill, D. D., officiating in the services. It was the first church built in the town and is out of debt. Rev. W. B. Corbett was the pastor from its organization till his death in 1894. For the last two years the pulpit has been supplied by Revs. Brearley, Gillespie and Arrowwood.

RED BLUFF.

Early in the present century there was a Presbyterian church at Red Bluff. It has been shown elsewhere in these pages that a good many Scotch people came to this county soon after the Revolution, and settled mainly in the eastern portion of the county along the Little Pee Dee River; and, having brought the Presbyterian faith along with them, they would naturally soon want a church of that faith to worship in. The first church was situated on the bank of the stream at Red Bluff. It is well authenticated that it stood there as far back as 1817, and might have been built some years previous to that date. The old building was not torn down till about 1860. For a good many years before that (perhaps twenty or more) the congregation had not worshipped there, but had moved their membership to Smyrna, a church in Robeson County only a few miles distant. Near the site of the old church is the burying ground, where the Scotch people of that community have been interred, and McLaurins and others have been carried there from other communities to find their last resting place.

The second church, bearing the name of Red Bluff, occupied a site two miles or more west from the old one, and was built about 1857 or 1859. The land upon which it stood was conveyed by Solomon L. McColl for that purpose, and when no longer used as the site for the church, was to revert back to his heirs. It was a new organization, the members of the old church, as already mentioned, having gone to Smyrna. It was organized and built, perhaps, through the instrumentality of Rev. P. E. Bishop, who for several years previously had been pastor of the Bennettsville church. The land upon which the church stood is now owned by D. D. McColl, of Bennettsville, who recently deeded a spot of ground near by for a burial ground.

Soon after the founding of the town of McColl (about 1886) it was determined to constitute a church at that place. It was accordingly done, and the membership of the new organization was made made up largely of members of the Red Bluff church. From members originally forming Red Bluff, McColl and Tatum Presbyterian churches have both been organized.

Within the last few years a new Presbyterian church has been built at Dunbar, a station on the Latta & Clio branch of the Atlantic Coast Line Railroad.

Capt. T. E. Dudley, Dr. J. C. McKenzie and others have given assistance much appreciated in the preparation of this chapter.

CHAPTER XXXIV.

McColl.

The prosperous and thriving town of McColl is situated on the eastern border of Marlboro County, only one and a half miles from the North Carolina line, and about ten miles from Bennettsville. It lies between Beaverdam and Panther Creeks, and is immediately upon the C. F. & Y. V. R. R. Eleven years ago, in 1884, the people in that community had no idea that a town of such considerable proportions would grow up in their midst so soon, but about that time the railroad was being built from Fayetteville in the direction of Bennettsville, and T. B. Gibson and J. F. McLaurin, in order to induce them to locate a depot at this point, offered to build a depot and subscribe to the stock of the company. They were ably assisted in their efforts by others in the community. In 1884, therefore, the depot was built, which was the first house erected in the town. Mr. Gibson had some time previously exchanged places with his brother, I. P. Gibson, and the railroad passed across the lower end of his tract, and a site for the depot was selected and located on his land, and so the town of McColl had its beginning. It was named in honor of D. D. McColl, of Bennettsville, who during the time of building and for a while afterwards, was the president of the S. C. Pacific Ry., the South Carolina division of the C. F. & Y. V. R. R. A little less than a dozen years ago, where Mr. Gibson was growing fine corn and cotton, to-day stands the growing and prosperous, plucky and pushing town of McColl. In proportion to its size and age, the town of McColl has, perhaps, more strikingly handsome and well-appointed houses than any town in the State. "One is struck with the fact at McColl that the proper start was made in most things." This is particularly true of the churches and schools. Three comfortable and commodious churches, Methodist, Presbyterian and Baptist, adorn the town; while "the McColl High School was organized about the time the town was founded and has grown up with the town." The school building is large, well built and comfortable, and is under the supervision and control of Prof. Craven. Nothing in the community commands a greater share of the interest of the citizens than the McColl High School.

The town of McColl is lucky in having a number of men of fine business capacity who do thoroughly and well what they undertake. Mr. Frank P. Tatum, a native of North Carolina, is one of the leaders in enterprises calculated to help the town. He located in Marlboro about 1867, and is now a farmer, merchant, cotton-buyer, liveryman, and president of the McColl Manufacturing Co. He runs a farm of eighteen plows, and conducts a very large and successful mercantile business. T. B. Gibson, his son-in-law, was born not very many years ago, within a few hundred yards of the business center of the town; and though comparatively a young man, has a mature business head set firmly on his shoulders. He is one of the leading successful merchants of the place. Mr. P. Mangum came from Chesterfield to Marlboro a number of years ago, and lived a few miles north of McColl, but judiciously decided to make McColl his home. He manufactured the brick from which his handsome and imposing residence was built. Mr. Arch K. Odom is his partner in the mercantile business. Mr. J. F. McLaurin was born in the immediate neighborhood of McColl, and is a son of the late Capt. Loch McLaurin. He represented the county in the Legislature during the last term, and has been re-elected for the term of 1897-98. Mr. McLaurin has been merchandising about eight years,

History of Marlboro County. 265

and is doing business in a handsome two-story brick store, built of brick manufactured at his yards. A. W. Morrison & Co. may be ranked among the leading business establishments of the town. Mr. Jeff D. Morrison is the junior member of the firm. Among the other business houses in McColl may be mentioned J. E. Willis, Luther McLaurin, Lane & Bristow, W. M. Gibson, Lester Sisters, J. I. Vick, J. F. Stubbs, and W. T. Smith.

One of the chief reasons, and perhaps the principal one, why McColl has grown so rapidly and prospered so well, is the fact that magnificent farming lands, rarely equaled for productiveness and fertility, stretch out on every hand, and this, with the further important consideration that the people who own those lands *work* them judiciously, intelligently and industriously. Bounteous harvests, as a natural consequence of well-ordered and intelligent labor, bring prosperity and content. Thrift, prosperity, fine management, and a proper regard to comfort and convenience, are all shown in the "fine orchards, splendid stock," magnificent cotton and corn fields, numerous and large out-buildings, and handsome, convenient and well-arranged dwelling-houses. Farming in the McColl neighborhood means a bounteous and generous home support, and a handsome surplus for sale, and consequently but *few* of the farmers trade on time. The merchants therefore handle *cash*, instead of bad accounts, and hence they prosper. Marlboro lands, Marlboro methods, and McColl farmers make success and prosperity sure for the town of McColl. The Gibsons, McLaurins, Fletchers, Willises, Tatums, Parkers, farm to some purpose and profit.

The McColl Manufacturing Company, located in the town of McColl, the only cotton mill in Marlboro, is owned and managed almost entirely by citizens of Marlboro. It is spinning Marlboro cotton into a fine grade of yarn at the rate of fifty bales a day. "In the spring of 1892 the first wing of the main building was completed, and the machinery put in motion. The main building is now a brick structure 88 by 303 feet, with opening and lapper room 50 by 80 feet, packing room 40 by 40 feet, and machine shops 30 by 50 feet." It is run by a Corliss engine of 250 horse-power, having three large boilers of 100 horse-power each. The finest English and American machinery was purchased. It is supplied with all the latest and most improved devices for insuring safety against fire, and illuminated throughout by electricity. Three hundred operatives are employed, who live in comfortable cottages, erected on land belonging to the mill. The mill runs day and night, and a ready market is found for the entire product of the mill. Mr. F. P. Tatum is the President of the mill, and T. B. Gibson its Secretary and Treasurer, who, together with D. D. McColl, C. S. McColl, E. Strudwick, W. W. Goodman, Eli Willis, T. H. Bethea, and A. W. Morrison are the directors, whose work have accomplished such satisfactorily results. "Messrs. F. P. Tatum and T. B. Gibson, and a few other citizens of McColl are the men who hesitated not to navigate this large undertaking to its present successful condition. It took pluck, ability and money more than once to overcome the obstacles, but one of the best managed and most successful mills in South Carolina to-day tells the story of the fight and victory." The court-house town no longer dominates the whole county, or absorbs all its business. Towns grow up at the railroad stations, and at the site of a cotton mill, and by reason of their churches and schools, and by reason of their more intimate connection and association with the surrounding community, are becoming centers of influence and trade, and are able and willing to enter into business competition with the county seat, though often larger and more pretentious.

While the McColl Manufacturing Company is the

only cotton mill in Marlboro to-day, yet two others have been built. The first cotton mill built in Marlboro was at the "Burnt Factory," lately the property of Mr. Aaron Manship. It was built by a joint stock company composed of Col. Williams, of Society Hill; John Taylor, of Cheraw; John McQueen and William T. Ellerbe, of Marlboro, in the year 1836. In 1840 Meekin Townsend, father of R. E., C. P. and Walter, acquired an interest in the "factory," as it was called, and about 1845 he purchased it. It was burned in 1852, and the same year Mr. Townsend died. Another cotton mill was erected a few years after the war, at what has been known as Medlin's Spring (property now owned by Rev. Mr. Kirton) by a man named Cameron, but the mill was burnt about the time of its completion. It is hoped that other mills will be erected and operated in the county, for where the staple is grown there it should be manufactured; and the pluck of the McColl people ought to be a stimulus to others to do as they have done.

It has been mentioned elsewhere in these pages that William Leggett, the grandfather of James S. Leggett, of Clio, lived about the time of the Revolutionary War at or near what is now McLaurin's Mill, and owned land lying between Beaverdam and Panther Creeks. It would be interesting if we could show how much of the land lying south of the town of McColl he owned, and to whom he sold, and the changes that have taken place in the ownership of the land since his time. The land lying south of the town, and now in the possession of John F. McLaurin was once owned by Robert Hamer and conveyed by him to Bennett R. Jackson and from him to the late Captain Lock McLaurin, the father of John F. Esquire Pipkin, the father of Mrs. N. M. Gibson, owned several hundred acres of land, a part of which land Mr. N. M. Gibson purchased at the partition sale of the estate of Esquire Pipkin and the central and northern portion of the town is located upon that land. Lying north and east from the lands formerly owned by Esquire Pipkin and extending to and even beyond the Adamsville road, covering several square miles and several thousand acres of land, Moses Parker, the grandfather of Capt. John R. Parker, claimed as his own. Capt. Parker now lives on lands set off as dower to his grandmother, and has no intention of transferring his possessions to other hands. Mr. F. P. Tatum purchased his plantation lying just east from McColl from the late Isaac Pipkin, and while Mr. Pipkin might have sometimes regretted the sale, it is safe to say that Mr. Tatum has not regretted the purchase. Lying west from McColl are the beautiful plantations of H. L. B. McColl, T. H. Bethea, W. P. Lester, and then the plantation of R. J. Tatum. Then you come to the thriving town of Tatum, so named from Richard J. Tatum, who a number of years ago came from North Carolina and made his home in Marlboro. He married the daughter of the late Jesse Bethea, of Adamsville, and settled where he now resides. The town grew up at his very door; the depot and most of the town being on Hamer lands. There are two handsome churches, a large, roomy school building, a half dozen store houses and quite a number of comfortable residences. Fine farms lie all around the town, and Mr. Tatum, the Easterlings, Hamers and Manships know how to work them. Two doctors, McKenzie and Reese, attend to the sick when there is any sickness to attend. They do not need a lawyer, because they all behave themselves and pay their debts.

The "write-up" of McColl by J. E. Norment of the *News and Courier* has been freely used in preparing this chapter.

CHAPTER XXXV.

ADAMSVILLE.

Adamsville township is not so named because *all* the people living within its bounds are named Adams, but a goodly number do bear that name, and most of those bearing the names of Newton, Fletcher and Gibson are related to the Adams family either by blood or marriage; so that it is not inappropriate that the township should take its name from the Adams family. The township lies in the northeastern portion of the county and in every respect is a favored land. The farmers in no section of Marlboro excel those of Adamsville in successful, careful, remunerative farming. Nowhere are more comfortable dwellings and neater out-buildings seen than in Adamsville. A large proportion of the land is under cultivation and hence you can often have in sight several different farms, the handsome dwellings, well-kept out-buildings, and fruit-laden orchards indicating thrift and prosperity. By painstaking methods and the intensive system of culture, the farmers of Adamsville have made themselves equal, if not superior to any other section of the county, in successful, remunerative, "all-round farming." Mr. John C. Fletcher, one of the young farmers of Adamsville, has just been awarded a prize of one hundred dollars by the *News and Courier* for the best "all-round farming" in the State of South Carolina for the year 1896, where the contestants were allowed to produce "anything and everything that can be grown or raised on a farm and consumed on a farm or sold for profit." The purpose of the contest, as explained by the *News and Courier*, "was to prove that diversified and all-round farming pays in South Carolina; to exhibit the proof, and give public recognition to the farmer who makes the best showing." It is quite complimentary to Adamsville, and especially so to John C. Fletcher, to carry off the prize where all the farmers of the State might have been contestants. It is to be hoped that his success in "diversified, all-round farming," may be an incentive to others to adopt the same method pursued by him, and thus bring prosperity to themselves and to the county.

The plantation now owned by B. F. Moore, when purchased by his father, had been "run down" by slipshod methods of farming till it produced only a few "nubbins" per acre; and Wm. Moore was doubtless warned by his friends that starvation would be his certain fate if he undertook to make a living on the place. He not only made a living, but prospered, and "Ben Frank" is to-day making as much cotton and fine corn per acre as any of his neighbors, and constantly bringing his land up to a higher degree of cultivation. Capt. Breeden's father, Lindsay Breeden, "in his day was considered a *good* farmer." But it is, perhaps, safe to say, that Capt. Breeden on the same land cultivated by his father, makes ten bales of cotton where his father produced one; and other crops doubtless in the same proportion. For a continuous stretch of four miles or more along the Bennettsville and Adamsville road the land is owned by the Breeden family. Sheriff Green's plantation is included, but he married a Breeden. On plantations embraced in that stretch Andrew and Wm. K. Breeden lived and died. Their plantations were admirably and judiciously worked by them, and now by their sons after them. Capt. Breeden, J. L. Breeden and T. J. Breeden, while not residing in Adamsville, are partial to Adamsville dirt. The late James B. Breeden was a native of Adamsville. No man perhaps who has lived in the county has had a more abiding faith in Marlboro land than he. He continually bought land, but seldom sold it. When he purchased a plantation he immediately built comfortable tenant houses, stocked it with mules and began to farm it at a profit. While he was successful as a merchant, yet he had practically retired from active mercantile pursuits, and at his death, March 3d, 1891, was devoting his fine talent to farming on a very large scale. And he made it pay, for, according to his own valuation, his estate was worth one hundred and seventy-five thousand dollars. He was among the first farmers, if not the very first, to try the lavish use of fertilizers under crops. It must have paid him or he would have discontinued it. Chief among the many plantations which he owned when he died was the beautiful "Beauty Spot" plantation in Adamsville, a large part of which is now owned by his nephew, J. Frank Breeden, who knows as well how to work it as did his Uncle, James B.

But there are other fine plantations in Adamsville besides those named. The lack of time and space will forbid the mention of others. The truth is they are nearly all fine and well worked, and the owners drive sleek, fat horses, plow fine mules, kill fat hogs, and have barns filled with home-raised corn.

This chapter would not be complete without a sketch of the Adams family. Jonathan Adams, the first of the name to place his feet upon Marlboro soil, came from Ireland prior to the Revolutionary War, and was of Scotch-Irish descent. He married Miss Mary —— and lived not far from the "burnt factory," a few miles above Bennettsville. He fought through the Revolutionary War as a Whig, and after the struggle had ended, and when within two days' march of home, sickened and died. He left three sons, William, Shockley and John, to perpetuate the name, and a daughter, Divinity.

William Adams was married four times. His wives were Mary Marine, Julia Bullard, Elizabeth Gibson and Patsy Easterling. William and Mary Marine had three sons, Jonathan, John P. and William, and three daughters,

Bede, Hannah and Mary. Jonathan married Mary Bright, and was the father of the venerable Rev. Andrew Adams, a local preacher in the M. E. church who married Miss Margaret Smith. Andrew Adams had several sisters who have married and left many respectable representatives among the Fletchers, Gibsons, and others. John P. married Julia Newton, sister of Rev. Cornelius Newton, and daughter of Younger Newton, Sr. Their son, Jackson, also married a Newton, Miss Elizabeth. The daughters of John P. married Newtons, Pates, etc. There are none of the Adams of this branch living except a grandson, Archie Adams and his family. The only surviving child of John P. is Mrs. Ann Pate, widow of Travis Pate, deceased, and mother of John A. Pate. William (called "Branch Billie") of Adamsville, married Sallie Newton and Sallie Fletcher, and Jonathan and Eb. are his sons. His daughters married among their neighbors and kinfolk. Robertson married Miss Betsey Fletcher and lived near Boykin church, of which church he was a consistent member. His son lives at the old homestead. Shockley married Miss Martha Fletcher, who left several children living in North Carolina. Shockley belongs to the ministry of the M. E. church. Jephtha also married a Fletcher, Miss Annie, making four brothers who went to the same house to get wives. Jephtha's children are found in the communities of Gibson Station and McColl. Wyatt Adams married Miss Nancy Leggett and lived in Robeson County, North Carolina. The daughters of William Adams, Sr., have descendants in Marlboro and Richmond counties. The descendants of Shockley Adams, son of the first Jonathan, are found among the Malloys and McIntyres, of Richmond County, North Carolina. John Adams, son of Jonathan, and brother to William and Shockley just mentioned, has descendants in Marlboro. His children were Welcome, Mrs. W. K. Breeden and Mrs. Bethea, mother of B. F. and Welcome A. Moore.

Robert Peele came from Wayne County, North Carolina, with Joshua Fletcher about 1817. He married Mary, the daughter of William Adams. This couple had sixteen children, and now they are so numerous one of the family remarked that it would be impossible to count them. They are thrifty, industrious people and have much force of character, and, being of Irish extraction, they have their share of wit and humor, as well as intellect. They live in upper Marlboro and lower Richmond. The Adams were formerly Quakers but now are mostly Methodists.

XXXVI.

Educational Matters.

Our forefathers began to take an interest in educational matters at an early date. It is fair to presume that school-houses and churches went up simultaneously, and that soon after they had erected their rude log dwelling-places, log churches, and log school-houses were built. It is significant that the school-house was found near by a church. At Brownsville, Parnassus, Salem, Hebron, Smyrna, Pine Grove, Boykin, Beaverdam, and other churches, school-houses are seen. It shows that education and religion go hand in hand, and our forefathers recognized the fact. They also knew that the erection of churches and school-houses would have the effect to bring into their locality other settlers of good character. The lively bidding of towns and cities for the location and erection of educational institutions in their midst shows that the same idea is entertained to-day. The building of school-houses in Bennettsville antedated the churches. On December 12, 1830, an Academical Society was organized and the following signed the constitution governing it: John McCollum, Nathan B. Thomas, Joshua David, Hartwell Ayer, John McQueen, Jas. E. David, C. W. Dudley, Campbell Stubbs, Jas. C. Thomas, Geo. Bristow, Wm. T. Ellerbe, John H. David, Thomas Cook, E. L. Henegan, and several other. A board of trustees, consisting of John McCollum, John McQueen, C. W, Dudley, Nathan B. Thomas and E. W. Jones was elected, and they in turn elected as the first teacher of the Bennettsville Male Academy, A. C. Sinclair, with John W. Covington, assistant. Sinclair was succeeded by C. W. Dudley, and after him, Duncan McLaurin, C. Davy, and others. The first teachers for the

Female Academy were Miss Jane McKay, afterwards Mrs. John McCollum, Miss Sarah Richards, Miss Simpson, and others followed.

The female academy stood on the lot of land across the street from the Methodist church, now occupied by W. S. Townsend. The land was originally owned by James Cook, the grandfather of Mesdames Breeden and Moore. The house was perhaps 100 feet in length, one-story high, and with folding doors, was divided into two rooms, and as occasion required, could be turned into one large room for public entertainments. The male academy was adjacent to the Baptist church, and where it stood is now seen the Bennettsville graded school building for white children of both sexes. The Academical Society owns the school property, and convenes biennially to elect a new board of trustees, who have general supervision of the school, and whose duty it is to elect the teachers. The buildings are ample and well-arranged. The trustees have been fortunate in their selection of teachers, and the teachers have had the hearty encouragement and support of the patrons. Hence little or no friction arises, and large numbers of children attend. Additional room has recently been obtained by the purchase of the old Baptist church building, and with slight improvement, four or five hundred children may be accommodated. Messrs. Chase, Paisley, Thomson, Britton, Sheridan, Root, Graeser, Rast, Stackhouse, Wilcox, Brodie, and others have managed and taught the children. The school is now under the control of Prof. Cork.

The colored graded school has been managed by competent men like E. J. Sawyer, Cain, and others. They have been much hampered in their work on account of lack of room. But steps are being taken looking to the enlargement of accommodation. The large livery stable recently owned by Capt. P. L. Breeden has been purchased, and is being erected in West Bennettsville, where the colored children, in their laudable and earnest desire for education, may be taught.

In ante-bellum days the male academy in Bennettsville was in charge of good teachers. Such men as D. McD. McLeod, J. H. Hudson, R. H. McKinnon, E. H. Graham, Daniel White and Neill D. Johnson, Leary, and Anderson, endeavored to impart knowledge to the boys. At the female academy the girls were taught by Mrs. Ann Crosland, Mrs. C. A. Thornwell, Mrs. A. J. Johnson, Mrs. B. D. Townsend, Mrs. W. P. Emanuel, Mrs. J. B. Jennings and Mrs. B. D. McLeod. It must be understood by the *young* readers of this chapter, that these ladies all came to Bennettsville bearing *other* names, but decided to change *them* for the names here given. The list might be extended by mentioning Mrs. J. P. Campbell, Mrs. P. A. Hodges, Mrs. J. N. Weatherly, Mrs. W. P. Emanuel, Jr., and Mrs. R. A. Douglas. So that it is seen that a goodly number of female teachers who came to teach have become permanent residents. Marlboro feels justly proud of the long list of competent educators who have done faithful work in her schoolrooms. But especial mention must be made of the services of Mrs. B. D. McLeod and Mr. and Mrs. John S. Moore, who are residents of the county. Mrs. B. D. McLeod taught before and after the war in Bennettsville. Later for quite a number of years she had a large, flourishing school at Blenheim, where many young ladies and youths were prepared to take high stands in the colleges of this and other States. She was subsequently engaged in teaching near her home at the residence of the late Dr. A. McLeod. It may truly be said that Mrs. McLeod's whole life in Marlboro has been devoted to teaching and assisting in the rearing of her half brothers and nieces and nephews. A woman of high culture, broad-minded and kind-hearted, the good she has done in Marlboro can never be estimated.

Mr. and Mrs. Moore taught before, during and after

the war in Bennettsville, covering a longer period than ever did any other teachers in the town. After the war they taught for a number of years at Hebron. We suppose it is safe to say that no one teacher in Marlboro has left a stronger and more lasting influence on the minds and lives of so great a number of pupils as has Mrs. Moore. Her methods were gentle and so thorough that few passed from under her care without receiving a fine rudimentary education and many have become successful teachers who received no other advantages than such as the fine schools of Mr. and Mrs. John S. Moore furnished.

In the country the schools have generally been well sustained. With men like Donald Matheson and W. R. Smith at Parnassus; L. M. Hamer and Harris Covington at Hebron; the Johnson brothers at Pine Grove, and others like them at other places, it is easy to understand why the schools in a former day prospered. And with conscientious, competent teachers in charge and a united support of the patrons, they are prospering still. While the youth of the county enjoy the advantages of good schools at home, yet large numbers are not satisfied to accept what they offer, but very properly seek schools of higher learning where a collegiate education may be obtained. The number of college graduates is constantly increasing, and while it is scarcely to be hoped that another Thornwell will ever be sent forth in the world, yet some obscure boy born on Marlboro soil may come to the front and even rival Dr. Thornwell.

It is a laudable and praiseworthy ambition to strive for a collegiate education, for such striving will place others besides Thornwell and Robt. McIntyre in the college president's chair. Let the youth of Marlboro educate themselves, for as competition in all lines of human thought and action increases more and more will the educated mind hold sway. Some other Marlboro boy may follow John L. McLaurin into the U. S. Senate.

The incentive and necessity for a finished education is greater to-day than ever before. Because your countrymen, C. S. McColl and D. D. McColl, have succeeded in their lines of business and made handsome fortunes without the advantage of college training—youth of Marlboro, do not undertake to do the same! Because Peter T. Smith could, with no college training, amass a snug fortune on his farm—farmer boy, do not take for granted that you could do likewise!

CHAPTER XXXVII.

THE COLORED PEOPLE.

About sixty per cent. of the population of Marlboro County is of the negro or African race, and their coming to this country was as slaves. This county had very few previous to the Revolutionary War, but, as the culture of rice and cotton increased and became the principal crops, the demand for negro labor increased. About 1830 a negro man would sell for say three or four hundred dollars; a young woman probably for less. But about the beginning of the war prices for similar slaves would be at least three times as much. This was, no doubt, largely owing to the growing demand for this labor for the new Western States, and the prohibition of further importation to this country about the year 1820. The bringing of these people to this country as slaves, has proved a great blessing to their descendants, in giving them civilization and Christianity, and has also greatly blessed the South in giving to it the best labor in the world, adapted to its peculiarities as to climate and products. The negroes of this county previous to and during the war were well cared for and protected by their owners, and seldom during those times was anything actually cleared from the result of the year's work upon the farm, further than was expended in the care, clothing, etc., of the whites and blacks upon the place. The main property in considering wealth was the number of slaves owned, and the principal idea in obtaining wealth in the South previous to the war was to take care of the negroes and let them multiply. During the war the negroes were entirely docile, doing the work of making the crops in the absence of their masters, and being faithful and obedient.

With the close of the war came the freedom of the negro as one of the results of the conflict, and it was seriously felt by the former masters that this was a calamity indeed, principally as they could not conceive of such a state of things as that a negro would work unless made to do so as a slave; and also that the two races would not be able to remain together in any other relationship than as master and servant. Neither the masters nor slaves were prepared for the new situation, and, as was natural, both made mistakes. The new freedman could not fully realize that he was free unless he moved from his old home and confidently expected to be set up with "forty acres and a mule." Then came reconstruction and the conferring of suffrage upon the colored people, which caused political aspirations. During that exciting and stormy period immediately following reconstruction, to their credit it must be said that no outbreaking act of violence occurred in this county, as in some others.

The conduct of the slaves of Marlboro during the war, when the able-bodied whites were at the front in the army, was commendable indeed. No instance during the whole four years is remembered where the blacks were other than faithful to the home and family. It is not too much to say that no other race of people under similar circumstances would have been so loyal and true.

The present development of Marlboro is largely the result of negro labor. The colored people largely work as tenants and share-owners of crops, and any disagreement or litigation with their employers is very uncommon. The stores of the county are largely supported by the patronage of the colored people, and it is rare indeed that credit extended by a merchant to a colored farmer or tenant is not promptly paid in the early fall.

Quite a goodly number of colored people in Marlboro own their own farms and know how to work them. The following colored men own valuable farms and have excellent credit in their respective communities: Alex. L. Ivy, Silas Easterling, C. C. McRae, George Pearson, Lewis Emanuel, Thomas Green, J. Evans Quick, January Johnson, Richard Reese, Richard Gibson, Rufus Tatum, Amos Tatum, Handford David, Noah Melloy, Edward Ware, G. W. Steel, Washington Bright, Robert McColl, Tony Lide, Moses McLeod, Benjamin F. Quick, Nicholas Kollock, the Cook brothers, the McKay brothers, Moses Hodges, H. W. Hines, Henry Bradford and Dennis David.

Among the colored population there are a few well-to-do farmers and business men. J. C. Allman has a large plantation, which he cultivates very successfully, making from 125 to 150 bales of cotton annually. Peter Banks, living near McColl, is another good farmer and has an excellent plantation, which might, perhaps, sell for forty dollars per acre. He runs a four or five horse farm.

E. J. Sawyer came to Bennettsville about twenty-five years ago. He has had good educational opportunities and has received thorough college training. He served as principal of the Colored Graded School for a number of years, and has also been engaged in mercantile and farming pursuits. He has served two terms as postmaster at Bennettsville. He is a resident of the town, owning an attractive home, and numerous other town lots, together with valuable farms in the country. His property is worth perhaps $20,000.

The *Pee Dee Educator* is the name of a paper owned and edited by E. J. Sawyer, and is creditably supported by the colored people of the county. Its circulation is about two thousand, and with one exception is the oldest colored paper in the country, being in its seventh year.

The churches of the colored people will compare favorably with those of other sections. At the town of McColl there is a small Presbyterian church. With this single exception all the others are Baptist and Methodist. The colored Baptist church in town has a larger seating capacity than any other church in town. It is a substantial frame building, neatly painted and well furnished. The building is worth about $3,000, and was built chiefly through the contributions of the colored people through the efforts of the present pastor, Rev. F. W. Prince, who received his training at Benedict College, Columbia, South Carolina. The Methodists have a church in Bennettsville, known as "St. Michael's M. E. Church." For comfort, convenience, beauty and situation, it is all that could be desired by any congregation. This church is worth about $2,500. Both churches have comfortable parsonages attached. When we remember that so many, and such comfortable churches, have been erected through the contributions of the colored people chiefly, we are amazed at their liberality and religious zeal. As an illustration of this, Tony Lide, a few years ago, mortgaged his home and thirty acres of land, all he owned, in order to make the purchase of one of the parsonages spoken of above. Below we give the names of twenty of their country churches, all of which are well-built frame structures, completed, painted and furnished, the average value of each being about $1,000: Hopewell, Sarian, Spears, Clio M. E., Clio A. M. E. Z., Asbury, Pee Dee, Sardis, Macedonia, Saw Mill, Level Green, Smyrna, Pine Plains, Galilee, Wesley Chapel, Ebenezer, Cedar Fall, Shiloh, Goodwin Chapel, and Dyer's Hill. There are others of less value, but neat and comfortable.

As a rule the colored people avail themselves of every opportunity for education, frequently keeping up private schools at their own expense when the limit for the public schools has expired. Many parents by much sacrifice send their sons and daughters to colleges. Benedict, Shaw and Claflin being usually patronized. More detailed allusion is made to the schools and school buildings in the chapter on education. When we consider the rapid strides that have been made by the negro race along financial, social, religious and educational lines, we are amazed. Time nor space will admit of a more extended chapter in this work. Nor is any pen adequate to the task of bestowing the just meeds of praise upon them to which they are entitled, for having so successfully overcome adverse fortunes. Their progress and improvement as a race in the last thirty years has been without a parallel in the world's history, and their motto is, "Onward still, to yet better achievements."

CHAPTER XXXVIII.

1886.

The following poem was found among the papers of J. A. W. Thomas at his death. He evidently wrote it for one of his grandchildren. It may very appropriately appear as a chapter on the eventful year 1886:

Another mile-post in the march of time, soon we shall have passed,
  And deeply marked the footprints its rapid tread has made ;
Its entrance icy cold, 'mid winter's storms and howling blast,
  The ground hard frozen oft, in sunshine and in shade.
In vain we sought the hot-house in which to hide our rare and precious plants;
  Cold entered there, and hope and flowers both withered 'neath its frosted breath.
The growing grain was killed by arctic winter's blast,
  The anxious farmer hoped that summer's heat would atone for winter's death.
Spring came and summer, but alas ; such mighty floods of rain,
  The earth was drenched, the lowland crops were drowned,
O'errun with grass and weeds men toiled but toiled in vain;
  A scanty meager harvest was all the little gain.
And then as August numbered out its last long weary day,
While sons and daughters, worn and weary sought their evening rest,
  A new and startling voice was heard which seemed to say :
Stand still, O child of clay, till Mother Earth shall find her rest.
      Sleep fled from mortal eyes,
        Strong men grew faint from fear,
      Brave women sent up piteous cries,
        And all were filled with awe.
Strong buildings rocked, as solid earth upon her stable pillars shook;
  Fair city by the sea! almost destroyed, sent up her wail of woe,
As scores of people only waked to meet death's cruel stroke.
  And full many a time since that dread night of anxious fear
    The strange and solemn sound, unlike all else we ever heard or felt before,
  Has come at intervals to remind the myriads far and near
    Of Power that shakes the earth, uplifts the isles and makes the ocean roar.

And now as chill December comes,
And makes a three days' march upon her rapid way,
For three successive days the fleecy snow descends
To clothe the ground, adorn the leafless forest trees,
And cause the bells of cheer and joy to ring.
One day or less of snow has often come before,
But three successive days in this fair southern clime
Is quite a new event to old and young.
    Therefore, my dear child, we say without fear
    "1886, an eventful, earthquake year."

CHAPTER XXXIX.

Down to the Twentieth Century.

"Love thou thy land with love far brought
From out the storied Past, and used
Within the Present; but transfused
To future time, by power of thought."

From many evident causes the author has in a very desultory manner covered over a space of one hundred and seventy-six years in the history of Marlboro. In these pages we have been carried back to primitive forests whose solitude was disturbed only by the twittering of birds and the hunting songs of the red men, whose rights there were none to dispute. At the coming of the white man we have seen the dusky Indian fleeing farther and yet farther into the wild woods, until he disappeared forever.

We have seen the struggle for subsistence of the early settlers of this section of South Carolina. Later, their growing discontent at the hardships and tyrannies imposed upon the feeble colonists by the mother country We have learned that our forefathers of the Pee Dee section bore their share of taxation; gave of their meager subsistence; took up their guns and fought and died for the independence that was bequeathed to their posterity, as the result of the Revolutionary War. We have seen under what almost insurmountable difficulties the infant republic was born. Had the straggling population been unanimous for a colonial government it would have still been difficult. But a portion of the population were loyal to British rule, and conscientiously opposed all measures looking towards the establishment of American government, and later were engaged in predatory hostilities against what they honestly believed rebellion in the colonists. The early struggles of the infant republic were serious and discouraging. But true and tried men stood at the helm. Numbers of them bore our names. Many sons and daughters of Marlboro to-day may justly be proud of the part their ancestry took in establishing peace and prosperity in this fair land.

In the march of years we find Marlboro grown to be a fine, flourishing district. Prosperity and civilization had rewarded the industry of those sturdy sons of the soil, our forefathers of a later generation. Again we find Marlboro's sons, buckling on the sword in defense of principles as dear to them as were those of their Revolutionary sires. Bidding adieu to homes of luxury, and loved ones, they endured for years the hardships and privations of war. The noble women of the South became not only the bread-winners for their families, but by their devotion and assistance food and clothing were supplied to the armies, to a large extent. The mothers and daughters of the South with their lily hands toiled and spun; spun and sung; prayed and waited. Waited for the husbands and sons who never came home; who had fought and lost—lost not only life and property, but principles and institutions that had been bequeathed from sire to son. Institutions and principles so interwoven with their industrial and political life, that the result of the Civil War left our State and county in almost as impoverished a condition as were our forefathers after their struggle for liberty. Among the many disasters of war one of the hardest was that our county had been invaded by the enemy. Traditions of the future will tell many a sad story of experiences and scenes enacted during Sherman's raid. Hidden spoons and trinkets, buried demijohns, and incised feather-beds may figure in these recitals. But these legends rightly belong to those who were the participants in those fearful times, and through them to their descendants. So, as a fair historian, we will not trespass on family matters. We have never ceased to wonder, however, if that little pest and destroyer known as the Sherman bug was really left behind as an ever-present reminder of Sherman's raid. If so, by what process of incubation were the bugs hatched the year after the raid? If these are not actual facts, would it not be fair to the distinguished Sherman family to trace the pedigree of the yellow bug to the name of some other destroyer. As remembered at this late day, there may have been some amusing and ridiculous incidents connected with the terrors of Sherman's raid. Yet the realities and distress were pathetic in the extreme. In many cases, a bed of smouldering coals was all that was left of once happy homes. In other families there was not food enough left for the next meal, and everywhere there was desolation and devastation. But bread for the hungry children had to be won in some way. Sadly and slowly our stricken and impoverished people rallied their energies. Hope and Faith lifted them out of the depths of Despair; crushed and kneeling in the dust of defeat and humiliation, they implored the Ruler of Destinies for strength to again start the struggle for life and home. Turning their faces to a future that was uncertain of all but toil and tears they gathered up their scattered agricultural implements—it was all that was left—and went resolutely to work. Truly they started from the bottom. Former methods were useless to them now.

Henceforth their efforts were a matter of experiment. Eking out what few provisions they had with a painful economy, and wearing their remnants of clothing they went cautiously on, a step at a time. Through the sad, strange days just after the war, through the uncertain, perilous times of reconstruction, the people of Marlboro passed quietly and peacefully. No acts of lawlessness or bloodshed stained the fair name of our county, as was the

case in some of the other counties. The men who had
been brave enough to face the cannon's mouth in war were
wise enough in defeat to courteously, if silently, pass
the United States garrison of troops whose presence proclaimed our county for awhile under military rule.

Gradually our people grew stronger. Year by year the
most successful methods of agriculture under the new
system of labor have been discovered. New enterprises
have been the outgrowth of the changed conditions.
There are two distinct generations among us to-day. The
older, who succeeded under the system in ante-bellum days
and who gathered up the scattered threads and strove
patiently and humbly to disentangle the web that war had
left. The younger, who have been born in that New South
where all men are free and equal, and in which the greatest
success comes to him who strives the hardest. Both generations, assisted by the freedman, have contributed their
full share of work on that wonderful structure, the New
South. Without fear of challenge we make the proud
boast that Marlboro, in all the mutations of the past century, has kept pace with the most prosperous of her sister
counties. Peace, contentment and plenty reign throughout our land. Fine crops of varied products are the reward of industry. The skillful, painstaking methods of
the farmers, both colored and white, have brought the lands
up to a high state of cultivation never dreamed of by our
forefathers. Farms that produce more than one bale of cotton to the acre are not uncommon. And Marlboro stands
to-day the proud champion of the world in the produc-
tion of the greatest amount of corn to the acre.

As we ride over these fine level fields that so easily
yield a support to all who work, and see the hundreds of
elegant homes, and notice the improved machinery and
commodious farm buildings, we wonder at the strides that
have been made in prosperity in the last thirty years.
Yet some are heard to wish that the fortunes of war had

been otherwise. Indeed, the passing away of the blot of slavery is felt to be not only the grandest moral act ever performed by a nation, but it has proven a blessing to all and none the less to those who felt most injured at the time. The habits of industry and the strength gained by individual effort have led to greater prosperity as to individuals and as to the country than could ever have been hoped for under the old system. Marlboro's sons and daughters review the events of the past century with tender, chastened emotions, but none the less with gratitude, for the years so fraught with trials and sorrow brought many blessings.

But true it is that our faces are turned cheerfully and hopefully to the light that precedes the dawn of the twentieth century. Our fond prayer is that the generations who will make the history of the twentieth century may make as much of their improved opportunities as their forefathers did of their limited ones. But let them be urged here to ever more look back reverently at the trials, sorrows and struggles of those who cut out and smoothed the pathway for them to tread.

> "Gently and without grief the old shall glide
> Into the new ; the eternal flow of things
> Like a bright river of the fields of heaven
> Shall journey onward in perpetual peace."

THOMAS MEMORIAL BAPTIST CHURCH.

The foundations of this building were laid about one year ago, and many read the name through a mist of tears. Every brick that has gone into that stately pile has been a tribute of love for him whose memory it perpetuates. They have builded wisely. Solid walls have been reared that tell of the strength with which he stood for right. Beautiful arches suggest the gentleness that made even little children love him. The tall graceful spire that crowns this magnificent edifice will for ages to come, point the weary, careworn sinner to a haven of rest. The old bell in the tower for more than thirty years called the people of Marlboro to the old church to listen to the counsels and receive the benedictions of one who loved them as a father. During the ministrations of almost fifty years, he had rejoiced with friends on nuptial occasions; he had helped to soothe their bed in sickness and had wept with them when their hearts were stricken. The years came and went, the summers bringing more weariness to his lagging footsteps and the winters more frost to his honored head. Yet his loving hands and aching heart found ever more and more work among the flock he loved as a tender shepherd. At last there came a long midsummer day when his work wearied him past mortal endurance. It was a Sabbath, but his rest came not till nightfall.

> "He knelt, all his service complete,
>   His duties accomplished, and then
> Finished his orisons sweet
>   With a trustful and joyous 'Amen!'
> And softly, when slumber was deep,
>   Unwarned by a shadow before,
> From a halcyon pillow of sleep
>   He went to the thitherward shore.
> Without a farewell or a tear,
>   A sob or a flutter of breath,
> Unharmed by the phantom of fear,
>   He glided through the darkness of death."

The old bell, whose Sabbath morning peals had been sweetest music to his ear, called the people of Marlboro together once more. But in solemn tones it tolled a requiem over the loved and honored father, J. A. W. Thomas.

The first Sunday in August, 1897, was the first anniversary of the day on which "God's finger touched him and he slept." On that day the old bell rang in a new, magnificent edifice and the "Thomas Memorial Baptist Church" was dedicated to the worship of God with appropriate ceremonies. Rev. Lansing Burrows, D. D., of Augusta, Ga., preached the dedicatory sermon. Many ministers, life-long friends of him so honored, assisted the pastor, Rev. Rufus Ford, in the services. They wove a memorial chaplet to crown this grand monument that the people of Marlboro have erected to the memory of J. A. W. Thomas. This stately monument will proclaim to unborn generations the respect and devotion of Marlboro's people to their friend and fellow citizen. If he left no memory which will "grow greener with years, and blossom through the flight of ages," yet would his feeble effort at leaving the History of Marlboro to future generations prove his devotion to his friends and neighbors.

Sad was it that before his pen could complete the work in his own better style, Death, all too soon, wrote on the pages of his perfect life

FINIS.

INDEX

ADAMS, 249 269 A H 242
Andrew 249 272 Andrew J 220
Ann 183 Annie 272 Archie 272
Bede 272 Betsy 272 Branch
Billie 272 Branch Billy 88
Divinity 271 Eb 272 Elijah 196
Elizabeth 271-272 Hannah 272
Harris 196 J B 25 225 J R 211
Jackson 272 Jeptha 88-89 247
272 John 271-272 John P 271-
272 John Tyler 196 Jonathan
220 271-272 Joshua 211 Julia
89 271-272 Lizzie 25 Martha
272 Mary 186 271-273 Mrs
174 Mrs Jeptha 88-89 Mrs S J
183 Nancy 272 Patsy 271 Peter
L 220 Robert 88 Robertson
247 272 Sallie 272 Shockley
88 271-272 T M 225 W H 211
W L 211 Welcome 272
William 111 271-273 William
Sr 272 Wyatt 272

ALDRICH, Mrs Judge A P 36 108
ALFORD, Berry 157 243 J M 224
Jacob 153 Jas M 200 M M 200
Margaret 153 Margaret C 156
Mrs 152 Nathan T 200 Sion H
219
ALLEN, 49 239 ---- 255 Elmore
200 223 J 223 Jacob S 169 Joel
49 238 Mr 148 Mrs 148 T W
135 203 Thompson 49
ALLISON, 37 Ann 72 Catherine
30-31 Elizabeth 34 Isabella 24
Miss 24 35 39 Mrs 34 Robert
57 72 126 133 Tom 34
ALLMAN, J C 281 Jacob 133
ALLSTON, ---- 256
AMMONS, Allen 216 Alpheus
216 Joshua 83 87 Mr 148 Mrs
Joshua 87 Silas 203 Thos 216
ANDERSON, 276 George 220
J G 211
W T 211

293

ANDREWS, John 135
    Stephen D 196
ANSON, Commodore 155
ANTHONY, Jacob B 255
ARIAIL, J W 255
ARMSTRONG, Miss 60
ARNETT, Benj 216
ARROWWOOD, Rev 260
ASBURY, Bishop 241
ASKEW, John 47
AULD, F 254
AUNT, Kissy 44
AYER, 109 Hartwell 36 96 175
    180 258 274
    L M 36 108 Lewis M 39
    Lewis Malone 36 97 108
    Mr 108 175 Mrs 97
    Thomas 36 95-96
    William 36 Zaccheus 97
AYERS, Thomas 70
BAGGETT, Nellie 101 Wm 101
BALDWIN, Harvey J 174
BANKS, M L 256 Peter 281
BARBER, R W 254
BARENTINE,
    Duncan 182
    J M 225
    Miranda 182
BARNES, Mrs 23 254
BARNETT, Thomas 244
BARNWELL, R W 115
BARRENTINE, G 216
    Philip 251
    Thomas 247
BARRINGTON, Alex H 208
    Ebby W 208
    Goodwin 184 208
    Harris 200 P L 211
    Philip 211
    Sion R 208
    Thomas 184 W 211
BARROW, J L 215

BARRY, D F 223
BARTON, J 223
BASS, Ann B 42 Richard 216
    Wade H 220
BATTLE, 239 Katie 152
BAXTER, Robert 125
BAY, 162
BEALANCUA, Augustus 208
BEARD, J E 256
BEASELEY, J S 257
BEATTIE, 72 R Q 236 W Q 235-
    236 238 252
BEATY, L F 255
BEDGEGOOD, 37 Mr 229-230
    Nicholas 58 229
BEDINGFIELD, Charles 57
BENJAMIN, Dr 174
BENNETT, Ellen 92 F 211
    G W 216 Gov 168 171
    J J 216 Joseph 93
    Mr 93 Mrs W 24
    Nevil 93 Thos 211
    William 93
BENTON, 105 110 Col 126-127
    Lem 126 Lemuel 121 125-126
    Maj 95 Mary 91 Miss 125
BETHEA, A J 216 Catharine 34
    David 102 Deborah 62 186 Ed
    C 31 James 62 James R 156
    Jesse 268 Jessie 86 John 61
    John C 31 34 Margaret 61
    Mary 156 Mrs 272 Mrs John C
    31 P W 203 Philip 61 Rachel
    61 Samuel 186 Sarah 186 T H
    91 266 268 T T 216 Tristram
    42 Truss 91
BEVERLY, Robert 216 W R 200
BINGHAM, Thomas 71
BISHOP, P E 250 259-261
    Pierpont E 259 Samuel E 259
BISSELL, J C 254
BITTLE, James H 207

BLACK, Kenneth 50
BLAIR, Miss 129
BLAKENY, Gen 115 James W 188
BLANDING, Col 40
BOAN, B F 203
BODIFORD, Isabella 156
BOLTON, Britton 207 Frank 117 J F 170 223 Jas H 242 Mary 117 Robert 242 T M 176 William 117
BONCHIER, Mrs Dr 106
BONE, Leonard D 220 Nicholas P 220
BOOTH, Sarah 24
BOSEMAN, ---- 255
BOSWELL, John 255
BOTSFORD, Edmund 230
BOUCHIER, 166
BOUNDS, Mr 242
BOWEN, C 211 F C 211
BOWYER, Lizzie 182 Peter 182 T M 216
BOYD, D A 258 G M 254-255 George M 257
BOYKIN, Lemuel 246
BRADFORD, Henry 281
BRADLEY, Jackey M 255-256
BRAZIER, Pleasant 186 Rebecca 186
BREARLEY, Martin 260 Rev 260
BREEDEN, Aaron 119 150 Andrew 119 270 Capt 270 J B 77 178 J F 77 225 252 J Frank 271 J L 135 270 James B 119 178 270-271 John 119 John L 119 220 Joseph L 119 Lindsay 119 270 Miss 86 Mr 119 251 Mrs 275 Mrs J B 175 Mrs J F 24 Mrs J L 171 Mrs John 119 Mrs W K 272 Nancy 62 P L 173 178 195 219 275

BREEDEN (cont'd) Peter L. 119 219 R J 203 T J 270 Thomas 119 W K 89 Wm K 119 242 249 251 270
BREVARD, 59 162
BRIDGES, Eliza 24 Elizabeth 103 Frank 102 John 102-103 Judge 102 Mary 24 101 Miss 62 Mollie 103 Mr 103 Mrs 24 102-103 Nancy 103 Sallie 103 William 24 103 118 Wm D 24
BRIGHT, Charles 182 Chas 181 Mary 272 Mr 181 Washington 281
BRIGMAN, 49 Alex 220 B F 203 Eli 207 Evander 220 Frank 203 Geo 211 Henry 207-208 J A 224 J Curtis 207 Jacob C 208 John 220 L 216 Madison 203 Moses 208 William 208 Wm 220
BRISTOW, 179 265 A E 135 177 185 195 A N 136 235 Alexander E 207 Celia 185 Chesley D 196 D M 211 E H 203 Edmund D 196 Geo 135 274 George 185 J M 203 J W 223 Lucy 117 Mr 117-118 Mrs 154 Mrs A E 179 R W 211 T C 216 W J 211 W M 146 William 135 William M 146 Wm 135 171 Wm M 219
BRITT, James 220 Thos P 220
BRITTON, Hugh 47 Jacky 25 John 25 Mary 25 Mr 47 275 Mrs 47
BROCKY, Athalinda 114
BRODIE, Mr 275
BROWN, 50 110 232 Alex R 172-173 Alexander R 244 Caroline 34 Charles 34 39 James 39 Jeremiah 38 John 38 228

BROWN (cont'd)
  Morgan 122-123 125-126 132-133 161 Morgan J 135 Mr 38 Mrs Charles 39 S A 180 Samuel 38-39 125 William 38-39 167
BROWNFIELD, R 126 Robert 126
BRUCE, Caleb 49 Joseph 49 Joseph D 200 Mrs 47 T R 203 Thomas 200 Thos 201 Wright 49
BUIST, E H 259
BULL, Gov 57
BULLARD, Charles 224 Geo W 224 Henry 196 Julia 271
BUNCH, J P 134
BUNDY, G W 211 Mrs Axey 88 Wm 196 220
BURKETT, 111
BURKITT, Ephraim 49 Samuel 49
BURN, Mrs 124
BURROWS, Lansing 292
BUTLER, Andrew Pickens 163 Elijah 196 211 Miss 31 W 211 Wm 196 211
BYRD, Levi 220
CAIN, 275
CALDER, Arthur 203 225 Boswell 203 Daniel 208 H 216 Henry 208 J D 211 Peter 220 R 216 Robt 224 Stamford 208 Stanford 212 225 Tobias 247 W J 203 Wm 224
CALDWELL, James J 163
CALHOUN, 147 A L 203
  Alexander 149
  D A 225
  Dougald 149
  H H 204
  J C 204 John 149
  John A 195 203
  John C 200

CAMERON, 267 Jeannette 140 John 140 Mary 140 Miss 139
CAMPBELL, A D 258-260 Capt 129 Col 130 J 196 J B 256 James 129 James P 130 Jane 125 130 John 125 129-130 164 Maria 129 260 Mr 130 Mrs J P 276 Robert 129-130 Robert B 129 132 135 164 259 Robt B 129
CANNON, Henry 126
CAPEL, Mrs B A 235
CAPERS, Samuel W 255
CARGILL, Martha 61 Thomas 61
CARLISLE, J A 225 J M 250 John M 256 T F 203
CARLOS, Robeson 171
CARLOSS, 41 Mr 131 Mrs Robeson 40 131 Robeson 40 131-132 Robeson A 174 Squire 40
CARMICHAEL, Mrs Duncan 153
CARRIBO, Henry 203
CARROLL, Chancellor 163 H W 174 178
CARTER, W J 203
CASTON, 166
CAULK, Daniel 196 J C 216 James 216
CHANDLER, Mr 228
CHASE, Mr 275
CHAVIS, Alfred 208 Bithel 208 Bytha J 208 Calvin 208 Eli 208 Eliab 208 Geo 216 J 216 James 208 John 208 Levi 208 Murray 226 Nelson 208 William 208 Willis J 208 Wm 216
CHERRY, George 29 125 Sarah 29

CHILD, R A 254
CHURCHILL, John 15
CLARK, ---- 203 B 224 Daniel
  203 Elsey 203 Jesse 226 Jno C
  212 Joseph 200 William 208
  Wm C 255
CLARKE, Archie 212
CLAYTON, John 208
CLINE, J M 256
CLYDE, T J 169 242 Thomas J
  256-257
COBB, J G W 177
COCHRAN, C 160 Nancy 93
COCHRANE, C M 61 Claudius M
  61 Ellen 61 Louisa 61
  Margaret 61 Martha 61 Mary
  61 Mr 61 Mrs Thomas 61
  Rachel 61 Robt 62 Robt C 61
  Thomas 61-62
COIT, D G 260 David G 129 J C
  129 Jno C 258 Maria 129 260
COLCOCK, 162
COLE, James 203 William 208
CONNER, Mr 101 Nancy 103 119
  Polly 101 Rebecca 184 Widow
  119
CONNOR, Mary 101 Mr 101 Robt
  T D 196
COOK, 177 179 Bros 281 James
  171 174 176 275 Jno R 196
  Mrs James 120 Nancy 50
  Olivia 171 Sallie 101 171
  Sarah 245 Thomas 174 196
  242 244-245 274 W D 211 W J
  133 176 242 Wm J 244-245
COOPER, Vernon H 196 Widow
  49 Wm C 196
COPE, Daniel 220 E 216
  Elijah 203
  J F 224
  John 216
  Thomas 200

CORBETT, W B 170 259-260
CORK, James 221 John 149 221
  Prof 275
CORNWALLIS, 105 112
COTTINGHAM, Andrew 117
  Charles 118 Chas 200 Conner
  117-118 David 117 Elkana 117
  F 212 James 118 Jonathan 103
  118 150 203 Nancy 117 Sallie
  103 Thos 221 Turbet 241 Ucal
  221
COUNCIL, Miss 61
COUSAR, 260
COVINGTON, ---- 223 A B 212 A
  D 212 Caleb 100 Col 86 102
  151 Eli T 200 Elizabeth 100
  Fannie 189 H 216 H H 166
  Harris 101 133 164 207 277
  Henry 61 101 174 208 248 Ira
  101 J A 204 J T 104 James 101
  Jas T 134 200 John 100-101
  John W 274 Louisa 61 Mary
  101 Miss 92 Mrs Henry 149
  Nancy 101 103 Nellie 101
  Noah 189 Polly 101 Robert
  101 Sallie 101 Thomas 101
  Thos S 242 Tristram 86 101
  169 Truss 101 William 101
  118 Wm 101 Wm W 202
COWAN, 224
COWARD, J H 212 Lewis 221
  Louis M 196
COX, C A 203 Elvin 203 Ely 203
  M C 203 W E 203
COXE, 111 Aaron 43 62 Ann 42
  Benjamin 41 Charles 42
  Daniel 42 Edwin 224 Edwin M
  42 Eli 42 Emanuel 41-43
  Ezekiel 41 Ezra 42 Fanny 42
  Hugh 42 James 41 43 James E
  41-42 173 Jas E 41 Jeremiah
  43 Jesse 41 John 41-42

COXE (cont'd)
    Josiah 41 Michael 43 Moses E
    42 Mr 42 Mrs Aaron 43 62
    Mrs Eli 42 Mrs James 43 Mrs
    John 42 R A 224 Robt A 42
    Samuel 41 43 William 41 43
CRABB, H S 224
CRAVEN, 253 Prof 264
CRAWFORD, G G 216 H B 216
    W H 216
CREECH, David 212
CRIDER, John W 256
CROSLAND, 175 179 Ann 276
    Charles 152 173 Chas 224
    Daniel M 35-36 60 David 36
    Dr 173 176 245 Edward 35
    173 Eliza 61 George 36 173
    Israel 36 John 35 Mr 35 Mrs
    John 35 Mrs Sam 29 Mrs T L
    34 39 Philip 36 Sam 29
    Samuel 35 196 Sarah 60 T L
    61 224 Throop 173 177 W A
    60 W E 225 William 36 168
    173 Wm 61 173 Wm A 160
    196
CROWLEY, Robert 224 Robt C
    200 Wm 200
CROWLY, W 203
CULLY, C W 203
CULVERHOUSE, ---- 255
CUMMINGS, Elijah 212
CURRIE, N R 212
CURRY, Miss 138
CURTIN, ---- 200
CURTIS, E 235 Mrs Caleb 93
DABBS, Joseph 107
DANIEL, J W 245 254 Thos
    Sumter 255
DANTZLER, D D 254 D G 256
DARGAN, 238
    E C 230
    G W 163-164

DAVID, 73 A Judson 23 Aiken L
    197 Alex H 23 Ann 22-23
    Azariah 23-24 Benjamin 22-23
    60 Betsy 23 Catherine 22
    Charles 23 David 22 David
    Bevan 22 Dennis 281 Dinah
    22-23 E 235 Eliza 24 103
    Elizabeth 23 Ephraim C 197
    Evander 23 Handford 281
    Isabella 24 J 224 J H 169 J O
    235 James 21 James E 23 132-
    133 164 James F 23 Jas E 274
    Jenkin 22-25 Jesse 23 29 John
    22-24 103 John H 23 119 274
    John O 23 Joseph H 23 197
    Joshua 22-23 25 112 135-136
    173 274 Josiah 22-23 Lucy 22-
    23 25 Lydia 22 Mary 23-24
    Mollie 103 Mr 24 Mrs 24 Mrs
    Jesse 23 29 Owen 22-25
    Rachel 24 Rebecca 62 Richard
    21 Robt J 197 Sarah 22-24 60
    Susanna 23 Tennant 21
    Thomas 22 W J 23 62 119 176
    212 Washington W 207
    Welcome 23 William J 23 Wm
    R 23 226
DAVIS, Columbus 201
    James M 207
    M C 256 Mrs 186
    Rev Mr 186 Younger 208
DAVY, C 274
DAWKINS, Elisha A 208
DAY, Wm 216
DEBERRY, Henry Mrs 34
DEPOELNITZ, Baron 130-131
DEVONALD, Daniel 21
    Mrs Daniel 21
DEW, H C 204
DEWITT, Miss 26
    William 112 121 126 132
DIAL, Jacob 212

DONALDSON, 77 Mrs 47 Mrs W Z 243
DOTY, A 224
DOUGLAS, 72 176 Hugh J 196 Mrs R A 276
DRAKE, 260 Ancil 201 Jas A 136 Jno N 133 Maj 192 Preston 202 Susan 63 Z J 192 225
DRAYTON, 70 Gov 162 Judge 67 Wm Henry 67
DRIGGERS, ---- 216 Aaron T 221 Abner 221 Alex 204 C O 216 Eli 208 Gage 208 J H 204 224 Jesse 197 Jesse G 197 M C 216 Matthew 149 Peter 208 Philip 221 Robt S 201 Thomas 208 Whit 216
DUDLEY, 73 C W 132-133 164 174-175 177 180 274 Col 176 Geo 192 258 George 173 258 James 197 Mrs 175 179 Mrs T E 192 R 160 T E 40 160 166 175-176 179 195 234 262 William 173 Wm 173 244-245
DUNBAR, Daniel 149 J C 149
DUNFORD, John 204
DUNKIN, Francis Wardlaw 163
DUNN, Alexander 216 Thomas 212 Wm 212
DUPRE, T J 204 Thomas J 221 Thomas J J 49
DUPREE, Thos J 201
DURANT, H H 253 Henry H 255
EARL, Elijah 221 Jesse 204
EARLE, Baylis J 163 Senator 165
EASTERLING, 239 268 A B 211 A J 212 Alfred R 197 Betsy 92 C D 195 215 Crawford 242 David 201 242 Elijah 197 Ellen 92 Fannie 245 G W 212 H R 212 Henry 92 186 221 233 J L 135 J N 217 J T 217

EASTERLING (cont'd)
Jas T 212 Jesse A 212 Jno A 212 Jno L 88 212 Joel A 212 Joel L 24 Josiah K 197 Lewis R 201 Mary 186 Mintie 186 Mr 92 Mrs C D 63 Mrs Crawford 119 Mrs Joel 46 Mrs Joel L 24 N A 210 Nancy 101 Patsy 271 Robt C 197 Shadrach 92 Silas 281 Thos 196 W B 217 W L 212 217 William 92 124 133 136 Wm 186 Wm T 197 W T 212
EDENS, Alfred 103 Allen 103 146 219-220 242 Ann 104 Asa 103 H L 225 Henry 103 219 J N 225 Joseph 201 Mrs T N 148 R M 250 Rev 104 Richard 103 T 201 T N 133 146 148 T Nelson 103 Thos H 201 Thos W 197 221
EDMUND, Lewis 21
EDWARDS, 110 Evan 21 John 21 Joshua 228 Mr 229 Mrs 106 Sam 93
ELLEN, W B 216
ELLERBE, 75 135 160 Ann 75 John C 75 Maria 75 Mrs John C 33 Thomas 75-76 122 W T 133 William 75-76 William E 75 William T 75 125 132 Wm H 75 Wm T 133 274
ELLERBY, John 75 Obedience 75 Thomas 75 William 75 William T 267
ELLIOTT, Bishop 115
ELLIS, Miss 77
ELLISON, Robert 126 132
ELMORE, Capt 138
EMANUEL, ---- 223 Chas L 197 221 Columbus 204 F M 174 177 Frank 204 Frank W 207

EMANUEL (cont'd)
  J. 160 James M 201 Joel 179
  Lewis 281 Mrs 77 Mrs Joel 77
  Mrs Simon 61 Mrs W P 276
  Mrs W P Jr 276 P C 179 R C
  202 Simon 49 179 W P 136
  179 Wm P 219
ENGLAND, J F 256
ENGLISH, Alex 208 Chas 204 Eli
  208 James 204 John 204
  Welcome 208 Wm 201
ERVIN, 93 Col 129 E P 129 133 G
  W 225 James R 128 132-133
  164 167
ERVINS, 162
ERWIN, 135
EVANS, 107 Bettie 64 C D 221
  Catharine 64 156 Charles 126
  Col 27 40 Col Tom 27 Daniel
  64 Eleanor 64 236 Elizabeth
  29 63-64 J A 133 J J 162 John
  64 John A 135 Joseph 259
  Josiah J 26 133 Judge 26-27
  29-31 40 Lucy 64 Mrs 40 Mrs
  Samuel 22 Mrs Thomas 21 Old
  Col Tom 26 30 Rebecca 30
  Samuel 22 Thomas 21 26 64
  123 126-127 132-133 135 161
  Thos A 64 W D 133 W Dewitt
  27 William 63-64 Wm 22
FAIRLY, Robert 246
FALCONER, 162
FEAGAN, E J 211 Neddy 118 W
  G 118 167
FERNISS, Mary 60
FIELDS, Mr 77 Mrs 77 P 217
  Silas 212 William 77 135
FINLAYSON, A E 224
FLETCHER, 249 265 Ann 89
  Annie 272 Betsy 272 J D 225
  John 88 John C 269-270 John
  K 225 John S 88 208

FLETCHER (cont'd)
  Joshua 88 273 Joshua D 197
  Julia 89 Lewis 88 Martha 272
  Mr 88 N 217 Nancy 88
  Nicholas 88 Raiford 88 Sallie
  88 272 Thomas 88 Thos 212
  W R 201 William 88
FORD, 239 R 238 Rufus 292
FORNISS, James 76 167 Mrs 76
  William 76 109
FOWLER, W D 224
FRANKS, Robert P 256
FRASER, John 221
FRASIER, Chas 224 Sam 224
FREEDEN, J B 36 Mrs J B 36
FREEMAN, Benj 201 221 James
  221 L D 201 Lorenzo 204
FRIPP, J E W 256
FULLER, Aunt Betsy 119 Henry
  103 119 145 Mary 23 Miss
  103 Shadrach 23 119
GADDY, J W 217 Wm 217
GADSDEN, Bishop 116
GADSEN, Bishop 115 Gen 74
GALESPY, Francis 74 James 74
GALLOWAY, 45 James 244 Jno C
  204 Jos S 204 Moses P 202
  Mrs 46 W A 204
GALPIN, 174 Amos 174 Amos A
  172
GANTT, Richard 162
GARDNER, Miss 31
GARNER, Wm 204
GATES, Gen 98
GAY, P W 212
GEORGE, Iii King Of England
  113
GIBSON, 249 269 272 A H 212
  Ann 89 Eli 208 247-248
  Elizabeth 271 Francis B 248
  Frank B 209 I P 225 263 J M
  88 211 J P 189

GIBSON (cont'd)
    James M. 247-248 James W
247 John 209 Miss 48 Mr 263
Mrs 89 Mrs Frank B 187 Mrs
N M 91 267 Mrs Noah 88-89
Nathaniel 247 Nelson M 247-
248 Noah 88 247-248 Richard
281 Simeon 133 T B 263-264
266 Thomas 247 Thos 221 W
M 265 William 247 Wm L 197
Ziba 247
GILBERT, Robt 204 Simeon 208
    Thomas E 256
GILLESPIE, 135 Francis 74 Gen
72-74 167 James 74 98 133
135 171 May 74 O H 196
Obedience 75 Rev 260 Samuel
74 197 Sarah 74
GLOVER, 163
GOOCH, Joseph H 225
GOODMAN, W W 266
GOODSON, J 235
GOODWIN, E W 181 185 193
    Ebenezer W 247 Lucy 185 Mrs
E W 35 Mrs E W Jr 187
Samuel 181
GORDON, Justice 59
GRAESER, Mr 275
GRAHAM, ---- 256 Ananias 72
251 Daniel 138 E 201 E H 276
Henry C 197 J J 204 224
Martha 72 Mrs Ananias 251
Windsor 204
GRANT, Barnabas 221 J G 133
James T 209 Jeremiah 136 Jno
S 197
GRAY, Calvin 204 Robt 204
    William 204
GREEN, Bishop 116 Geo 217 J B
136 217 Sheriff 270 Thomas
281 W J 215
GREENE, Gen 59 99 105

GREGG, 21 28 54 Alexander 114
    Athalinda 114 Bishop 16 22 27
36 41 72 80 108 114 116 184
Charlotte 115 David 114 G C
258 James 114 John 114
Joseph 114 Mr 115-116
GREGORY, Justice 70
GRICE, E G 212 J D 224
GRIER, B M 254
GRIFFIN, John 217 Mary 32 Miss
    61 Wm 215
GRIFFITH, Elizabeth 21 Thomas
    20
GRIGGS, Henry 208
GRIMKE, 162 Judge 121
GROOMS, E 201 Evander 209
    221
GROOVER, ---- 255
GUINN, Anderson 209 Geo 212
    Thommas 226
GUNTER, John 200
GUZZARD, John W 201
HAITCHCOCK, Thos 201
HAITHCOCK, R 204 217 R F 204
    Samuel 204 Wm 221
HALE, 162 Senator 27
HALL, Alexander 207 Esther 183
    James 217 Joel 183-184 251
John 183 Mr 183-184 251
William 183 209 Wm 221
HAMBRICK, Amos 197
HAMER, 268 A C 212 Alfred 93
    C H 212 C T 171 Daniel H 93
204 E C 212 Henry C 93 J C
212 James 93 John 61 93 171
John H 242 L D 171 242 L M
253 277 Lewis M 93-94 242
Mary 61 Mrs 93 Nancy 93 P M
94 133 169 212 224 242 Philip
94 Philip M 93 R H 212
Robert 93 267 T C 213 T M
166 Thos C 93 William 93

HAMILTON, 253
HAMMER, L M 256 P M 133
HAMMOND, Haynes L 207
   Stephen 209
HAMPTON, Wade 138
HANNA, 164
HARGROVE, Daniel 200
HARGROVES, James 201
HARLLEE, W W 188
HARMON, A H 256 G T 254 J A 257
HARPER, Chancellor 40 William 163
HARRIL, Tristram 201
HARRINGTON, 77 Capt 81 Henry W 70 Henry Wm 66 J W 133 John W 195 William Henry 79
HARRISON, Wm T 255
HARROLL, John 180
HARRY, Ann 29 35 Daniel 22 28 David 28 John 22 28 Miss 23 29 Mrs Daniel 22 Mrs John 22 Mrs Thomas 22 Thomas 22 28
HART, Oliver 80
HARTLEY, J 255
HARVEL, John 197
HARWELL, Elizabeth 25 L 235 Londen 25 Londen Jr 25 Loudon 176 Mary 25
HASKEW, Ann 42 John 47 John W 201 Mrs 46 Thomas H 47 Zacheus 47
HATCHER, Aaron 209 Abner 209
HAUSER, F 256
HAWLEY, Joseph 144 Mr 145
HAYES, James M 207
HAYS, J J 201 Robt W 201
HAYWOOD, Anderson 213 Isham 213 Wm 213
HEARSEY, George R 199

HENAGAN, Amanda 49 B K 33 47 128 134 Barnabas K 132 C S 176 Dr 48 134 E L 135 274 Ephraim L 48 J W 133 James 47 Jas M 197 Jno W 135 John W 48 199 M I 176 Mrs 48 Mrs A B 64 Mrs B K 33 Nancy 48 Robert 48
HERBERT, T G Sr 255
HERNDON, David 213 John J 219
HERSEY, G R 204 George 75
HEUSTISS, 63 A J 204 225 Alex 104 Ann 62 G W 213 James 204 M 235 Mathew 62 Mrs Alex 104 Sarah 150
HEYWARD, Isham 197
HICKS, 37 Benj 126 Benjamin 125 133 Benny 127 Col 95 Geo 161 George 54 57-58 77 122-123 James 77 Maj 79-80 Miss 93 Mrs 77 Mrs James 77
HILL, H G 260
HILSON, Miss 63
HINDS, J D 224
HINES, H W 281
HINSHAW, 146 Capt 147
HINSON, E D 217 H P 217 J P 216 John B 197 Philip H 197
HODGE, Lucy 22 25 Mary 25 T C 201 Thomas 22 25 William 176
HODGES, ---- 223 Adeline 60 Capt 29 39 Elizabeth 29 George 29 J H 217 J L 30 John L 226 Moses 281 Mrs 30 Mrs P A 276 P A 30 179 R 217 R H 30 Sarah 29 T C 224
HOLLIWAY, Sallie 88
HOOD, Fanny 42 John 42 204 Miss 73 Wellington 204 Wiley 204
HORN, Daniel 156 Isabella 156

HOWARD, John 213
HOYLE, Abel 255
HUBBARD, E G 204 Elizabeth
    185 Feribe 185 Martin 217
    Miss 43 Peter 185 Rebecca
    185 S G 204 Wm 185
HUCKABE, John 201
HUCKABEE, Allen 188 Capt 188-
    189 Fannie 189 John J 197
    Mrs Tally 189 Nancy 188
    Penelope 189 Tally 189
    Thomas 188-189 Thomas W
    188 246
HUDSON, J H 25 133 166 169
    176 207 213 276 Judge 175-
    176 245 254 Mary 25 Narcissa
    25 Wilson 114
HUGER, Daniel Elliott 163
HUGGINS, Betsy 64 Theophilus
    255
HULL, Hope 241
HUMBERT, ---- 255
HUNTER, Andrew 125 Jane 155
    Lady 155 Widow 61
INDIAN, Chief Morrison 18
INGLIS, Chancellor 115 John A
    163
IRBY, 77 Annie 76 Catharine 34
    Catherine 30 Charles 30 76
    133 Chas 133 Elizabeth 76
    Fannie 76 James 76 John 30 34
    40 M L 76 Mehitabel 76 Miss
    76 Mr 30-31 Mrs 31 Mrs John
    192 Mrs M L 76 Rebecca 30
    Wm W 197
IRVIN, J R 40
IVEY, Gadi 144 Joe 144 Levi 144
    W H 224
IVY, Alex L 281 Gadi 144 H M
    204 H W 201
    Joe 144
    Levi 144 201-202

JACKSON, A W 205 Abner 204
    Bennett R 267 Chas 221 Enos
    197 J M 172 178 James A L
    197 John 205 John C 201
    Joseph 221 Laban M 221 Sam'l
    133 Wm 205
JACOBS, Archie 209 Asbury 217
    B L 213 Bethel 221 Curtis J
    209 David 221 J Frost 201 J P
    217 Robt 201 Samuel 209 221
    Snowden 213
JAMES, Abel 21 Ann 60 David 22
    J J 126 James 21 John 21 John
    J 126 John Jones 126 Miss 60
    Mr 126 228 Mrs Abel 21 Mrs
    James 21 Mrs John 21 Mrs
    Phillip 21 Philip 38 60 77 228
    Phillip 21 Thomas 22 Wm 22
JEFFERSON, President 162
JENNINGS, Douglas 173 177 J B
    176 260 J Beatty 258 J T 176
    250 Mrs J B 276 W Beatty 259
JERRY, J L 255
JOHN, D C 225 D S 202 Daniel 51
    60 63 192 244 Daniel C 201
    Griffith 22 J T 225 Mary 21 63
    150 Mrs Griffith 22 P M 225
JOHNS, 46
JOHNSON, 49 A G 48 133 Bros
    277 Daniel 198 David 163 H P
    175 180 Hugh T 198 J 217 J M
    164-165 J Monroe 253 January
    281 Job 163 Mrs A G 48 Mrs
    A J 276 Neill D 164 197 276 R
    215 Robert 253 W D 163-165
    176 205 213 258 260 Wm 162
    Wm D 133 193
JONES, David 21-22 Dr 77 173 E
    W 274 Edward W 173 J A 217
    J H 136 J J 133 James 133
    James H 197 209 John 186 221
    242 250 John C 201 John J 133

JONES (cont'd)
  Martin 201 Mary 24 Mary A
  186 Mr 258 Mrs David 22 Mrs
  Thomas 22 Thomas 22 W W
  217 Widow 186 William 209
JORDAN, 239 J L 25 Narcissa 25
KEITT, L M 35 Lawrence M 179
  Mrs 35 179
KENNEDY, F M 39 J E 224
  William 39
KERSHAW, Eli 58
KILGO, J T 254 John C 256
KING, 224 Wm 255
KINNEY, F W 40 133 223 Frank
  44 Mrs 44 Mrs W F 192
  Thomas 244
KIRBY, H 201
KIRKWOOD, E H 225 R L 172 R
  Lee 178
KIRTON, Rev Mr 267 W H 255
  257
KISTLER, P F 250 Paul F 250 256
  Rev Mr 250
KNIGHT, A H 136
KOLB, 108 Abel 60 110 Ann 60
  Col 39 60 105-107 109 232
  Henry 60 Jacob 60 Lt-col 95
  Martin 60 Mehitabel 76 Mrs
  106 Peter 60 Sarah 60
KOLLOCK, 77 Charlotte Wilson
  115 Nicholas 281
KOSCIUSKO, 130
LAFAYETTE, Marquis 87
LAMB, A 235
LANE, 265 J H 29
LANY, Noah 255
LAURENS, Henry 80 Mr 81
LAVINER, Harris 209 Hiram 209
LAVINGER, Daniel 198 Geo W
  198
LAW, Mr 38 Mrs 38
LAWRENCE, Willie 117

LEARY, 276
LEE, 129 209 Francis 32 Mason
  40-41 Mr 258 Mrs Francis 32
  William 62
LEGGETT, A J 213 James 91
  James S 267 Nancy 272
  Salathiel 91 202 Sherrad 91 W
  L 210 William 91 267
LEITNER, Maj 18
LESTER, Bright 90 Isaac B 195
  Mrs William 91 Nimrod 90 T
  C 211 Thomas 90 W P 268
  William 90
LEWIS, 37 John 225 Joshua 230
  Mr 230 W S 217
LIDE, 37 Annie 76 C J 133
  Charles M 124 Charles Motte
  124 Chas 133 Chas J 133
  Colonel 124 Elizabeth 39
  Hugh 39 132 230 James 124
  John 124 Mr 124 Mrs Hugh
  230 R W 230 Robert 124
  Thomas 58 71 124 Tony 281-
  282 William 221
LILES, B I 184-185 Elizabeth 185
  Holden 185 James S 209 Jas S
  185 Joseph R 185 198 Mrs J S
  23 S H 217
LIMEHOUSE, Robt J 255
LINDER, 224
LIPSCOMB, 224
LITTLE, Lewis M 256 Miss 125
  Mrs 245 Robt W 176
LIVINGSTON, Duncan 160 Knox
  44 133-134 136 166 175
LOCHLIER, John 205
LOCHLIN, A 213
LOCKLIER, Alex 213
LONG, Henry A 198 219-220 Mrs
  36 176
LOUIS, Xiv King Of France 190
LOWE, 224

LUCAS, H G 233 244 247 252
LUKE, 37
MAGEE, Hartwell 39 James 39 109-110 Martha 39 230 Mr 39 William 39 Zacheus 39
MAHONEY, Thomas 209
MAJOR, Ben 33
MALLONIE, J C 215
MALLOY, 272
MALONE, John C 207
MANDEVILLE, David 29 Mrs David 29
MANGUM, P 264
MANNING, E 224 Frank 199 Holland 226 Houston 225 J 224 John 223
MANSHIP, 268 A 213 Charles 90 Chas 242 John 202 Mrs Charles 90
MARINE, Mary 271
MARION, 105 Francis 188 Gen 102
MARSHALL, John 222 Mrs 36
MARTIN, W S 257
MASSEY, 173 Joseph D 172
MASTIN, Jeremiah 241
MATHESON, 260 A J 191 226 Donald 50 190-191 277 Hugh 202 Margaret 191 Mr 190
MATHIAS, Margaret 21
MAXWELL, H J 133
MCALISTER, 260 Chas 205 D S 259 John 205
MCARTHUR, 97-98 Maj 96
MCCALL, Alex 201 C S 133 138 173 178 195 Cameron 201 Crawford 200 David 138 Flora 188 Hugh B 200 J N 213 John 138-139 242 John L 137 Lock B 139 Mr 134 138 Nancy 188 Peter 135 Stumpy Duncan 139 T D 138

MCCASKILL, R 224
MCCOLL, Alex 140 Big Solomon 138-139 C S 225 266 278 Christian 139 D D 139 164-165 179 261 263 266 278 Daniel 138 140 205 David 139 David R 141 Dougald 140 Duncan 205 Effie 142 Flora 141 Granny 141 H L B 268 Hugh 139-140 Hugh D 139 Hugh G 138 Hugh S 222 J L 146 James 141 Jeannette 140 Jno S 205 John 138-140 142 255 John A 140 John C 138 John Gurly 139 John S 141 220 222 Joseph 139 Katy 141 L H 224 Little Solomon 139 Lock 139 Long Hugh 138 Malcom 139 Margaret 140 Miss 142 Mr 137 146 Nancy 138 140 Peter 139 172 Robert 281 Roderick 158 Samuel S 222 Silas 205 Solomon 139 Solomon L 261 Steady Hugh 139 W M 206 Wellington 140
MCCOLLUM, Charles T 154 Farquar 154 H 217 Hugh 154 Jno H 198 John 129 173 176 191 244-245 274 Miss 145 Mrs 47 Mrs John 275
MCCORQUODALE, A 256 Allen 255
MCCOY, James 91 John 90-91
MCCRIMMON, John A 222
MCDANIEL, Ann 104 Fred 101 120 George 120 I W 213 J R 224 Jas R 201 John B 120 145 Joseph 118 120 Mary 117 Mr 146 Mrs Fred 101 Nancy 101 Thomas 120 Toler 118 W H 224 William 120
MCDIARMID, Mr 156

MCDONALD, 155 D J 145 Mr 145
MCEACHERN, John 205 Niell 205
MCGEE, Henry 209 Wesley M 209 William 39
MCGILVRAY, B F 135 205 219
MCINNIS, A C 141 187 Angus 187 Archie 188 Flora 141 188 James 222 James A 188 John 222 Mr 187-188 Nancy 48 S J 141 188 Simeon J 198 Squire 188
MCINTOSH, 137 Alex 66 126 198 Alexander 70 132 Col 83 Ellen 156 Mr 156 Nicholas H 198
MCINTYRE, 272 Capt 120 J T 213 Robt 277
MCIVER, 115 137 Evander 107 John 126 132 Mrs R D W 28
MCIVERS, 164
MCKASKILL, N C 213
MCKAY, 91 Bros 281 Jane 275
MCKELLAR, John R 25 Martha 25
MCKENZIE, Alex 198 Dr 268 J C 213 262 R H 205
MCKIBBEN, Marcus A 256
MCKINNON, Cameron 200 Lauchlin 160 R H 276
MCLAURIN, 137 141 261 Alex L 221 D Mcq 205 D P 133 221 D W 205 Daniel 143 Daniel C 142-143 Duncan 142 274 Effie 139 142 Geo 205 H L 205 Hugh 142-143 205 Hugh L 139 Hurricane Daniel 142 J B 133 205 J F 134 225 263-264 J J 205 Jack 142 Jas R 142 Jas W 221 Jno L 134 John 142-143 John B 142 John F 139 202 267 John J 142-143

MCLAURIN (cont'd)
John L. 63 142-143 165 277 L B 142 L L 139 Lauchlin A 200 221 Laughlin 142-143 Little Hugh 142 Loch 264 Loch B 222 Lock 142 267 Luther 139 265 Milton 136 Mr 264 N D 205 P B 133 142 164-165 W B 139
MCLEAN, 137 224
MCLEOD, 260 A 193 276 Alex 155-156 Alexander 32 191 Aunt Isabella 157 B F 224 Betsy 156 Catharine 156 D M D 155-156 199 D Mcd 243 276 Daniel 62 156 Donald 243 Donald Mcdiarmid 156 Dr 32 Ellen 156 Isabella 156-157 J C 224 Jane 155 John 156 Katie 156 Lady 155 M 224 M D 64 Margaret 156 191 Martha 32 Mary 156 Moses 281 Mrs 276 Mrs B D 276 Mrs M C 153 155 Mrs W C 153 Murdock 202 Uncle 157 William 156
MCLUCAS, Archie 201 Daniel 157 Hugh 157 200 John 157 John D 158 199 Mrs 153 Mrs Hugh 153 R S 225
MCMACKIN, John 255
MCNAB, 50
MCNAIR, Miss 142
MCNEIL, Neil 168 258
MCPHERSON, Angus 148 202 Arch 226 Dougald 147 Malcom 202 255 Mr 148
MCQUAGE, J R 213 John J 200
MCQUAIG, H 217
MCQUEEN, 73 Archibald 259-260 F Sarius 199 Gen 32 154 174 James 129 Jane 125 130 John 164 173 191 198 267 274

MCQUEEN (cont'd)
   Maria 129 Miss 33 Mr 260
   Mrs 32
MCRAE, A D 201 A L 202 Alex
   153 Alexander 152 Angus 222
   Barbara 63 152 C C 281 C M
   200 Charles 154 157 Charles T
   149 Chas 205 Christian
   Bristow 152 Christopher 152-
   153 Colon 152 154 Daniel C
   222 Duncan 154 Duncan D
   152 Frank 200 Ian 152 J 224 J
   Calvin 222 Jack 192 James
   154 222 James A 222 James C
   220 Jno A 153 Jno C 201 Jno
   R 154 John A 146 John D 152
   201 222 John L 152 244 John
   T 153 205 Katie 152-153 Katy
   154 Margaret 62 Mr 137 Mrs
   153 Mrs Charles T 149 Mrs
   James 154 Mrs Philip 153
   Murdoch 153 Philip 154 192
   Polly 152 Roderic 152-154 157
   Sallie 64 152 Squire 154 T F
   195 225 Uncle Charley 157 W
   J 217 William 226
MCSWAIN, Wm A 255
MCTIER, Betsy 34 Mr 34 Robert
   34 William 34
MEDLIN, 147 Jas 217 John 217
   Jonathan 217 W C 146
MEEKINS, John 153 Jonathan 104
   118 148 Lidia 62 Mr 104
   Oscar 217 P J 205 P P 217
   Philip P 104 W E 217
MELLOY, Noah 281
MENDENHALL, 90
MILES, Amanda 49 Francis 48-49
   G W 224 Lucretia 48
MILLER, Alexander J 244 Anna
   25 Elizabeth 25 George 25 H
   217 Henry 25 198 John 25

MILLER (cont'd)
   John M 198 Joyce 13 Lizzie 25
   Martha 25 Mary 25 Mrs 25
   179 Mrs John M 185 Philip 25
   173 Sue 25
MILLS, Wm Henry 59
MITCHELL, T 256 Thomas 256
MIXON, Miss 42
MONROE, President 168
MOOD, Henry M 256 John A 256
MOODY, G W 224 Geo 205
MOON, Benjamin 251 James 251
   Joseph 255
MOORE, A W 186 211 Alfred Y
   186 B E 186 B F 186 270 272
   B J 213 Ben Frank 270
   Benjamin 186 Benjamin Sr
   185-186 C F 187 Carey 186
   Catharine 186 Drucilla 185-
   186 Duncan 62 Duncan W
   186-187 Elizabeth 186 Francis
   185 J Alex 187 J Alexander W
   185 J D 187 J R 211 James
   135 185-186 John R 186 John
   S 276-277 M A J 187 Martha
   62 186 Mary 186 Mary A 186
   Mintie 186 Mr 186 276 Mrs
   275-277 Mrs Jno S 171 Mrs
   John S 276-277 Nancy 186 P B
   186 Parmilia 186 Rebecca 186
   Sarah 186 T B 215 Thomas B
   186 W A 186 Welcome A 272
   William 186 Wm 270
MORGAN, Enoch 21
MORRIS, Campbell 209
   Tennant 21
   Thos J 222
MORRISON, A W 265-266 Jeff D
   265
MULLIGAN, James 222
MUMFORD, James 209
MUNFORD, Wm 205

MUNNERLYN, C T 136 Chas T 172 198 Wm 172 174 236
MUNRO, 163
MURCHISON, John D 178 Mrs 154 Wm 176 178
MURDOCH, Jno T 196 John 242
MURDOCK, Alexander 120 Andrew 120 Daniel C 132 David 120 James 120 Jno 160 John 120 133 John T 222
MURPHY, 37 105 Elizabeth 31 Marcia 31 Miss 229
MURRAH, Wm 255
MURRAY, J W 256 Justice 59 P A 254 P B 256
NAPIER, Joel E 205
NAPOLEON, I 50
NELSON, Ervin 213
NEVIL, Bennett 220
NEWBERRY, John 22
NEWTON, 269 Anderson 247 B J 226 C Dudley 226 Cornelius 242 246 248-249 252 272 Cornelius D 182 222 249 David C 247 Dorcas 249 Elizabeth 272 Giles 247 Giles Sr 248 H H 133 164-166 169 253 Hope 253 Hope Hull 222 249 Hope Jr 180 Ira 184 J C 213 J R 25 Joseph 220 222 249 Julia 272 Martha 182 Mrs H H 138 Peyton V 222 Richard D 222 Sallie 272 Smith 226 Sue 25 Thos B 222 Younger 247-248 Younger Sr 272
NEY, Peter Stuart 50
NICHOLAS, Griffith 20-21
NICHOLLS, Mrs 93
NOBLE, Gov 48 128
NORMAN, Jeremiah 255
NORMENT, J E 268
NORTHROP, Mr 48 Mrs 48

NORTON, Elias 217 Jas 217 Samuel 217
NOTT, 162
O'NAILS, James 222
O'NEAL, Judge 28 122 128 163 Lark 255
O'TUALL, Gus 184
ODOM, 248 Abram 182 186 Alexander 209 Arch K 264 Betsy 92 182 Catharine 186 Chloe 182 D A 213 218 D C 119 Daniel 182 Daniel J 222 Dorcas 183 Drucilla 186 Durant 183 Elizabeth 186 Evander W 222 Godfrey 182 H E 217 H K 182 H King 222 Henry 213 J E 213 J G 217 James 182 248 Jas Thomas 222 Jennie 182 John 182 222 Josiah 198 L 218 Leggett 196 Nancy 182 186 Nehemiah 222 Noah 209 222 P E 218 Philip 183 186 Philip W 198 Robt H 222 S D 213 S W 217 Sam 183 Samuel Sr 247 Sion 182-183 Sion W 198 Theophilus 182 186 Thos Q 222 Tristram 182 W B 211 William 182 Wm 186
ODOMS, D A 217
OGBORNE, Rev Mr 226
OWEN, John 254
OWENS, Jno 213
OXENDINE, Leonard C 209 Manny 209
PAISLEY, Mr 275
PARHAM, A 218 Alex K 207 Avery 118 Daniel 101 H 224 Henry 205 J H 224 James 118 Lemuel 118 Malcom 226 Mrs 118 Nellie 101 Robt 205 Samuel 218 Wesley 118 William 209

PARISH, Alfred 62 117 Caleb 118
　　David 118 Ellen 117 Henry
　　117 205 Joel 117 224 John 117
　　220 Lucy 117 119 Mary 117
　　Milton 118 Mr 117-120 Nancy
　　117 Noel 117 Willey 118
　　Willie 117
PARKER, 265 Andrew 222
　　Andrews 209 Capt 268 Elijah
　　222 Harrison 198 222 J R 133
　　John 87 John R 195 268 Moses
　　86-88 268 Mr 90-91 Mrs 88
　　Mrs Lewis 91 Mrs Moses 86
　　Peter 207 Philip 88-89 Sam
　　224 Wm 218
PARKHAM, Daniel 117 Ellen 117
PARKS, Alex 209
PARROTT, B F 182 James 182
　　222 Mary 182 Matilda 182
PATE, 272 A D 213 Ann 272 John
　　A 272 Penelope 189 Travis
　　272 Willis 189 213
PAWLEY, George 54 66
PEARCE, E L 186 Jesse 161
　　Martha 35 Mrs E L 186 W 235
PEARSON, 45 Aaron 46 63 Aaron
　　1st 46 Aaron 2nd 46 61 Ann
　　46 63 Elizabeth 186 George
　　281 John 46 63 186 John D 24
　　46 Lemuel 24 Mary 24 Moses
　　41 46 111 122-123 161-162
　　Mr 32 Mrs 24 32 185 Mrs
　　Aaron 2nd 61 Rachel 24 Robt
　　C 198 Thomas 46 William 24
　　Wm 252 Zacheus 46
PEEL, Eli F 213 Freeman 218
　　Thos 213 William 247
PEELE, Mary 273 Robert 273
PEGUES, Capt 112 Christopher 31
　　Claudius 31 57 66 71 79 112
　　121 123 161 Claudius Jr 123
　　161 Elizabeth 31 J K 226

PEGUES (cont'd)
　　Marcia 31 Mr 31 Mrs
　　Christopher 31 R R 256
　　Randolph 31 Wesley 31
　　William 31 112 121
PERKINS, Miles 209 Wm 209
PETERKIN, Alex 60 Alexander 63
　　Barbara 63 152 Elizabeth 63 J
　　A 64 James 63 James A 223-
　　224 Jesse 63-64 John A 200
　　Mrs Alex 60 Mrs Jessie 153
　　Sallie 64 154
PEUGUES, Claudius 133
PIPKIN, E C 62 Elisha C 202 Eliza
　　62 Emily 62 Esquire 267-268
　　Isaac 62 91 268 John F 267
　　Mary 91 Mr 268 Squire 91-92
PLEDGER, 61 Aggy 160 Elizabeth
　　76 John 77 Joseph 77 Mary 60
　　Miss 63 P W 77 Philip 54 57
　　60 76-77 112 122 Sarah 60
　　William 76-77 135 Wm 135
POELNITZ, 130 Baron 40 Julius
　　131
POLSON, Alex 205 Chas 224
　　David 205 Jerry 224 W 213
　　Wm 224
POPE, Bennett J 222
PORTER, J A 255-256 John A 256
POTTER, Ira L 255 Solomon 198
POUNCEY, Adeline 60 Ann 61
　　Anthony 60 Eliza 61 Ellen 61
　　James 60 John 60 Maj 60-61
　　106 Mary 60-61 Mrs 106 Mrs
　　John 60 Peter 60 Sarah 60
　　William 60 71
POUNCY, Ann 60 Mrs William
　　35 William 35 Wm 135
POWE, Thomas 121 132
POWELL, 59 Col 66
　　Gabriel 66
　　Wm R 209

POWERS, Ellison 222 Ervin 214 J
   F 226
PRATT, 239
PRESTON, Wm C 40
PREVATT, Angus 222 Evander
   209 James 222
PREVOST, Gen 83
PRICE, E G 257
PRICHARD, Claudus H 256
PRINCE, F W 282 Jno T 198 L B
   258
PRIVATT, Evander 198
PROCTER, 49
PROCTOR, Aaron 205 Frederick
   205 Thos A 223
PUCKET, Miles 255
PUGH, 232 Elizabeth 39 Evan 39
   126 229 Martha 39 230 Mr 83
   230 Rev Mr 111 229
PULASKI, 130
PURNELL, Dorcas 249 Mr 148
   Robert 148 241 Robt 248-249
QUICK, 248 A 218 A W 206 224
   Aaron T 209 Alfred 205 Angus
   214 Benjamin F 281 Bennie
   183 Chas D 210 Daniel 205 E
   B 206 Ebby 209 Evander 209
   Giles 205 H T 211 Henry 205
   214 J Evans 281 J F 226 J W
   226 James 149 218 225 Jas H
   205 Jno B 214 Leggett 223 M
   218 Madison 210 Philip 205
   Pleasant 206 Robert 207 Robt
   W 209 Stephen 209 Thomas
   112 Thomas P 207 Welcome
   226 Wyatt 210
RAE, A P 206
RAINWATERS, Joshua 223
   Samuel 210
RASCOE, Alex 214
   Daniel 202 H 218
   Wm 206 214 224

RAST, Mr 275
REED, 89
REESE, Dr 268 J D 215
   Richard 281
RICE, John A 257
RICHARDS, 260 Sarah 275
RICHARDSON, A 255 John S 163
ROBBINS, 115 162 M 255 Mr 73
ROBERSON, John H 255
ROBERTSON, 37 D 133 Drury
   125-126 133 135 167 181 185
   Maj 125
ROBESON, John H 255
ROBINSON, Ann 75 Mrs Jephtha
   93
ROGERS, 72 166 B A 136 195
   199 B B 34 133 B N 33 191
   260 Ben 32-34 111 Benjamin
   32-33 58 71 132 135 C B 226
   Caroline 34 Catharine 34 Col
   131 Eliza 34 Elizabeth 34 F B
   192 Frank A 202 Henry 31 J T
   225 James 22 John 32 34 61
   133 John M 32 133 Maj 34
   Martha 24 32 Mary 32 Miss 75
   Mrs B N 33 Mrs Henry 31 Mrs
   John 61 Nicholas 24 32
   Pinckney 210 Rachel 24
   Robert 32 T I 75 134 136
   Thomas Irby 31 William 145
   Wm 223 Wm T 199
ROLLER, Benjamin 210 Henry T
   210 John 207 210
ROOT, Mr 275
ROPER, 147 Caswell 223 Dan C
   134 J W 142
ROSCOE, Geo W 198 John 198
ROUNTREE, Moses 198
ROWE, ---- 223 A J 178 Bros 173
   178 J H 218 J J 173 176
   Joseph H 198 Mrs 245 W D
   218

ROWLAND, Mrs 93
RUTLEDGE, Col 27 Gov 112 John 27
RYAL, Needham 247
SANDERS, J 218 Moses 225 Moses P 223
SANDS, Mary 85
SARRIS, A L 202
SAWYER, E J 275 281 Joel 206 John H 223 Levi 206
SCOTT, Benjamin 210 Wash 214
SEALS, James 206
SELLERS, Bryant J 223 W W 164
SERVANT, Nero 112
SHERIDAN, Mr 275
SHERMAN, 288
SIMMONS, Dennis J 256 Mr 228
SIMPSON, Miss 275
SINCLAIR, 50 A C 274 Archie 137 D C 206 D M 211 Daniel C 225 Elias 255 John 243
SISTERS, Lester 265
SKIPPER, Josiah 198
SMITH, A D 207 Ann 61 183 Betsy 156 183 C 214 Frank 183 H 224 Herbert 183 223 J Wesley 136 James 210 Jennie 182 John 149 John L 255 John W 200 Joseph R 223 Margaret 272 Mr 61 Mrs Dr 28 Mrs Simon 149 Nancy 88 Peter T 278 Simon 149 Stephen 210 T C 183 W D 202 W R 237 244 277 W T 255 265 William 183 William R 149 Wm Benjamin 220 Wm R 156
SNEAD, Samuel 35
SNEED, Israel 198
SORENCY, Samuel 22
SOUTHERLAND, Alexander 176 258 260 Thos A 199

SPARKS, 106 260 A D 35 223 Alex D 179 Ann 29 35 Charles 34-35 Daniel 34-35 Harry 34-35 105 Lucy 35 Martha 35 Mr 35 252 Mrs 29 195 Mrs Samuel 35 Sam'l 160 Samuel 29 34-35 179 191 252 Sarah 60
SPEARS, Andrew 62 Ann 62 Bettie 44 David 61-62 Deborah 62 186 Edwin 62 Eliza 62 Elizabeth 63 Emily 62 Harris 43 62 119 Harris N 206 J A 214 J E 225 J Edwin 215 James 62 104 168 186 192 244 James Sr 62 191 Lewis 43 62 101 119 Lidia 61-62 Margaret 62 153 Martha 62 186 Mary 63 Meekins 62 Miss 43 46 Mr 61-62 Mrs 62 153 Mrs Lewis 140 Nancy 62 119 Nathaniel 61-62 Nellie 101 Rebecca 62 Silas 202 William 62 117 119 Wm 206
SPENCER, Calvin 125-126 Capt 127 T D 224
SPORT, George 202
SPORTS, John 206 W B 206
STACKHOUSE, E T 165 H M 133-134 H Milton 223 John 223 Mr 275 Robt Boyd 223
STANTON, 63 147 A A 202 A J 184 Alexander J 246 E G 218 Evander 150 Handy 150 183 J 224 J H 206 John 150 210 John A 198 M 218 Milton 199 N 218 Noah 198 Peter 150 206 Sarah 150 Thomas 150 W G 206 W Godfrey 150 W H 206
STARKE, Mr 122
STEED, W H 206
STEEL, G W 281

STEEN, A 214 Esther 183 Morgan 210
STEPHENS, J E 214 Reuben 214 Sarah 24
STERGIS, John 206 Joseph 206
STERNBERGER, 147
STEWART, David 126 James 246 Mr 131 Mrs 131
STOGNER, John 206 Tom 214 Wm 206 214
STOKES, J L 245 253-254 256
STOLL, James C 257
STOUT, John 228
STRAUSS, Simon 178
STRICKLAND, ---- 223 Henry 210 Mrs S J 183 S J 183
STROTHER, Chas S 135 William 121 125
STROUD, Miss 42
STRUDWICK, E 266
STUART, Charles 40 David 133 Mrs Charles 40
STUBBS, 120 A A 214 Albert 103 Alex 35 Alexander 184 Ann 62 Benjamin 185 Big Jim 185 C 235 C E 214 Campbell 184 274 Celia 185 D D 183 214 Daniel 218 David 184 Dorcas 183 Elizabeth 103 185 Feribe 185 Francis 185 J B 214 J F 265 J L 216 Jackson 181 184-185 James 119 184-185 Jas 206 Joel 206 John 24 103 184-185 206 John J 184 John W 184-185 247 L D 226 Lewis 103 184 Lewis E 136 184 Lucius 202 Lucy 35 185 M W 214 Mary 24 Mrs 62 Mrs J L 24 Mrs James 119 Mrs Lewis E 47 Mrs Mastin 184 Peter 184-185 Rebecca 184-185 S. F. 214 Silas 184 T E 214

STUBBS (cont'd) T. P. 133 184 214 Thomas 35 184-185 235 Thomas E 62 Thos 218 Thos A 223 W H 235 W J 235 Widow 24 William 103 184-185 William F 184-185 Wm 185 Wyriott 103
STUCKEY, Ben N 223
STURGIS, Milton 226
STURNISS, David 160
SUMMERFORD, T M J 202
SUMTER, Gen 96
SWEAT, Aaron 161 Benjamin 210 Ellis 226 Harris 218 Henry 223 J W 218 James 97 Jas 218 John 210 Leonard 210 Mr 97 Nathan 97 Sam 218 Saml 223 Sandford 223 Simeon 218 William 210 Wm K 223
SWEENEY, B K 47 Barney 47 Darby 47 Ephraim L 47 James 47 John 47
TARBOX, J W 256
TARELL, William 72
TART, W J 214
TATUM, 265 Amos 281 F P 215 266 268 Frank P 264 Mr 268 R J 196 268 Richard J 268 Rufus 281
TAYLOR, 176 James 203 John 226 267 S 126 Samuel 127
TERREL, Jno 235
TERRELL, Ann 72 Capt 72 John 72 77 Martha 72 Samuel 72 W T 214 William 72 77 Wm 22
THOMAS, 224 A W 284 Alexander 125 Ann 104 Caleb 100 Carey J 199 Eleanor 64 Eli 86 93 145 242 Elisha 21 Elizabeth 100 Gen 123 126 Gumfoot 100 Horace 174 Horace B 172-173

THOMAS (cont'd)
　J. A. W. 169 210 234 236-237
　239 250 292 J W 133 James
　223 James C 85 135 245 Jane
　125 130 Jas C 244 274 Jno 235
　Joe 214 John 135 John S 86
　167 171-172 174-175 Joseph
　M 199 Lewis 85-86 Maj 127
　Margaret 62 Mary 21 61 85
　Miss 87 Mrs 62 Mrs Eli 93
　Mrs Jas C 245 Mrs William 39
　Nathan 86 93 100-101 104 111
　118 Nathan B 167 175 180 274
　Nathan S 223 Philemon 85-86
　Philip 206 R S 61 Rachel 120
　Robert 62 85-86 100 234
　Robert W 86 Robt D 135 199
　Stephen 85-86 T 133 Tristram
　85-86 95 98 112 121 123 126
　132-133 160-161 W E 136 W
　L 130 William 39 64 86 124-
　126 132 236 William L 125
THOMLINSON, L 224
THOMPSON, Mrs 154 T J 218
THOMSON, Lucy 64 Mr 64 275
THORNWELL, C A 133 Charles
　A 73 Chas A 133 164 199 258
　Dr 72-73 258 277 J H 73
　James 72 James H 72 258
　Martha 72 Mrs 73 Mrs C A
　276
THWING, E F 256
TILLER, Dove 256
TIMMONS, 224
TOMLINSON, Jas 224
TOWNSEND, 176 B D 44
　Benjamin 44 Bettie 44 C P 24
　44 133-134 162 165 169 176
　187 Chas P 195 Elizabeth 63
　Henry E 196 J R 40 243 Jabish
　44 63 Jabish N 44
　Jabish T 44

TOWNSEND (cont'd)
　Joel W 255 John 43-44 John C
　44 244 John R 192 Light 43-45
　192 M 135 168 Maj 245
　Meekin 24 44 73 Mr 190-191
　267 Mrs B D 276 Mrs Jabish
　N 44 Mrs Light 40 R E 24 210
　Rachel 24 46 Rhoda 43-44 S J
　133 174 176 Samuel 44
　Samuel J 44 164 W S 216 275
　Walter 24 Walter S 210
TRADWELL, ---- 255
TRAWICK, Lidia 61 Mr 61 Ned
　107 Peter 218
TRAYWICK, J B 254
TREZEVANT, 162
TURLINGTON, Elizabeth 186
　Willis 186
TURNAGE, Luke 214
TURNER, Aaron 210 248 D 218
　Isham 182 Jack 218 James 248
　Jas 218 John 224 L 218 Nancy
　182
TURRENTINE, Morgan C 255
TWITTY, Mrs 124
UNCLE, John 44 Sandy 64
UNDERWOOD, Dinah 22
USHER, Chas 218 M 214
VANCE, Chloe 182
VANDIVER, John W 255
VAUGHAN, Catherine 22 Evan 22
VICK, J I 265
VINING, Ann 46 63 Bettie 64
　Elizabeth 63-64 Jeptha 63
　Jesse 63 John 63 Thomas 63
WADDILL, G W 136
WADE, Holden 127
WALKER, A W 255 Chas S 255
WALLACE, Barnabas 182 246-
　247 Barney 184 186 Evander
　182 J A 258 J B 218 Jennie
　182 John W 182 207

WALLACE (cont'd)
  Lizzie 182 Martha 182 Mary 182 Matilda 182 Miranda 182 Murray C 182 Parmilia 186 S 224 Stephen 182 186 T G 214 Thos G 186 224 W T 224 Washington 206 William 182 Wm D 176
WALSH, ---- 223 T R 256 Tracy R 256
WALTER, C P 267 R E 267
WANNAMAKER, T E 245 254
WARDEN, Eli 206
WARE, ---- 223 Edward 281 Nicholas 243 255
WATERS, J 218 Reuben 214
WATIES, 59 162
WATSON, Coleman 210 E O 245 254 257 Sam 224
WATTS, John 255
WAYNE, Gen 23
WAYS, 90
WEATHERFORD, Jas 214
WEATHERLY, 224 A W 202 C A 220 C M 32 136 170 172 178 195 E A 206 Isaac 223 J N 178 219 Miss 149 Mr 137 Mrs C M 32 Mrs J N 276 Robt T 220 Sallie 152 T C 133 135 146
WEATON, D D 211
WEBB, Alex 206 David 206
WEBSTER, Chas T 199 George 118 George M 250 Hartwell 199 Henry D 199 J 224 Jas 224 Miss 23 Mr 118 Robert 118 Thos M 199 W R 202 William 118 Wm 185
WELBORN, J W 255
WELCH, 147
  J W 225
  Richard 206 242
WELLS, P B 255

WEMYS, 96
WEST, Annie 25 Mary 25 William 223
WHITBY, Wm 255
WHITE, Daniel 164 276
WHITFIELD, G R 133 Geo R 133 William 126 132-133
WHITNER, 163
WHITTINGTON, Betsy 34
WICKAM, Mrs 33
WICKER, Allen 182 Betsy 182
WICKHAM, Maria 75
WIGGINS, 40 Ham 206
WIGHTMAN, James W 256 W M 255 W S 245 254
WILCOX, Mr 275
WILDON, John Lide 128
WILDS, 162 Abel 27 Col 27 John 27-28 Judge 28 74 Miss 74 Mrs 28 107-108 Mrs Samuel 22 Peter 28 Samuel 22 27-28
WILKINS, J T 206
WILKINSON, Gorman 210
WILLIAM, Earl Of Craven 20
WILLIAMS, 232 Chas 210 Col 267 David 199 David R 229 H H 251 Henry 214 Jno 214 Joseph 218 L 218 Lazarus 202 Paul A M 255 Robt 229 S V 224 Sam 214 T J 133 Thos 218 Thos J 133
WILLIAMSON, Capt 139
WILLIS, 107-108 265 Allen 214 Eli 93 200 266 J E 265 Jas B 93 Milby 93 Mrs J B 93
WILLOUGHBY, J P 225 R 218
WILOUGHBY, J P 206 R 224
WILSON, 37 162 C W 260 Charlton W 259
  John 135
  John Lide 124 Wright 149 242
WINCHESTER, Elhanan 80 230

WINFIELD, Jno 135 Joel 135-136
WISE, Capt 79 81 Jonathan 58
 Lidia 61 Sam'l 71 Samuel 66
 79 83 W W 214
WITHERS, 163-164
WITHERSPOON, 162
WOODLE, Allen 225 E 218
 Hinson 218 Ransom 214
WOODLEY, 147 Alex 202 James
 150 John C 150 Jonathan 150-
 151 218 Mary 150 Mr 150-151
WRIGHT, Daniel 218 Daniel G
 199 Ellerbe 199 Geo W 199
 James 152 Miss 76
YOUNG, Jackson 223 Miss 74
ZIMMERMAN, John H 256

www.ingramcontent.com/pod-product-compliance
Lightning Source LLC
Chambersburg PA
CBHW060554230426
43670CB00011B/1817